The Hebrew Republic

The Hebrew Republic

Jewish Sources and the Transformation of
European Political Thought

ERIC NELSON

Harvard University Press
Cambridge, Massachusetts • London, England

First Harvard University Press paperback edition, 2011

Library of Congress Cataloging-in-Publication Data
Nelson, Eric, 1977–
The Hebrew republic : Jewish sources and the transformation of European
political thought / Eric Nelson.
p.   cm.
Includes bibliographical references and index.
ISBN 978-0-674-05058-7 (cloth : alk. paper)
ISBN 978-0-674-06213-9 (pbk.)
1. Jews—Politics and government—To 70 A.D.   2. Judaism and politics—
History of doctrines.   3. Politics in rabbinical literature.   4. Political science—
Europe—History.   5. Europe—Civilization—Jewish influences.   I. Title.
JC67.N45   2010
320.01'1—dc22   2009038615

To Cela and Jack Sarna,
to Renee Nelson,
and to the memory of Howard Nelson

"One who teaches his grandson the Torah is regarded as if he himself
received it from Sinai."

כל המלמד את בן בנו תורה מעלה עליו הכתוב כאילו
קבלה מהר סיני.

Talmud, Kiddushin

Contents

The Hebrew Republic

Introduction

I T HAS BECOME COMMONPLACE to attribute the rise of modern political thought in the West to a process of secularization. In Medieval and
Renaissance Europe, so the story goes, political thought was fundamentally Christian, an exercise in applied theology. To ask what form our
political lives should take was, during this period, inevitably to ask what
form God wished for them to take. Questions about politics quickly became questions about Revelation, about the proper understanding of
God's commands as reflected in Scripture. It was, in short, an age of *political theology*. In the sixteenth century, however, this worldview began
to erode and, in the seventeenth, to collapse. The new science of Galileo
and Bacon, along with the strident philosophical skepticism of Montaigne
and Charron, provoked a radical reconfiguration of European thought.
Philosophers of the period no longer recognized religious claims as authoritative and, given the horrors of the Wars of Religion, came to regard
them instead as inherently dangerous to civil peace. The result of this
intellectual upheaval has been called "the Great Separation," by which
is meant the epoch-making exclusion of religious arguments from the
sphere of political discourse.[1] It is this separation, we are told, that is responsible for producing the distinctive features of modern European
political thought, including (but by no means limited to) its particular

notion of individual rights, its account of the state, and its embrace of religious toleration. These innovations could not appear on the scene until religion had effectively been sequestered from political science. It is, then, the peculiar achievement of the seventeenth century to have bequeathed us a tradition of political thought that has been purged of political theology.[2]

This book begins from the conviction that the traditional story I have just sketched puts things almost exactly backward. Leaving aside its overly schematic characterization of Medieval political thought,[3] it is clear that this narrative seriously misrepresents the relationship between Renaissance political thought and the political thought of the seventeenth century. Renaissance humanism, structured as it was by the pagan inheritance of Greek and Roman antiquity, generated an approach to politics that was remarkably secular in character. The political science of the humanists did not rely on appeals to Revelation, but rather on the sort of prudential knowledge to be found in the study of history and in the writings of the wise. It was, rather, in the seventeenth century, in the full fervor of the Reformation, that political theology reentered the mainstream of European intellectual life. The Protestant summons to return to the Biblical text brought with it incessant appeals to God's constitutional preferences as embodied in Scripture.[4] To use a crude but revealing measure: if one compares the average number of Biblical citations in the political works of Petrarch, Bruni, Machiavelli, More, and Guicciardini with the number in the political works of Grotius, Selden, Milton, Pufendorf, and Locke, one can be in no doubt about the direction in which the discourse is moving.* It is, indeed, not for nothing that seventeenth-century historians have dubbed their period "the Biblical Century." Yet it is also unmistakably the case that many of the central ideas we associate with the emergence of modern political thought did

---

* To take just two examples, there are fewer than ten Biblical citations in the entire course of Petrarch's *Qualis esse debeat qui rem publicam regit;* and there are none at all in Bruni's *Laudatio fiorentinae urbis.* See Francesco Petrarch, *Letters of Old Age,* 2 vols., trans. Aldo S. Bernardo, Saul Levin, and Reta A. Bernardo (New York, 2005), vol. 2, pp. 521–552; and Leonardo Bruni, *Opere letterarie e politiche di Leonardo Bruni,* ed. Paolo Viti (Turin, 1996), pp. 566–647. In contrast, there is hardly a page in any of the seventeenth-century texts I just mentioned that does not contain several Biblical citations.

indeed develop in the seventeenth century. What we are in need of, then, is an explanation of how these ideas might have been generated, not as a by-product of advancing secularization, but rather out of the deeply theologized context of the Biblical Century.

In what follows, I attempt to offer such an account.[5] It centers on the sixteenth- and seventeenth-century revival of the Hebrew language and on the consequences of that cultural and intellectual phenomenon for the development of European political theory. During this period, Christians began to regard the Hebrew Bible as a political constitution, designed by God himself for the children of Israel. They also came to see the full array of newly available rabbinic materials as authoritative guides to the institutions and practices of this perfect republic. My argument, in brief, is that the Christian encounter with these materials transformed political thought along several important dimensions. The first of these has to do with the idea of political science itself. Before the middle of the seventeenth century, European political thought was characterized by the complete hegemony of what we might call "constitutional pluralism." Following Aristotle and other classical authors, political theorists acknowledged the existence of several correct constitutional forms—monarchy, aristocracy, and polity (later called "republican" government)[6]—which they distinguished from the corresponding incorrect or degenerate forms: tyranny, oligarchy, and democracy.[7] Although each theorist often had a view about the *best* constitution (either the best absolutely, or the best under particular circumstances), it was taken for granted that each of the correct forms was legitimate and even desirable under particular circumstances. In the middle of the seventeenth century, however, we find republican authors making a new and revolutionary argument: they now began to claim that monarchy per se is an illicit constitutional form and that all legitimate constitutions are republican. In Chapter 1 I make the case that this rupture was provoked by the Protestant reception of a radical tradition of rabbinic Biblical exegesis, which understood the Israelite request for a king in I Samuel as an instance of the sin of idolatry. This embrace of "republican exclusivism" heralded the decline of constitutional pluralism and therefore marks a crucial turning point in the history of European political thought.

The second dimension has to do with the early-modern understanding of the state and its purposes. Before the seventeenth century, it had been an unchallenged orthodoxy of republican political theory that a free state ought not to use its coercive power to redistribute wealth. Renaissance republicans learned from their Roman authorities that the most famous ancient attempt at the redistribution of wealth—the Roman agrarian laws—had been unjust, seditious, and ultimately responsible for the collapse of the Roman republic. Even those republicans who rejected the Roman inheritance and instead derived their political commitments from Greek philosophy nonetheless accepted this orthodoxy. These dissenters were occasionally prepared to argue for the *abolition* of private property, but never for redistribution, which they continued to regard as both dangerous and impolitic. By the middle of the seventeenth century, however, a dramatic transformation was under way. Quite suddenly, republican authors began placing redistribution (in the form of agrarian laws) at the very center of republican politics. My suggestion, which I defend in Chapter 2, is that it was the meditation on Biblical land law—seen through the prism of rabbinic commentaries—that convinced a new generation of republican writers to reexamine the antipathy toward redistribution they had inherited from their forebears. The result was a major reconfiguration of the republican tradition, with consequences extending into our own time.

The third and final dimension concerns the relationship between church and state and, in particular, the question of religious toleration. It is in this context that the traditional narrative has been perhaps most influential. We are told that the rise of toleration depended upon the advance of secularization, both historically and at the level of theory; that only when religion had finally lost its grip on the European imagination could theorists begin to contemplate broad protection for nonconformist religious belief and practice. We are also told that toleration depended upon, and emerged out of, the belief that church and state should remain fundamentally separate, neither encroaching on the prerogatives of the other. My argument in Chapter 3 is that both of these assertions are largely mistaken. The pursuit of toleration was primarily nurtured by deeply felt religious convictions, not by their absence; and it emerged to a very great extent out of the Erastian effort to unify church and state, not out of the desire to keep them separate. Once again, I argue that the Hebrew revival played a crucial role in forging this nexus between a pious Erastianism and toleration. It was a particular understanding of what the Jewish historian Josephus had meant by the term *theocracy*, mediated through a series of rabbinic sources, that convinced a wide range of seventeenth-century authors that God's own thoroughly Erastian republic had embraced toleration.

The combined significance of these three transformations is clear enough. Once we are talking about a world in which a republican constitution is seen as a requirement of legitimacy, in which the state uses its coercive power to redistribute wealth, and in which broad toleration is the rule, we are recognizably talking about the modern world. And if that world was, to an important degree, called into being, not by the retreat of religious conviction, but rather by the deeply held religious belief that the creation of such a world is God's will, then the traditional narrative will have to be significantly revised, if not discarded. In short, it may well be that we live, as Charles Taylor tells us, in a "secular age," but if so, we nonetheless owe several of our most central political commitments to an age that was anything but.[8] And it seems reasonable to suppose that we will not be able to understand the peculiar fault lines and dissonances of our contemporary political discourse until we come to terms with that basic, paradoxical fact.

This is, then, a book about the transformative impact of an encounter between readers and texts, and like all such studies, it must navigate between two simplistic pictures of how authoritative sources operate in the history of ideas. According to the first, texts do all of the work: intellectual history should be regarded as a kind of ballistic display in which thinkers at rest are set in motion by collisions with newly discovered sources. On this view, readers bring very little to the table; they are empty vessels waiting to be filled by the arguments they read. According to the second picture, in contrast, texts do none of the work. They are, rather, deployed instrumentally by readers whose ideological commitments are to be regarded as fully formed in advance—shaped perhaps by their political circumstances, economic situation, or psychological profile. In the case of the Hebrew revival (as in most other cases), neither of these pictures will do. To be sure, the encounter between Protestant theorists and Hebrew sources did not take place in a vacuum. It is, for example, undoubtedly the case that the intensifying fury of the English Revolution, and the ultimate execution of an English king in 1649, prompted English republicans to consider radical new arguments about the proper form of political life—arguments that they would never have seriously considered even five years earlier. But it is equally clear that these arguments came from somewhere. The Hebrew revival made republican exclusivism possible by introducing into Protestant Europe the claim that monarchy is sin. It legitimized redistribution by teaching that God had incorporated agrarian laws into his own perfect constitution. And, by disseminating the Josephan account of Israelite theocracy, it rendered the practice of toleration not merely *politique* but also pious.

Having now said a bit about what this book is, it might be helpful for me to say a few words about what it is not. It is, first and foremost, not a history of what has come to be called *political Hebraism*—let alone of Christian Hebraism more broadly. A history of the former would set itself the task of chronicling the various political uses to which Hebrew materials were put throughout the early-modern period; a history of the latter would, even more monumentally, attempt to tell the full story of the recovery and deployment of the Hebrew language and Hebraica in the Christian West.[9] This book does not pretend to do either. It is, instead, an attempt to identify what I take to be the most important ways in which the recovery of Hebraica reoriented European political thought. A brief example should illustrate the difference between these projects. It became common in the late 1640s and 1650s, in the midst of the English Revolution, for defenders of the regicide to cite a ruling of Maimonides's that kings may be judged, and even whipped, if they commit crimes.[10] The use of this commonplace would, presumably, be a subject of interest in a history of political Hebraism; yet, because this rabbinic text was simply deployed to lend further authority to an old and ubiquitous argument in European political thought (familiar from Medieval conciliarism and from the monarchomach writings of the sixteenth century), it is not a focus of this study. My aim is to explore how the Hebrew revival *changed* what it was possible for Europeans to argue, either by making available an argument that was simply foreign to previous generations of political theorists (Chapter 1); or by taking a disreputable political position and rendering it suddenly respectable (Chapter 2); or by bringing together a series of claims that had never been brought together before and fusing them into a new and powerful whole (Chapter 3). A further consequence of this narrowly defined mission is that certain authors who would, presumably, feature quite prominently in any history of political Hebraism (Jean Bodin, for instance) receive relatively little attention in this book, while others who would not figure much at all in such a history (Wilhelm Schickard, for example) receive quite a lot.

It is also worth pointing out that this book is not, in the usual sense, a work in the field of Jewish Studies—although I certainly hope that scholars in that field will find it interesting. My story is about how European Christians in the sixteenth and seventeenth centuries interacted with a foreign corpus of political and theological writings. Although (as we shall see) Jews played an important role in the dissemination of the Hebrew texts with which this study is concerned, the political debates that these texts came to structure took place among Christians—Christians who, it must be said, had for the most part never met a Jew, and who were (again for the most part) anything but *philo-semites*. This book is intended as a contribution to the history of early-modern political thought, and it is part of my purpose to insist that one can no more understand that history without reckoning with the Hebrew revival than one can without taking seriously the revival of Greek and Roman antiquity. Before that reckoning can begin, however, I need to offer a brief account of the origins and progress of this cultural phenomenon, as well as an anatomy of its fateful brush with political theory.[11]

The Hebrew Revival

On September 22, 1626, Sixtinus Amama, professor of Hebrew, ascended the podium at the University of Franeker to offer both congratulations and a warning to his Dutch compatriots. Only eight years earlier, he reminded his audience, the University had celebrated the centenary of the Reformation. In doing so, it had also commemorated the rebirth of Hebrew studies in the Christian West, for, as he insisted, the great crusade of the "incomparable heroes" Luther and Melanchthon—and that of their progenitors, Erasmus and Reuchlin—had been intrinsically tied to the revival of the Hebrew language.[12] Luther's conviction that the way of a true Christian was to seek salvation through the Bible—and only through the Bible—had, for the very first time, placed the study of the original Biblical languages at the heart of the Christian ministry. If one could no longer rely on commentaries, translations, or the authority of the institutional Church for guidance in the life of the spirit, then it became a matter of the utmost urgency to understand the Biblical text correctly, to read the Hebrew Bible in its original language. The result, Amama explained, was a great revival of Hebraic learning, undertaken in defiance of the "barbarians" who wished to silence scholarship and thereby repress the memory of the true, primitive Christian church. The linguistic ignorance and scholarly infirmity of the Middle Ages had at last been transcended; the corrupt Aristotelianism of the scholastics (in which "he who was more learned was more wretched"),[13] and their near idolatrous veneration of Thomas Aquinas and Peter Lombard, had finally come to an end. Or so Amama had thought. Surveying the intellectual landscape of his home university, and of the United Provinces more broadly, he now detected worrying signs of backsliding and retreat. Theologians were once again concerning themselves with abstruse metaphysical speculation; scholasticism threatened to return; and the study of the Biblical tongues, particularly Hebrew, was no longer honored and valued to the appropriate degree.[14] At the close of his oration, Amama entreated his audience to reaffirm the principles of the Reformation, to direct their attention once again to the study of Hebrew, and to defeat the encroaching threat of Catholic barbarism.[15]

Amama's version of this story, according to which the Reformation straightforwardly gave birth to Christian Hebraism, is not, alas, one that we can fully accept. Christian fascination with the Hebrew language goes back to Origen and Jerome among the church fathers and never entirely disappeared.[16] Already in the twelfth century, Christian exegetes in the Abbey of St. Victor in Paris were using Biblical commentaries by Rabbi Solomon ben Isaac of Troyes (known as Rashi, 1040–1105) and other rabbinic authorities in order to understand the literal sense of the Hebrew Bible (which was already being called the *Hebraica Veritas,* or Hebrew Truth),[17] and Maimonides's *Moreh Nevukhim* (Guide for the Perplexed) was translated into Latin in the middle of the thirteenth century.[18] Moreover, it was also in the Medieval period—scorned by Amama as a linguistic wilderness—that scholars made the first systematic attempts to use Hebrew texts in order to refute Judaism and advance the cause of Jewish conversion. The most famous instrument of this project was the *Pugio fidei adversos Mauros et Judaeos* (1278), composed by the Dominican Raymund Martini. Martini had been taught by fellow Dominican Raymund of Peñafort (1176–1275), whose broad program of Christian proselytization focused particularly on the Jews. Martini used his knowledge of Hebrew to great effect, deploying a full array of rabbinic sources to defend the claim that the Talmud,* the ancient midrashim (rabbinic homiletical writings), and the targumim (Aramaic paraphrases of the Hebrew Bible) *themselves* refuted the beliefs and practices of contemporary Jews.[19] Although the *Pugio fidei* was not printed until 1651,[20] it circulated widely in manuscript, and its arguments structured a large number of Christian apologetical works (both Catholic and Protestant) over the next four centuries. It inspired, among others, the anti-Jewish polemics in the Franciscan Nicholas of Lyra's *Postillae perpetuae in universam S. Scripturam* (first printed in 1471),[21] the converso Paul of Burgos's *Scrutinium Scripturarum libris duabus contra perfidium Judaeorum* (first printed in 1475), Petrus Galatinus's *De arcanis catholicae veritatis* (1518), and the Calvinist Philippe Du Plessis Mornay's *De veritate religionis christianae* (1583).

Yet, to admit that Amama's account is not completely accurate is not to say that it is wholly mistaken. For while Christian Hebraism was by no means absent from Medieval Europe, its great flowering did indeed take place during the late Renaissance and Reformation. One can see this most clearly by looking at the history of European universities. Although the Council of Vienne (1311–1312) had formally decided to create professorships in oriental languages at Bologna, Oxford, Paris, and Salamanca in order to facilitate the conversion of Jews and Muslims, this

---

* The Talmud is the great compendium of rabbinic law and exegetical writing. It is composed of two parts: the Mishnah (redacted c. 200 CE), which digests the "oral law" (or *torah she-ba'al peh*), and the Gemara (completed c. 500 CE), which consists (broadly) of commentary on the Mishnah. The Gemara itself is often referred to as the Talmud. There are two different versions of the Talmud, the Babylonian *(Bavli)* and the Palestinian *(Yerushalmi)*. The Babylonian is far more authoritative and influential, and when Christian writers refer to "the Talmud," it is usually this that they have in mind.

commitment went more or less unfulfilled until the sixteenth century.[22] The first trilingual college (at Alcalá de Henares, northeast of Madrid) opened its doors in 1508, and its more famous rival in Louvain was not founded until 1516; Regius professorships in Hebrew only arrived in Paris in 1530, and it was not until 1540 that Henry VIII endowed similar chairs at Oxford and Cambridge. The two great Dutch centers of Hebraic study, Leiden University and the University of Franeker, were founded in 1575 and 1585, respectively, and the other Continental centers (Basel, Leipzig, Tübingen, Heidelberg, Zurich, Strasbourg, etc.) did not establish their important dynasties of Hebrew scholarship until the period of the Reformation.[23]

Moreover, it was not until the late fifteenth century that Hebrew texts and grammars became widely available to Christian scholars. The first publishing firm dedicated to Hebraica was founded by Joshua Solomon, a Jew who took the name "Soncino," after the Italian town in which his father and uncle had settled. In 1484, the firm printed its first Hebrew book, an edition of the Talmudic tractate *Berakhot,* followed by a Jewish prayerbook, or *siddur,* according to the Roman Rite *(Mahzor Minhag Roma)* in 1486, and a text of the Hebrew Bible itself in 1488. When the Soncino family was forced to flee Italy in the early sixteenth century, their work was taken up by the Christian printer Daniel Bomberg. In 1517–1518, Bomberg published the first rabbinic Bible, the *Mikra'ot Gedolot,* assembled for him by a converted Jew, Felix Pratensis. This text, in four volumes, brought together a complete version of the Hebrew Bible, along with the Targum and the standard commentaries by Rashi, David Kimchi *(Radak,* c. 1160–1235), and Abraham Ibn Ezra (c. 1092–1167). Bomberg then published the first edition of the Babylonian and Palestinian Talmuds in 1520–1523, with the approval of Pope Leo X. Also published during this period were vital reference works, such as the Franciscan Conrad Pellican's *De modo legendi et intelligendi Hebraea* (1504); Alfonso de Zamora's Hebrew-Aramaic dictionary, published in the sixth volume of the Complutensian *Biblio Polyglotta* (1514–1517); the *Thesaurus Linguae Sanctae* (1523), compiled by the Dominican Santes Pagninus (a simple reworking of Kimchi's *Sefer ha-shorashim*);[24] and Johann Reuchlin's *De rudimentis hebraicis* (1509).

The appetite for these books among Christian scholars was fueled, initially, by the philological and theological preoccupations of what has been called the proto-reformation—the particular brand of humanism popularized by Pico della Mirandola and Marsilio Ficino in Italy, and then creatively reinterpreted by Erasmus, Thomas More, Johann Reuchlin, Jacques Lefèvre d'Étaples, and others in Northern Europe. One essential feature of this program was its absorption in the search for a *prisca theologia,* an ancient, pristine theology underlying all of the great religious systems of the world: pagan, Jewish, and Christian.[25] The search for this elusive ur-religion led these humanists to the study of Kabbalah, the Jewish mystical tradition most famously epitomized in the *Zohar* (*Splendor,* a work traditionally attributed to the second-century sage Simon bar Yochai, but actually written in thirteenth-century Spain), and other compendia such as the sixth-century *Sefer Yetzirah* (Book of Formation).[26] For Ficino (1433–1499), who produced the first complete Latin translation of the Platonic dialogues, the Kabbalah took its place alongside the Greek Hermetic corpus as vital evidence for the proposition that God had revealed the true theology to a series of inspired ancients, including Moses, Pythagoras, Hermes Trismegistus, Plato, Zoroaster, and the Hebrew prophets.[27] His fellow Florentine Pico della Mirandola went considerably further. Pico (1464–1494), unlike Ficino, actively studied Hebrew with a succession of Jewish teachers, including Elijah del Megido, Johanan Alemanno, and Flavius Mithridates (Raimundus Moncada);[28] and he placed the Kabbalah at the center of his notoriously heterodox theological project in the *Conclusiones* of 1480.[29] For Pico, "if any language is primal and not contingent, many interpretations show clearly that it is Hebrew," and one who knows this primal language "deeply and by the roots" will "have a pattern and a rule for the complete discovery of anything that can be known."[30] This comment reveals not only the extent of Pico's mystical preoccupation with the Hebrew language, but also the considerable degree to which, for both Ficino and Pico, theology and philology went hand in hand. The *prisca theologia* would reveal itself only to those who had mastered the study of ancient languages. One could only get to the bottom of nature by getting to the bottom of texts.[31]

The members of the Erasmian circle were deeply influenced by both of these Italian thinkers. Some (such as John Colet) corresponded with

Ficino directly, and Thomas More prepared an English translation of Pico's biography, the *Life of John Picus* (1510).[32] Erasmus himself carried on the work of Ficino's Greek revival by composing the monumental *Novum Instrumentum* (1516), a thorough critical examination of the Vulgate New Testament based on the Greek original. But of all the Christian humanists, it was certainly the German Johann Reuchlin who most energetically took up the banner of Pico's Hebraism.[33] Reuchlin, who studied Hebrew with Jacob ben Yechiel Loans (the Holy Roman Emperor's Jewish physician), as well as with two other Jews (Ovadiah Sforno of Cesena and Elias Levita),[34] composed two important kabbalistic works, the *De verbo mirifico* (1494) and the *De arte cabalistica libri tres* (1517). He also produced (as we have seen) an important Hebrew grammar and lexicon, the *De rudimentis hebraicis* (1509)—which was based to a considerable extent on the grammatical works of David Kimchi—as well as a study of Hebrew orthography and pronunciation, the *De accentibus et orthographia linguae hebraicae* (1518). Reuchlin also famously intervened in the acrimonious dispute over whether the Talmud and other rabbinic texts should be condemned as heretical by Christian authorities.[35] Under the influence of Johann Pfefferkorn (himself a converted Jew) as well as the Dominicans of Cologne, Emperor Maximilian I gave orders in 1509 to have all books directed against Christianity confiscated and destroyed. In 1510, Reuchlin was summoned by the emperor to give his opinion concerning which rabbinic texts might contain calumnies against Christianity, and, in his reply, offered an elaborate defense of the Talmud and other rabbinica. The dispute in which he participated—which, in effect, had begun in the twelfth century when Peter the Venerable of Cluny (1094–1156) declared the Talmud "heretical"[36]—would continue in Catholic Europe until the Roman Inquisition ordered the Talmud publicly burnt in 1553.[37]

None of the Christian humanists just mentioned embraced the Reformation when it came. Erasmus deeply regretted the degree to which he might have prepared the way for it; More became a zealous persecutor of Lutheran heresy; and Reuchlin tried in vain to rescue his grandnephew, Philip Melanchthon, from Luther's influence. Yet it is undeniable that, after the rupture of 1517, the story of Christian Hebraism becomes a disproportionately Protestant story, unfolding for the most part in the great centers of learning in the United Provinces, Northern Germany, and England. This is not, of course, to deny that there were Catholic Hebraists of great distinction. One thinks, for example, of Gilbert Génébrard (1537–1597), Regius Professor of Hebrew in Paris, who translated Rashi and Ibn Ezra into Latin; Guillaume Postel (1510–1581), who did the same for the *Sefer Yetzirah* and sections of the *Zohar* (although he was hardly an orthodox Catholic);[38] the Spanish Erasmian Arias Montanus, who produced the Royal Polyglot Bible (1572) under the auspices of Philip II of Spain;[39] and, somewhat later, Père Richard Simon and his *Histoire Critique du Vieux Testament* (1678). Many more such examples could be offered.[40] Yet the constitutive link between Reformation and Hebraism is real and readily comprehensible, in part for the reasons sketched out by Amama in his oration. Luther's clarion call of *sola scriptura* made the study of the Bible a Christian duty and led Protestants back to the original texts of the Hebrew Bible and the New Testament to an unprecedented degree. The contrast with Catholic Europe became even more pronounced after the Council of Trent (1545–1563) decreed that the Vulgate Latin was the authoritative Bible, and that no Biblical scholarship based on the original Hebrew and Greek text was relevant from the point of view of Church dogma or practice—and it became positively glaring after Clement VIII authorized the Sisto-Clementine Index of 1596, which banned even those editions of the Talmud that had been purged of "calumnies against Christianity" by the censors.[41]

Relatedly, the general Protestant hostility to received exegetical tradition made possible a radical break with the conventional Catholic view that the Hebrew Bible should be regarded as a typological prefiguration of the Gospel. On this traditional account, the Pentateuch was not to be read primarily as an account of Israelite history, but rather as an allegorized prophecy of Jesus's birth, death, and resurrection; its laws were not to be studied as the regulations of an actual human community, but rather as vatic intimations of the Christian sacraments.[42] Having moved away from this paradigm, Protestant scholars were more likely to regard the Hebrew Bible as worthy of study on its own terms.[43] Nor is it a coincidence that the most vital center of Christian Hebraic scholarship in early-modern Europe was to be found in the Protestant United Provinces. Beginning with the settlement of the Portuguese Jews in the 1590s, the Dutch Republic played host to a thriving Jewish community and, as a result, afforded easy access to Hebrew instruction and printed versions of Hebraica.[44] Moreover, the seventeenth-century Dutch (like the Calvinists more generally and the English Puritans in particular) came to regard themselves during this period as the "New Israelites" and increasingly saw the events of their own time as reenactments of Biblical history. The dominance of this paradigm guaranteed that the study of Hebrew would find itself at the center of Dutch intellectual life.[45]

For these and other reasons, the late sixteenth and seventeenth centuries witnessed a truly remarkable burgeoning of Hebrew scholarship across Europe. Its extent is captured by the 1694 *Bibliotheca Latino-Hebraica*—compiled in Rome by Carlo Giuseppe Imbonati—which lists over 1,300 works authored by Christian Hebraists during the period.[46] The publishing boom was fueled by the emergence of great dynasties of Hebrew scholarship at the major Continental universities: Sebastian Münster and the two Buxtorfs in Basel, the Vossiuses at Leiden, the Carpzovs at Leipzig, and several others. Münster, who was known as "the German Ezra," taught Hebrew to John Calvin and produced a series of Hebraist works, including an annotated Latin translation of the Hebrew Bible (1534); a compendium of the Mosaic law, the *Catalogus omnium praeceptorum legis Mosaicae* (1533); and a Latin translation of the tenth-century chronicle *Yosippon*, mistakenly attributed to Josephus (1541).[47] After the founding of Leiden University, the Huguenot Joseph Justus Scaliger (1540–1609) was imported as a professor, and his deep Hebrew learning inspired a generation of scholars, including Daniel Heinsius, Hugo Grotius, and Peter Cunaeus.[48] Another influence on this group of budding Hebraists was Johannes Drusius, who served as a professor of Hebrew at Leiden until 1584 (at which time he moved to Franeker).[49] Drusius composed the *Annotationes in totum Jesu Christi Testamentum . . . [quo] consensus ostenditur synagogae Israelitae cum ecclesia Christiana* (1612), one of the first Biblical commentaries to make extensive use of rabbinica. After 1592, his work at Leiden was carried on by yet another Huguenot, Franciscus Junius (1545–1602), who produced an important Hebrew grammar, the *Grammatica linguae Hebraeae* (1590), among other works.

One of the finest pupils of this first generation of Hebraists was Constantijn L'Empereur, professor of Hebrew at Leiden from 1627 to 1646. L'Empereur composed a vital guide for the study of Talmud, the *Halicoth Olam sive clavis Talmudica* (1634), as well as Latin translations of two important Talmudic tractates, *Middot* (1630) and *Bava Kamma* (1637). He also patronized the efforts of Johannes Coccejus, who produced Latin translations of the tractates *Sanhedrin* and *Makkot* (1629); and his Leiden colleague, Dionysius Vossius, translated the chapters on idolatry *(Hilkhot 'Avodah Zarah)* from Maimonides's great law code, the *Mishneh Torah* (1641).[50] It is important to recall that Dionysius's father, Gerardus Johannes Vossius (who founded the eponymous dynasty of Hebraists at Leiden) had been close friends with perhaps the greatest Jewish scholar of the Dutch seventeenth century, Menasseh ben Israel. Through Vossius, Menasseh had been introduced to a wide range of Christian Hebraists, including Grotius,[51] L'Empereur, and Claude de Saumaise (Salmasius)—the last of whom would become the great antagonist of John Milton after the regicide in 1649. Menasseh's own scholarship—most notably the *Conciliator, sive de convenientia locorum S. Scripturae, quae pugnare inter se videntur* (1633), which mustered a wide range of rabbinic materials to the task of harmonizing seemingly contradictory passages of Scripture—greatly influenced this circle, and he clearly served as a valued conduit of instruction in more advanced Hebrew. It was also at roughly this time that Johannes Buxtorf the Elder and the Younger released their heroic *Lexicon Chaldaicum Talmudicum et Rabbinicum* (1639–1640), which, for the first time, opened the riches of the Talmud (particularly the heavily Aramaic Gemara) to the wider republic of letters.[52]

By the end of this period, the *Zohar*, the Aramaic targums, numerous midrashic works, and fifteen tractates of the Talmud had been translated into Latin (the first complete Latin translation of the Mishnah, by Willem Surenhuis, would not be published until 1698–1703),[53] along with the major works of Maimonides, David Kimchi, Abraham Ibn Ezra, Levi ben Gershom (Gersonides), Isaac Abravanel, Judah Halevi, and others. And although vernacular translations of rabbinic materials were uncommon in the seventeenth century, the converted Jew Phillipe d'Aquin published an Italian version of the Talmudic tractate *Pirkei Avot* (Ethics of the Fathers) in 1620.[54] This explosion in the quantity of available Hebraica affected virtually every aspect of European intellectual life—not least in the British Isles, where such eminences as Edward Lively, Henry Ainsworth, John Lightfoot, Edward Pococke, Thomas Coleman, John Spencer, and, of course, John Selden, produced works of Hebraic learning that matched (and sometimes surpassed) the high standards set by their Dutch and German predecessors. The Hebrew revival transformed European literature and criticism, medicine and science, theology and ecclesiology, and philosophy and law. But this study is concerned with one aspect of the phenomenon in particular: its intersection with political thought.

The Invention of the *Respublica Hebraeorum*

Protestants of the late sixteenth century certainly did not inaugurate the practice of drawing political lessons from the text of the Hebrew Bible. Europeans had been engaged in this enterprise for centuries before.[55] Yet, in the wake of the Reformation, it is undoubtedly the case that the European relationship to this crucial text changed dramatically. Readers began to see in the five books of Moses not just political wisdom, but a political constitution.[56] No longer regarding the Hebrew Bible as the Old Law—a shadowy intimation of the truth, which had been rendered null and void by the New Dispensation—they increasingly came to see it as a set of political laws that God himself had given to the Israelites as their civil sovereign. Moses was now to be understood as a *lawgiver*, as the founder of a *politeia* in the Greek sense.[57] The consequences of this reorientation were staggering, for if God himself had designed a commonwealth, then the aims of political science would have to be radically reconceived. Previous authors had sought guidance in political affairs from ancient philosophers or from the schoolhouse of human history; now, however, they would have to look elsewhere—to the perfect constitution designed by the omniscient God. It became the central ambition of political science to approximate, as closely as possible, the paradigm of what European authors began to call the *respublica Hebraeorum* (republic of the Hebrews): to compare it both to ancient and modern constitutional designs and thereby to see where the latter were deficient.

Yet, given the parameters of this mission, a deep problem remained. How was one to know and understand the political constitution sketched

out in the Hebrew Bible? The Biblical text itself gave notoriously frag-
mentary and inexact (not to say contradictory) details about its operation. Where could one turn for guidance? This fundamental question,
as we have seen, had been answered by the Christian Hebraists: to understand the Hebrew Bible, they insisted, one should consult the full
array of rabbinic sources that were now available to the Christian West.
One should turn to the Talmud and the midrash, to the targums and
the medieval law codes. It may be that these texts were written by dei-
cides who had fallen from God's grace (to be a Hebraist, we should recall, was rarely to be any kind of philo-semite), but as Henry Ainsworth
put it in his *Annotations upon the five bookes of Moses* (written c. 1611–
1622), one must consult "Hebrew doctors of the ancienter sort, and some
later of best esteeme for learning" if one wishes "to give light to the ordinances of Moses touching the externall practice of them in the commonwealth of Israel, which the Rabbines did record, and without whose
helpe, many of those legall rites (especially in Exodus and Leviticus) will
not easily be understood."[58] The Jews may be "for the most part blinde,"
but they understand their own commonwealth.[59]

Accordingly, we see in the late sixteenth century the birth of what
would become perhaps the most dominant genre of European political
writing over the next century: texts that set themselves the task of studying the *respublica Hebraeorum* in light of the vast continent of newly re-
covered rabbinic materials. Imbonati's *Bibliotheca Latino-Hebraica* lists
over 100 such volumes published before 1694—and his list is conservative.[60] Few of these treatises were composed by genuine Hebrew scholars; some, indeed, were written by men who knew no Hebrew at all. Yet,
because of the remarkable proliferation of rabbinic texts in Latin translation (and analyses of these texts by eminent Hebraists), access to the
views of the rabbis was not restricted to great linguists. This genre had
important antecedents before the 1570s—notably Jean Bodin's *Methodus
ad facilem historiarum cognitionem* (1566), which offered a brief over-
view of the "form and alterations of the government of the Hebrews"
(status et conversiones imperii Hebraeorum)[61]—but the first full-length
treatment of the subject was the *De politia judaica tam civili quam ecclesiastica* (1574), authored by the Calvinist Bonaventure Cornelius Bertram. Bertram, who was professor of Hebrew at Geneva from 1566 to

1584, dedicated his treatise to Theodore Beza, Calvin's loyal lieutenant and successor. Bertram's contributions to Hebrew scholarship were quite extensive: the year 1574 also saw the release of his comparative grammar of Hebrew and Aramaic,[62] as well as his commentary on the Book of Job. A decade later he would collaborate with Beza on the first Protestant translation of the Bible into French, published in 1588,[63] and produce a harmonizing account of difficult or contradictory Biblical passages.[64] His treatise on the *respublica Hebraeorum* makes use of numerous rabbinic authorities, including Maimonides, Rashi, and Ibn Ezra, and he depicts the Mosaic commonwealth as a "mixed constitution," in the spirit of Polybius's analysis of the Roman republic.[65] Good Calvinist that he was, he also sharply distinguished between the *politia civilis* (or civil constitution) of ancient Israel and its *politia ecclesiastica* (or religious constitution). It was presumably for this reason that the impeccably orthodox Constantijn L'Empereur chose to release a new, annotated edition of Bertram's text in 1641.[66]

The next contribution to the genre came from a very different source, the Italian antiquarian Carlo Sigonio (1523–1584). Born in Modena, Sigonio made a career of studying the legal systems and constitutions of the ancient republics, first Rome, then Athens, and finally the most authoritative of all: Israel.[67] His *De republica Hebraeorum libri VII* was published in 1582, two years before his death.[68] It is difficult to overstate the contrast between this text and Bertram's. Whereas Bertram was, as we have seen, a trained Hebraist, Sigonio readily confessed that he knew no Hebrew. And while Bertram dedicated his labors to Beza, Sigonio addressed his own to Pope Gregory XIII—this despite, or perhaps because of, the fact that Sigonio had been a target of the Roman curia for over two decades (his gravest offense had been to agree with Lorenzo Valla that the "Donation of Constantine" was a forgery).[69] Yet, despite Sigonio's lack of Hebrew learning and his Catholicism,[70] the *De republica Hebraeorum* was deeply influential in Protestant Europe: it was reprinted in 1583, 1585, 1608, and 1609 at the Wechel Press and also in Cologne (1583), Speyer (1584), Middelburg (1678), and Leiden (1701).[71] And it would be a mistake to suppose that Sigonio's labors should be bracketed in any history of Christian Hebraism simply because he himself did not know Hebrew. Although he based a great deal of his exposition on Greek Jewish sources (chiefly Josephus and Philo), his reconstruction of the Jewish calendar in Book IV depended on the second-century Hebrew chronicle *Seder 'Olam* (traditionally attributed to Yose ben Halafta), which had been published in Mantua in 1514 and then translated into Latin by Gilbert Génébrard in 1577. In addition, his discussion of Jewish jurisprudence relied on the Talmudic passages excerpted in Petrus Galatinus's *De arcanis catholicae veritatis* (1518) (which, as we have seen, was heavily indebted to Martini's *Pugio fidei*).[72] Again, by the late sixteenth century, even scholars without any direct knowledge of Hebrew had extensive access to Hebraica.

After the release of the treatises by Bertram and Sigonio, the floodgates opened. Franciscus Junius, whom we have already met as a noted professor of Hebrew at Leiden, published his *De politiae Mosis observatione* in 1593; Wilhelm Zepper, Calvinist professor of theology at Herborn, released the *Legum Mosicarum forensium explanatio* in 1604; the Lutheran jurist Joachim Stephani produced his *De iurisdictione Judaeorum, Graecorum, Romanorum et Ecclesiasticorum libri IV* in the same year;[73] and sometime during the same decade, the young Hugo Grotius composed the manuscript treatise *De republica emendanda,* in which he put forward the Hebrew republic as the undoubted expression of God's own constitutional preferences.[74] This early text, although unpublished in Grotius's lifetime, laid the foundation for his extensive use of the Hebrew example (and a wide array of rabbinic materials) in his subsequent works of political theory, ecclesiology, and theology. However, the most important contribution to the genre in the period after Sigonio was undoubtedly the *De republica Hebraeorum libri III,* authored by the Dutch Remonstrant Peter van der Cun (Cunaeus) in 1617.[75] Cunaeus had been a student of Scaliger and was sent to Franeker to study Hebrew and rabbinics with Drusius.[76] A significant moment in his intellectual formation came in (or shortly before) 1615, when his friend Johannes Boreel presented him with the 1574 Venice edition of Maimonides's *Mishneh Torah.*[77] This text—which, unlike the *Guide,* had not been widely known to Christians before the seventeenth century—would organize Cunaeus's reconstruction of the Hebrew republic. From Maimonides, Cunaeus would draw the two fundamental theses of his treatise, each of them deeply significant: that God had established an agrarian law for ancient Israel, and that he had given plenary power over both civil and religious affairs to the civil magistrate. We shall have a great deal to say about each of these claims in due course.

After Cunaeus, the next noteworthy chapter in the history of the *respublica Hebraeorum* was written by the German Hebraist Wilhelm Schickard (1592–1635). Born in Herrenberg, the Lutheran Schickard studied oriental languages and theology at Tübingen and was appointed professor of Hebrew at his home university in 1619 (he served in that post until his untimely death from plague in 1635). He was also, it should be said, professor of astronomy at Tübingen beginning in 1631, and his scientific achievements were even more impressive than his philological ones: among other things, he has a plausible claim to being the inventor of the computer.[78] In 1625, he published a short book, *Mishpat ha-melekh, Jus regium Hebraeorum.*[79] This text (to which he gave a Hebrew title), unlike the contributions of Bertram, Sigonio, and Cunaeus, does not attempt to sketch the constitution of the Hebrew republic in the round. Its aim, as Schickard explained, was to establish the rights and prerogatives of Hebrew kingship by canvassing all of the important discussions of the subject in rabbinic literature. Accordingly, Schickard provided both Hebrew texts and Latin translations of a wide variety of rabbinic comments on monarchy—as well as an important digest of rabbinic texts that dispute the value of kingship. This treatise was remarkably influential throughout the Protestant world and made crucial statements of rabbinic political thought available to European readers who knew little or no Hebrew.

Turning now to the British Isles, we find the *respublica Hebraeorum* genre gaining momentum in the late 1620s.[80] In 1625, Thomas Godwyn, a schoolmaster and fellow of Pembroke College, Oxford, released one of the first vernacular contributions to the genre, his *Moses and Aaron: Civil and ecclesiastical rites Used by the Ancient Hebrews.* Godwyn was a competent Hebraist, and his text cites a wide range of rabbinic authorities, including the Talmud, the *Zohar*, Rashi, and Maimonides. In 1632, the Scottish Hebraist John Weemes added his *Explication of the iudiciall lawes of Moses*, followed several years later by *An exposition of the ceremoniall lawes of Moses* (1636). These texts were similarly festooned with references to rabbinic materials (Kimchi, Maimonides, and the

Targum were particular favorites of Weemes). Without question, however, the most significant seventeenth-century English works on the Hebrew republic were composed by John Selden (1584–1654). Selden, a lawyer and parliamentarian, was justly regarded as the greatest Hebraist of the age, and he published an extensive series of texts dealing with the *respublica Hebraeorum* and rabbinics more generally.[81] The series began in 1618 with his *History of Tithes* and continued with the *De successionibus in bona defuncti secundum leges Ebraeorum* (1631), a study of rabbinic inheritance law; the *De successione in pontificatum Ebraeorum* (1631), his analysis of the Israelite priesthood; the *Dissertatio de anno civili et calendario reipublicae Judaicae* (1644), a study of the Hebrew republic's calendar; and the *Uxor Hebraica,* his examination of rabbinic divorce law. This group of works—in which we find Selden taking positions on several of the most pressing political and ecclesiological questions facing England during the Personal Rule and the Civil War—culminated in the massive *De synedriis et prefecturis juridicis veterum Ebraeorum* (1650–1655), his elaborate case for the civil and religious supremacy of the Sanhedrin in the *respublica Hebraeorum.*

Selden's labors provoked an outpouring of literature on the Hebrew republic, including everything from formal treatises to brief pamphlets—such as an anonymous salvo of 1652 demanding that the English government should be "established, as the Commonwealth of Israel was in Mose's [*sic*] time."[82] His texts also provided those of his countrymen who did not know much Hebrew with a ready compendium of rabbinic materials, which they could easily study in Latin and quote in their own interventions. Two of Selden's acolytes deserve special attention, particularly because their works are rarely included in lists of texts on the *respublica Hebraeorum.* The first is the English republican James Harrington (1611–1677). Harrington, who readily confessed that he knew barely any Hebrew, was deeply influenced by the rabbinic sources he was able to study through the works of Grotius and Selden.[83] The second book of his *Art of Lawgiving* (1659) is entitled "The *Commonwealth of the Hebrews* As namely *Elohim* or the *Commonwealth of Israel* and *Cabala* or the *Commonwealth of the Jews*" and unambiguously represents his contribution to the *respublica Hebraeorum* genre. Selden's second important acolyte was Thomas Hobbes (1588–1679), who knew even less

Hebrew than Harrington. Nonetheless, Part III of *Leviathan,* which Hobbes called "Of a Christian Common-wealth," constitutes, as we shall see, his own extremely significant meditation on the Hebrew republic. Hobbes's approach to this paradigmatic constitution would, in turn, deeply influence what is perhaps the most famous seventeenth-century text on the *respublica Hebraeorum*—and the only one to have been written by a Jew—Baruch Spinoza's *Tractatus theologico-politicus* (1670).[84]

This brief tour of the genre makes clear, I hope, both its scope and its variety. Early-modern studies of the Hebrew republic were written by authors from different countries, different confessional backgrounds, and different political perspectives. Indeed, I have perhaps disguised the full extent of this diversity by opting to include in my summary only texts that are explicitly organized around an analysis of the Israelite constitution. Drawing the boundaries in this way leaves out a wide range of works that make serious and sustained political use of rabbinic materials, but do not take the *respublica Hebraeorum* for their primary subject. We shall be encountering many such texts, including Selden's own *De jure naturali et gentium iuxta disciplinam Ebraeorum* (1640); Salmasius's *Defensio regia* (1649); and a series of works by John Milton, including the *Pro populo Anglicano defensio* (1651), *The Readie and Easie Way to Establish a Free Common-Wealth* (1660), and, as I will argue, *Paradise Lost* itself. Taken together, these texts radically transformed European political thought and pushed it forcefully toward what we call *modernity.* That is the story I now want to tell.

CHAPTER 1

"Talmudical Commonwealthsmen" and the Rise of Republican Exclusivism

THE DEVELOPMENT OF republican political theory in the West presents something of a puzzle. In late Medieval and Renaissance Europe, republicanism was always a *relative* position. That is, it was characterized by the claim that republics are *better* than monarchies. Republicans could, of course, disagree sharply among themselves as to whether republics were always better, how much better they were, and why exactly they were better. But none had any interest in arguing that republics were the only legitimate or acceptable regimes. Even the most strident republican text of the period, Leonardo Bruni's oration in praise of Nanni Strozzi (1428), concedes that monarchy is "lawful" *(legitimus),* one of the "correct" constitutions identified by Aristotle in Book III of the *Politics.*[1] This commitment reflects the fundamental pluralism and modesty of the humanist persuasion; it follows from a deep skepticism concerning the ability of any principle to take sufficient account of all possible circumstances and situations, and from the conviction that there are always good arguments on both sides of any important question.[2] By the end of the seventeenth century, however, we see for the first time the appearance of what we might call republican *exclusivism,* the claim that republics are the only legitimate regimes. This transformation is largely responsible for the shape of political life and thought in the modern world, so we have good reason to ask why it took place. Our question quickly turns into a puzzle, however, once we recognize that the most obvious traditions of thought to which we might initially turn for an answer simply cannot provide one. There is nothing in the surviving sources from Greek or Roman antiquity that defends such a view (early-modern authors were quite aware of this fact),[3] nor is it explained by anything in the "social contract" tradition passing from Grotius through Pufendorf and Locke. Indeed, authors in what became known as the "modern school" of natural right were at pains to insist that there is nothing in the contractarian position that precludes monarchical government—most were, after all, monarchists of some stripe. So where should we look for the origins of republican exclusivism?

A valuable clue is to be found in a most improbable place: chapter 35 of Hobbes's *Leviathan* (1651), entitled "Of the Signification of the Kingdom of God." Hobbes's aim in this chapter is to refute the suggestion that the phrase "the kingdom of God" refers to a spiritual realm to which we are dispatched "after this life." His motivation is straightforward. As he had already explained in chapter 29, if belief in such a spiritual kingdom "moveth the Members of a Common-wealth, by the terrour of punishments, and hope of rewards" to disobey the orders of their civil sovereign, the state will be thrust "into the Fire of a Civill warre."[4] Hobbes therefore attempts to show that the phrase "kingdom of God" refers in the Bible, not to the world to come, but rather to the ancient commonwealth of the Hebrews, "wherein God was king."[5] He defends this claim with a three-paragraph discussion of a famous passage in I Samuel, chapter 8: "when the Elders of Israel . . . demanded a King, Samuel displeased therewith, prayed unto the Lord; and the Lord answering said unto him, *Hearken unto the voice of the People, for they have not rejected thee, but they have rejected me, that I should not reign over them.* Out of which it is evident that God himself was then their King."[6] Later, Hobbes adds that the prophets foretold the restoration of God's kingdom. He characterizes God's promise as follows: "I will reign over you, and make you to stand to that Covenant which you made with me by Moses, and brake in your rebellion against me in the days of Samuel, and in your election of another King." In short, Hobbes defends his claim that "the kingdom of God" refers to God's civil sovereignty over Israel by reading

I Sam. 8:7 to mean that, when the Israelites asked for a mortal king, they were in fact deposing God as their temporal ruler.

Two striking facts about this passage explain why it ought to be regarded as an important clue for our purposes. The first is the hostility with which it was greeted by Hobbes's contemporaries. Indeed, there are few passages in *Leviathan* that received as much direct criticism as this one in the first two decades of the book's reception. Robert Filmer, for example, attacked Hobbes by name on precisely this point in his 1652 *Observations Concerning the Originall of Government:* "I do not find," he observed, "that the desiring of a king was a breach of their contract or covenant, or disobedience to the voice of God. There is no such law extant."[7] Clarendon was even more insistent in his review of the English *Leviathan:* "We are not oblig'd," he wrote, "nor indeed have any reason to believe, that God was offended with the Children of Israel for desiring a King, which was a Government himself had instituted over them."[8] Hobbes's analysis had clearly touched a nerve. The second striking fact is that, when Hobbes translated *Leviathan* into Latin over a decade later (for inclusion in his 1668 *Opera philosophica quae latine scripsit omnia*), he excised this entire discussion.[9] It might initially seem as if the first fact is a sufficient explanation of the second: Hobbes responded to his critics by removing the offending passage. There is presumably an element of truth in this, but it is important to recall that Clarendon's *Brief View* was not published until 1676, and although Hobbes was certainly familiar with Filmer's polemic, this is, so far as I can tell, the only instance in which he actually removed an argument that offended his patriarchal antagonist.

My suggestion is that Hobbes's decision to strike this passage from the Latin *Leviathan* is not so much a capitulation to Filmer as it is an alarmed response to what had become of republican political theory in the 1650s. During that period, republican pamphleteers in England had taken the exclusivist turn and, on their own account, had been convinced to do so by a particular reading of the very same Biblical verses that Hobbes used to make his case in chapter 35. On this reading, God's rebuke in I Sam. 8:7 should be taken to mean that human kingship is inherently a usurpation of the kingdom of God, and that monarchy is therefore an instance of the sin of idolatry. This of course was not Hobbes's position—on his account, the civil kingship of God was unique to Israel, and so asking for a mortal king was only a sin in this one instance[10]—but, given the political circumstances of the Restoration, he evidently felt that it was too close for comfort.[11] The view from which Hobbes wished to distance himself was unprecedented in Christian Biblical criticism before the mid-seventeenth century (indeed, Hobbes's own less radical reading was itself exceedingly rare before 1600). It turned its back on every standard authority from Augustine to Aquinas, from the *glossa ordinaria* to Luther and Calvin. It was not contemplated by even the most militant resistance theorists of the late sixteenth century. The reason is simple: the reading in question derives from a tradition of rabbinic commentary on Deuteronomy and I Samuel that became available to the Christian West only during the Hebrew revival of the late sixteenth and early seventeenth centuries. The English pamphleteers who took up this position were very much aware of its provenance and enthusiastically endorsed what one of them called the tradition of the "Talmudical commonwealthsmen." In doing so, they transformed the politics of the modern world.

I

The Biblical account of monarchy had always been of immense interest to Christian exegetes, and all agreed that the challenge was to make sense of the relationship between two specific passages from the Hebrew Bible: Deuteronomy 17 and I Samuel 8. The central section of the Deuteronomy passage contains a set of instructions given by God to the Israelites; it reads as follows in the King James version:

> When thou art come unto the land which the LORD thy God giveth thee, and shalt possess it, and shalt dwell therein, and shalt say, I will set a king over me, like as all the nations that are about me; *15:* Thou shalt in any wise set him king over thee, whom the LORD thy God shall choose: one from among thy brethren shalt thou set king over thee: thou mayest not set a stranger over thee, which is not thy brother. *16:* But he shall not multiply horses to himself, nor cause the people to return to Egypt, to the end that he should multiply horses: forasmuch as the LORD hath said unto you, Ye shall henceforth re-

turn no more that way. *17:* Neither shall he multiply wives to him-self, that his heart turn not away: neither shall he greatly multiply to himself silver and gold. (Deut. 17:14–17)

The passage from I Samuel 8 stages the moment anticipated in Deuteronomy:

> Then all the elders of Israel gathered themselves together, and came to Samuel unto Ramah, *5:* And said unto him, Behold, thou art old, and thy sons walk not in thy ways: now make us a king to judge us like all the nations. *6:* But the thing displeased Samuel, when they said, Give us a king to judge us. And Samuel prayed unto the LORD. *7:* And the LORD said unto Samuel, Hearken unto the voice of the people in all that they say unto thee: for they have not rejected thee, but they have rejected me, that I should not reign over them. *8:* According to all the works which they have done since the day that I brought them up out of Egypt even unto this day, wherewith they have forsaken me, and served other gods, so do they also unto thee. *9:* Now therefore hearken unto their voice: howbeit yet protest solemnly unto them, and shew them the manner of the king that shall reign over them. (I Sam. 8:4–9)

Samuel then proceeds to tell the Israelites all of the terrible things that kings will do to them.

> This will be the manner of the king that shall reign over you: He will take your sons, and appoint them for himself, for his chariots, and to be his horsemen; and some shall run before his chariots. *12:* And he will appoint him captains over thousands, and captains over fifties; and will set them to ear his ground, and to reap his harvest, and to make his instruments of war, and instruments of his chariots. *13:* And he will take your daughters to be confectionaries, and to be cooks, and to be bakers. *14:* And he will take your fields, and your vineyards, and your oliveyards, even the best of them, and give them to his servants. *15:* And he will take the tenth of your seed, and of your vineyards, and give to his officers, and to his servants. *16:* And

he will take your menservants, and your maidservants, and your
goodliest young men, and your asses, and put them to his work. *17:*
He will take the tenth of your sheep: and ye shall be his servants. *18:*
And ye shall cry out in that day because of your king which ye shall
have chosen you; and the LORD will not hear you in that day.

The challenge for interpreters was to reconcile God's apparent acceptance
of kingly rule at Deut. 17:14 with his evident anger when the Israelites request a king in I Sam. 8.[12] Medieval and Renaissance exegetes tended to
pursue one of two strategies of harmonization. The first was to suggest
that the Israelites sinned in selecting kings who did not meet the criteria
established by God in the Deuteronomy passage. That is, the kings they
wished to institute over them were avaricious and tyrannical, quite unlike
the virtuous monarchs described in God's instructions. An influential
statement of this view is found in the *glossa ordinaria,* the standard Biblical commentary compiled in the twelfth century.[13] It reasons as follows at
Deut. 17:14: "It might be asked why the people displeased God when they
desired a king [in I Sam, 8], since here we find it permitted? But it should
be understood that it was certainly not according to God's will, because he
did not command that this should be done, but rather permitted it to the
people who desired it."[14] And why in particular was God angry? Because
"the inhabitants of the land constituted a king over themselves in a manner
contrary to God's instructions"—namely, kings who, like Solomon, took
numerous wives and concubines.[15] Another notable proponent of this
reading is John of Salisbury, who argues in the *Policraticus* (1159) that the
Israelites abandoned rule by "the authority of the law" when they asked
for kings with tyrannical powers.[16] Aquinas likewise appears to follow this
approach in the *De regimine principum,*[17] as does Erasmus in the *Institu-
tio principis christiani* (1516).[18]

The second strategy of reconciliation was to argue in a Pauline vein
that, in asking for a change of government, the Israelites committed the sin
of rebellion against God's established order.[19] All kings rule by divine appointment, and insurrection against them accordingly constitutes a rejection of God's sovereignty. This reading was particularly popular among
sixteenth-century Protestants.[20] It is, for example, Calvin's position in the
Institutes: those who preach disobedience and rebellion "do not reject

magistrates, but they reject God, 'that he should not reign over them' [I Sam. 8:7]. For if this was truly asserted by the Lord respecting the people of Israel, because they refused the government of Samuel, why shall it not now be affirmed with equal truth of those who take the liberty to outrage all the authorities which God has instituted?"[21] This Pauline account was not, however, limited to Protestants. Jean Bodin endorsed it strongly in his *Six livres de la république* (1576). "There is nothing greater on earth, after God," he argues, "than sovereign princes. . . . Contempt for one's sovereign prince is contempt toward God, of whom he is the earthly image. That is why God, speaking to Samuel, from whom the people had demanded a different prince, said 'It is me that they have wronged.'"[22] Neither this reading nor its counterpart suggested that kingship itself was the cause of God's displeasure.

One would, of course, expect to find such conservative readings in overtly monarchist works such as Bodin's. What is extraordinary is that even the most radical republican authors and resistance theorists writing before the seventeenth century tended to understand these passages in one of the two conventional ways and, even if they deviated from those readings, never understood I Sam. 8 to involve a critique of monarchy per se. Consider, for example, Ptolemy of Lucca, whose completion of Aquinas's *De regimine principum* is widely considered to be the most radical scholastic endorsement of republican politics. He is certainly willing to argue that kingship was "less fruitful" for the Israelites, which for him explains why Samuel went to such lengths to dissuade them from pursuing their request. But his gloss on the relevant section of I Sam. 8 is the following:

> Kings and rulers stand in the place of God on earth, and it is through them, as secondary causes, that God exercises governance over the world. Hence, when the Israelite people spurned the prophet Samuel's lordship and he laid his complaint before God, he received the response that they had not spurned him but God, in whose place he stood. As it is said in Proverbs: "Through me kings reign and those who institute laws decree what is just."[23]

This is the Pauline argument. For Ptolemy, God has been rejected in this passage only insofar as his royal designee, Samuel, has been rejected.

The sin of the Israelites was in asking for a *different* king from the one God had established among them.[24] Kingship remains a fully lawful form of government, instituted by God himself among the nations.

An even more instructive example is that provided by the Calvinist resistance theorist Theodore Beza in his *De iure magistratum* (1574). By the time Beza was writing, radicals had begun to read Deut. 17:14 and I Sam. 8 through the prism of a famous comment by the Jewish historian Josephus, taken from his attack on the Egyptian Apion:

> Some peoples have entrusted the supreme political power to monarchies, others to oligarchies, yet others to the masses. Our lawgiver, however, was attracted by none of these forms of polity, but gave to his constitution the form of what—if a forced expression be permitted—may be termed a "theocracy," placing all sovereignty and authority in the hands of God. To Him he persuaded all to look, as the author of all blessings, both those which are common to all mankind, and those which they had won for themselves by prayer in the crises of their history.[25]

This view of the ancient Hebrew commonwealth made it possible for Josephus to understand God's rejection in I Sam. 8 in the following terms: "they [the Israelites] deposed God from his kingly office."[26] God, not Samuel, had been king in Israel before the insurrection of I Sam. 8, and in asking for a mortal king, the Israelites had rebelled against God's sovereignty. This was indeed a radical reading, and was understood to be: it argued that kingship *itself* was inconsistent with God's plan for his chosen nation. It provided the foundation for the reading we encountered earlier in the English *Leviathan*. But—and this is the crucial point—it continued to treat Israel as a special case.[27] It had been a sin for the Israelites to ask for a king because they found themselves in the unique position of having God as their civil sovereign. It is this view, and nothing more sweeping, that we find in Beza:

> What raised [Israel] up above the very skies was that at its beginning the Eternal himself was its monarch, and not only in the sense that He is the sovereign Lord of all things, but in the more specific

sense as well, in that He visibly gave the Law through Moses, then brought the people to the promised land through Joshua, and, finally, governed through the judges whom He alone had chosen. In this period, Israel's government was truly a monarchy (although God made use of men as he saw fit). And if all kingdoms could be governed by this Monarch, or if kings would always be governed by Him who is sovereign of all the world, our present inquiry would be as superfluous as now it is necessary. But that happy government, which was given to no other people, was changed in a curious way. For whereas other monarchies change into tyrannies through the misdeed of the monarch, the Israelites, not appreciating their good fortune, constrained, so to speak, their true Monarch, who can never be a tyrant, to let them have a human king like other peoples. This was finally granted to them by the Lord, but granted in His wrath and anger, which was not because the monarchical state is of itself condemned by God, but because the people had insisted on a change.[28]

Even for Beza, monarchy itself is not at all unacceptable, and his fellow resistance theorists (including the author of the 1579 *Vindiciae, contra tyrannos)*[29] followed his lead.[30]

II

The European discovery of rabbinic sources dramatically reorganized this debate. To begin with, the central discussion of monarchy in the Talmud (BT Sanhedrin 20b)—also based on Deut. 17:14 and I Sam. 8—offered a powerful new perspective on the monarchist position. The point of entry for this Talmudic analysis is the question of whether the catalogue of frightening royal behaviors listed by Samuel in I Sam. 8:9–18 (which the rabbis referred to as the "section on the king," *parashat ha-melekh*) simply anticipates kingly abuses or actually establishes royal prerogatives. This question became particularly urgent in light of a rabbinic gloss on Deut. 17:14 ("When thou art come unto the land which the LORD thy God giveth thee . . . and shalt say, I will set a king over me, like as all the nations that are about me"). At issue is the phrase "and shalt say" *(ve-amarta)*. Although the syntax of the Hebrew sentence makes clear that this is purely descriptive, several rabbis pointed out that the same form of the verb could express the imperative.[31] That is, instead of "you will say" (or, better, "if you say") they chose to read "you shall say." As a result, these rabbis were prepared to argue that Deut. 17 did not simply offer a prophecy of what would happen when the Israelites entered the land (as both conventional Christian readings had assumed),[32] but rather expressed a positive commandment to establish monarchy. On this latter reading, the Israelites were actually *obliged* to ask for a king. The relevance of this new gloss for the controversy over I Sam. 8:11–18 is clear enough: one who believes that kingship is in fact commanded by God will tend not to believe that God meant for kings to behave tyrannically.[33] But it was also deeply relevant to the debate over the Israelite sin in I Sam. 8:4–7. If God had actually commanded the Israelites to ask for a king, then why did he become angry when they obeyed him? The Talmudic debate proceeds as follows:

> Rav Yehudah said, citing Shmu'el: All items mentioned in the section about the king are the king's prerogatives. Rav said: The section about the king was only pronounced in order to scare them.
>
> This [dispute] corresponds to a tannaitic dispute [i.e., a debate among certain "tannaim," rabbis of the Mishnah (c. 70–200 CE)]:[34]
>
> Rabbi Yose says: All items mentioned in the section about the king are the king's prerogatives. Rabbi Yehudah[35] says: The section was only pronounced in order to scare them.
>
> Rabbi Yehudah also used to say: There were three commandments that Israel were obligated to fulfill once they had entered the land: appointing a king, exterminating the offspring of Amalek, and building the temple.
>
> Rabbi Nehorai says: The section was only pronounced in response to their complaints, as written, "And you shall say, I will set a king over me, as do all the nations about me" (Deut. 17:14).
>
> Rabbi Eleazar b. Tzadok says: The wise men of that generation made a proper request, as written: "[All the elders of Israel assembled and came to Samuel . . . and they said to him,] . . . 'Appoint a king for us, to govern us' " (I. Sam 8:4–5). But the common people

['*ammei ha-'aretz*] amongst them spoke wrongly, as written, "that we may be like all the other nations" (I Sam. 8:19–20).[36]

The crucial position here is that of Rabbi Yehudah. He argues explicitly that Deut. 17:14 is a commandment and classes it with the commandments to take revenge on the Amalekites and to build the Temple. As a result, he also concludes that the *parashat ha-melekh* did not enumerate legitimate royal powers (God would never have enjoined tyranny), but had simply been designed to scare the Israelites. But if that is the case, then why is God angry, and why do the Israelites need to be scared in the first place? Rabbi Eleazar ben Tzadok provides the answer. The Israelites were indeed obliged to ask for a king, but they sinned in asking for a king "like all the other nations." There were, on Eleazar's account, actually *two* requests for a king in I Samuel: the first, by the wise elders *(zekenim)*, was appropriate because it emphasized the need for law and order, while the second, by the mob, was sinful because its aim was to imitate the surrounding idolatrous nations. The "section on the king" describes what having a king "like all the other nations" would look like; its aim is to dissuade the mob from pursuing a ruinous course. This view was taken up by the most important Medieval Jewish exegetes and therefore became a powerful orthodoxy in the European rabbinic tradition.

Christian commentators were quick to seize on these arguments as soon as they entered wide circulation during the second half of the sixteenth century. Indeed, perhaps more than any other source, the Talmud came to organize debates between Christian exegetes on the question of Biblical monarchy. The German scholar and Hebraist Sebastian Münster—who taught Hebrew to John Calvin—is representative. He simply reproduces the rabbinic discussion in his gloss on Deut. 17:14:

> The Hebrews observed that there were three commandments for the Israelites when they were going to enter the promised land, namely to constitute a king over them, to wipe out the seed of Amalek, and to build a Temple for the Lord. The Hebrews also pose this question, "Why did the Lord react with anger because they asked for a king in the time of Samuel, when in this place he either commands, or creates a right to constitute one?" Some respond to this

that the elders who lived at this time did not ask for a king wickedly and impiously when they said to Samuel "Give us a king who can judge us, etc.," but rather the mob sinned, because they did not wish to listen to the voice of Samuel, but said, "By no means; but let there be a king over us, so that we may be like the other nations."[37]

Claude de Saumaise (Salmasius), Milton's famous antagonist, likewise assigns great importance in his *Defensio regia* (1649) to the fact that "the rabbis of the Jews teach that there were three obligations for the Israelites which it was necessary for them fulfill after they were brought to the Holy Land, to constitute a king over themselves, to eliminate the Amalekites, and to build the Temple."[38] Salmasius continues by noting that "many of them [the rabbis] write that the elders of that time [i.e., the time of I Sam. 8] rightly and properly asked for a king, but the mob sinned in this, because they asked that he be given to them in the form of the kings which the other nations had."[39] Salmasius even quotes "Rabbi Jose in Gemara Sanhedrin" by name, to the effect that "that which is said in the section on the king is included in the rights of the king."[40]

There were, however, other Christian exegetes who endorsed the Talmudic reading of Deut. 17:14, but took their understanding of the Israelite sin, not from Rabbi Eleazar, but instead from a suggestion in Maimonides's *Mishneh Torah.* For Maimonides (who agreed that monarchy was a command), the problem was not the *sort* of king the Israelites asked for in I Sam. 8, but rather the *manner* in which they asked for one. The Dutch Hebraist Peter Cunaeus quotes him directly on this subject in the *De republica Hebraeorum* (1617):

> Maimonides answers learnedly, that the divine Indignation [over the request for a king in I Sam. 8] arose from hence, Because they desir'd a King by unfaithfull complaints and seditious murmurings, not that they might comply with Gods design in the Law, but out of a distast of the most holy Prophet Samuel: to whom it was spoken by the voice of God, They have not rejected thee, but me.[41]

Cunaeus's teacher, the Dutch exegete Johannes van den Driesche (Drusius), who held professorships in Hebrew at Oxford, Leiden, and

Franeker, concurred in his commentary on I Sam. 8: "Why then did this request [for a king] displease God? Because they petitioned him out of a wicked spirit, and not on account of the commandment [i.e., the presumed commandment in Deut. 17:14 to establish a king] . . . it was through murmuring, not so that [a king] might judge them, but so that he might fight their battles."[42] Another statement of this view is found in Edmund Bunny's *The Scepter of Iudah* (1584): it was necessary for the Israelites to ask for a king, "although on their parts it were very disorderly done."[43] Hugo Grotius puts it slightly differently, but in a similar vein. He accepts the Talmudic view that "the laws of the king, the temple, and the destruction of the Amalekites pertain to the time of possessing the Land,"[44] but his gloss on I Sam. 8:7 reads "at another time they could have erected a king for themselves without sin."[45] The problem was not asking for a king, but asking for one "during that time in which they had an interregnum established by God."[46]

The Talmud, then, exerted a powerful and radicalizing influence on numerous expositors of Biblical kingship, leading them to the conclusion that God had commanded, not simply permitted, monarchy in Israel. Indeed, these developments make sense of John Locke's claim in Chapter 8 of *The Second Treatise of Government* that Europeans "never dreamed of monarchy being *iure divino* . . . till it was revealed to us by the divinity of this last age."[47] Not until the proliferation of the Talmudic reading of Deut. 17:14 were Christian theologians prepared to argue that God requires monarchical government. But that is only half of the story. There was, after all, another important rabbinic discussion of Deut. 17:14 and I Sam. 8—one found, not in the Talmud, but in *Devarim Rabbah*, a compendium of classical Midrashim (rabbinic exegetical commentary) to Deuteronomy, most likely redacted at the end of the ninth century. This analysis took an entirely different view of Biblical monarchy. It appears as the gloss on Deut. 17:14 and is worth quoting at length.

> WHEN THOU ART COME UNTO THE LAND. . . . The Rabbis say: God said to Israel: "I planned that you should be free from kings." Whence this? As it is said, A wild ass used to the wilderness (Jer. 2:24): just as the wild ass grows up in the wilderness and has no fear of man, so too I planned that you should have no fear of kings;

but you did not desire so: "that snuffeth up the wind in her pleasure" (Jer. 2:24), and "wind" is nothing but kingship. Whence this? As it is said, And, behold, the four winds of the heaven broke forth upon the great sea (Dan. 7:2) [referring to Daniel's vision of the four world kingdoms]. God said: "Should you assert that I do not know that in the end you will forsake me, already long ago I have forewarned [you] through Moses, and said to him: 'Seeing that in the end they will ask for a mortal king, let them appoint one of their own as a king, not a foreigner.'" Whence this? From what we have read in the section, AND SHALT SAY: I WILL SET A KING OVER ME, etc. (Deut. 17:14).

. . . the Rabbis say: When kings arose over Israel and began to enslave them, God exclaimed: "Did you not forsake me and seek kings for yourselves?" Hence the force of, I WILL SET A KING OVER ME.

This bears out what Scripture says, Put not your trust in princes (Ps. 146:3). R. Simon said in the name of R. Joshua b. Levi: Whosoever puts his trust in the Holy One, blessed be He, is privileged to become like unto Him. Whence this? As it is said, Blessed is the man that trusteth in the Lord, and whose trust the Lord is (Jer. 17:7). But whosoever puts his trust in idolatry ['avodat kokhavim] condemns himself to become like [the idols]. Whence this? As it is written, They that make them shall be like unto them (Ps. 115:8). The Rabbis say: Whosoever puts his trust in flesh and blood passes away and his dignity[48] also passes away, as it is said, Nor in the son of man in whom there is no help (Ps. 146:3). What follows on this verse? His breath goeth forth, he returneth to his dust. God said: "Although they know that man is nought, yet they forsake my Glory and say: 'Set a king over us.' Why do they ask for a king? By your life, in the end you will learn to your cost what you will have to suffer from your king." Whence this? As it is written, All their kings are fallen, there is none among them that calleth unto Me (Hos. 7:7) . . .

Another comment on, I WILL SET A KING OVER ME. The Rabbis say: The Holy One, blessed be He, said, "In this world you asked for kings, and kings arose in Israel and caused you to fall by the sword." Saul caused them to fall on Mount Gilboa. Whence this? And the men of Israel fled from before the Philistines (I Sam. 31:1). David brought about a plague, as it is said, So the Lord sent a pestilence upon Israel (II Sam. 24:15). Ahab was the cause of the withholding of rain from them, as it is said, There shall not be dew nor rain these years, etc. (I Kings 17:1). Zedekiah was the cause of the destruction of the Temple. When Israel saw what befell them on account of their kings they all began to cry out: "We do not desire a king, we desire our first king [*malkenu ha-rishon*]," [as it is said], For the Lord is our Judge, the Lord is our Lawgiver, the Lord is our King; He will save us (Isa. 33:22). Whereupon God replied: "By your life, I will do so." Whence this? For it is said, And the Lord shall be king over all the earth, etc. (Zech. 14:9).[49]

On this view, monarchy itself is a sin; it is everywhere and always the act of bowing down to flesh and blood instead of God, and is therefore tantamount to idolatry.[50] Man inhaled the emptiness of monarchy like a desert mirage, worshipping kings in whom "there is no help," rather than the true, heavenly king, and his punishment has accordingly been great. It was this aspect of the rabbinic tradition that, in the hands of Christian exegetes, would transform republican political thought.

III

The first European political writer to make a straightforwardly exclusivist argument for republican government was John Milton. But, as many scholars have noted, Milton's attitude toward monarchy was by no means consistent over time.[51] When he published *The Tenure of Kings and Magistrates* in 1649, only weeks after the execution of Charles I, his brief was to defend the principle of resistance, not to dispute the legitimacy of monarchy.[52] Accordingly, he was happy to read Deut. 17:14 and I Sam. 8 in a relatively conventional manner, clearly indebted in the first instance to Josephus. God's remarks in Deuteronomy, he explains, were simply meant to underscore that

the right of choosing, yea of changing thir own Government is by the grant of God himself in the People. And therfore when they desir'd a King, though then under another form of government, and thir changing displeas'd him, yet he that was himself their King, and rejected by them, would not be a hindrance to what they intended, furder then by perswasion, but that they might doe therein as they saw good, 1 *Sam.* 8. onely he reserv'd to himself the nomination of who should reigne over them.[53]

The central issue for Milton is that the people choose their government, not God; if God is willing to allow even himself to be deposed, why not Charles I? There is no hint in this passage of an argument against kingship. God was "displeas'd" because the Israelites proposed to abandon their special relationship with him, not because kingship is inherently sinful. Indeed, Milton almost immediately softens his position yet further. "But som will say," he continues, "to both these examples [i.e., the deposition of Rehoboam and the earlier deposition of Samuel's sons], it was evilly don. I answer, that not the latter, because it was expressly allow'd them in the Law to set up a King if they pleas'd; and God himself joyn'd with them in the work; though in som sort it was at that time displeasing to him, in respect of old *Samuel* who had govern'd them uprightly."[54] Here Milton in effect moves from the more radical Josephan argument (according to which kingship itself is unacceptable for Israel, although acceptable for everyone else), back to a variant of the traditional argument. God was not angry at the Israelites because he did not want them to be governed by kings, but rather because they rebelled against Samuel. But that is not where Milton leaves matters in *Tenure.* Nearer the end of the text, he expresses his hope

> that as God was heretofore angry with the Jews who rejected him
> and his forme of Government to choose a King, so that he will bless
> us, and be propitious to us who reject a King to make him onely our
> leader and supreme governour in the conformity as neer as may be of
> his own ancient government.[55]

The crucial move here is Milton's suggestion that Israel is not a unique case. God, it now seems, can be enthroned as monarch in any commonwealth, and perhaps *must* be if, as Milton says, the kingdom of God is the "only just & rightful kingdom."[56] It is this revolutionary line of argument that Milton develops in the 1650s.

His most explicit discussion of this argument's provenance occurs in his great reply to Salmasius, the *Pro populo Anglicano defensio* of 1651. This text, however, is notoriously Janus-faced. On the one hand, Milton scrupulously reprises his primary argument from the *Tenure,* namely, that God gives all peoples the right to choose their form of government, and that monarchy, while inferior to a republican constitution, is a legitimate choice (here again, Milton faults Charles I for being a tyrant, not for being a monarch).[57] But only a few pages later, he begins to explore a very different argument. The context is his analysis of Salmasius's use of rabbinic arguments in favor of his monarchist position. Recall that Salmasius, in the *Defensio regia,* had quoted the Talmud to argue that God had given the Israelites a positive commandment to establish monarchy, and that he had intended the "section on the king" to catalog the legitimate powers of royal government.[58] Milton begins by addressing himself to the first argument. God did not order the Israelites to ask for a king, he insists, but on the contrary, "God was angry not only because they wanted a king in imitation of the gentiles, and not in accordance with his law, but clearly because they desired a king at all."[59] Here Milton explicitly rejects the Talmudic view and moves in a more radical direction. He then addresses the argument about kingly prerogatives, insisting that the *parashat ha-melekh* simply prophesied kingly abuses: "Such is the explanation of this passage by all the orthodox theologians and the jurisconsults, and as you might have learned from Sichardus, by many of the rabbis too, and no rabbi ever held that this passage treated of an absolute right of kings."[60]

This passage is interesting for two reasons. The first is the way in which Milton deals with the problem of Rabbi Yose, who had, after all, argued in the Talmud that the *parashat ha-melekh* enumerated legitimate powers. Milton tries to avoid the difficulty as follows: "It is obvious," he claims, "that the chapter about the king which Rabbi Jose spoke of as containing the rights of kings is in Deuteronomy and not in Samuel; and Rabbi Judas [i.e., Yehudah] declared quite correctly, contradicting you, that the passage in Samuel concerns only his putting fear into the people."[61] Milton argues, in short, that the "section on the king" Rabbi Yose had in mind was not the one in I Sam. 8, but rather the passage in Deuteronomy 17, where God lists the duties of an Israelite king. This is clearly false, but very clever.[62] The second point of interest is Milton's mention of "Sichardus." This is Wilhelm Schickard, the German Lutheran who became professor of Hebrew at the University of Tübingen in 1619. In 1625, he published the *Mishpat ha-melekh, Jus regium Hebraeorum,* his analysis of Biblical monarchy based on rabbinic materials. Milton knew this book well (he cites it in his Commonplace Book),[63] and he recognizes that Salmasius is getting all of his rabbinic references out of it. On the question of whether Israelite kings could be judged for their crimes, Milton writes "that Hebrew kings can be judged and even condemned to the lash is taught at length by Sichard from the rabbinical writings; and it is to him that you owe all this matter, though you are not ashamed to howl against him."[64] The reason this is so important is that it explains Milton's remarkable final verdict on Salmasius's reading of Deut. 17:14 and I Sam. 8:

> In order to show all that you have failed to prove in any way from the works of the Hebrews what you had undertaken to prove in this chapter, you freely admit that some of their rabbis deny that their fathers should have recognized any king but God, though such a king was given to punish them. I follow the opinion of these rabbis.[65]

These are the rabbis of the Midrash. Salmasius did indeed have to admit their existence, because Schickard had cataloged their opinions in his treatise, and anyone who read this influential work would have recognized Salmasius's omission. The question of Milton's direct access to the Midrashic account need not, therefore, depend on the notoriously vexed question of his level of reading fluency in rabbinic Hebrew.[66] The "opinion of these rabbis" had been translated into Latin in a text he knew intimately.

Schickard, like Salmasius, only mentions the Midrashic view in order to refute it, but in the course of doing so, he reproduces large sections of the discussion in *Devarim Rabbah.* He begins by endorsing the majority view in the Talmud: kingship was divinely ordained for Israel at

Deut. 17:14, and the Israelite sin in I. Sam. 8 was simply the act of asking for a king "like all the nations": "He [Samuel] did not upbraid the people because they asked for a King, but because they did not ask lawfully."[67] Before moving on, however, Schickard notes that "there is no lack among the Jews of those who contradict this position and believe that their fathers did not in the least require kings. Their reasons are diverse, and we will examine them carefully."[68] He begins by paraphrasing the view of Bahya ben Asher, a thirteenth-century kabbalist and exegete, whose commentary was deeply influenced by the Midrash:

> God the Master of the Universe was enough for them; nor did he grant them kings except as a punishment, perhaps just as Zeus gave the frogs a stork [as their ruler] in Aesop's fable. This is what he [Bahya] says in his commentary on *Parashat Shofetim* [Deut. 17:14]: "It was not the will of the most excellent and most great God that there should be any king in Israel apart from himself. For he is truly the highest king, who walks in the midst of their camp and carefully attends to all of their particular needs. Nor did they need any other king. For what would an elect nation whose king is the Lord of the Universe do with a king who is mere flesh and blood? . . . As it is written (Hos. 13.11), 'I give you a king in my anger.'"[69]

Schickard then adds an even more crucial passage, this time purporting to cite a figure he calls "Rabba B. Nachmoni,"[70] but, in actuality, quoting the Midrash verbatim:

> Rabba b. Nachmoni judges that this [institution of kingship] conflicts with the liberty of the Jewish people, whose condition should not involve being ruled by another, as cattle are ruled by a herdsman; but rather should let them wander free, like animals in the wild. . . . He says: "Thus said the Lord, Master of the Universe, to Israel, Oh my children! I meant for you to be free from masters. Whence this? Because it is said (Jerem. 2. v.24) 'A wild ass used to the wilderness.' Therefore just as a wild donkey who grows up in the wilderness is awed by no man above him, in the same way I intended that there should be no fear of kingship over you. But you did not

desire this. Rather (as comes next in the text) 'he sucked up the wind in the desire of his heart.' Nor is this 'wind' anything other than kingship. Whence this? Because it is said (Dan. 7.2), 'Behold the four heavenly winds broke forth on the great sea.' "[71]

In closing his discussion of these dissenting rabbis, Schickard then returns to Bahya, who paraphrases the last paragraph of the Midrashic commentary on Deut. 17:14:

Go and learn what befell us under the hand of the kings. . . . Saul fell at Mount Gilboah; David caused a plague, as it is said (2 Sam. 24.15) "and God sent Israel a plague"; Ahab kept the rains from them, as it is said (I Kings 17.1), "As God lives, if there will be dew or rain in these years," etc.; Zedekiah made the sanctuary desolate.[72]

Monarchy was not a command, but a fierce punishment for "sucking up" the emptiness of "flesh and blood" kingship. As Schickard puts it, quoting the fourteenth-century commentator Rabbi Levi ben Gershom (Gersonides), "the kings were the cause of the beguiling of Israel, so that they were alienated from the Lord their God, until they were taken away from their land into exile."[73]

Interestingly, the one paragraph of the Midrashic commentary that Schickard does *not* reproduce is the one that most explicitly draws the connection between monarchy and idolatry ("Whosoever puts his trust in flesh and blood passes away and his dignity also passes away, as it is said, 'Nor in the son of man in whom there is no help' (Ps. 146:3)."). But Milton had no trouble drawing the appropriate conclusion, either by inference, or, just as likely, because he had encountered the rest of the Midrash elsewhere (any number of sources were available to him).[74] Whatever the case, just after announcing that he was casting his vote with the rabbis of the Midrash, he proceeds to gloss I Sam. 8 in the Midrashic manner. As far as I am aware, this is the first appearance of this reading in Christian exegesis:[75]

God indeed gives evidence throughout of his great displeasure at their [the Israelites'] request for a king—thus in [I Sam. 8] verse 7:

"They have not rejected thee, but they have rejected me, that I
should not reign over them, according to all the works which they
have done wherewith they have forsaken me, and served other
gods." The meaning is that it is a form of idolatry to ask for a king,
who demands that he be worshipped and granted honors like those
of a god. Indeed he who sets an earthly master over him and above
all the laws is near to establishing a strange god for himself, one seldom reasonable, usually a brute beast who has scattered reason to
the winds. Thus in I Samuel 10:19 we read: "And ye have this day
rejected your God, who himself saved you out of all your adversities
and your tribulation, and ye have said unto him, Nay, but set a king
over us" . . . just as if he had been teaching them that it was not for
any man, but for God alone, to rule over men.[76]

Milton concludes with the obvious coda: "When at last the Jewish people came to their senses, they complained in Isaiah 26:13 that it had been
ruinous for them to have other lords than God. This evidence all proves
that the Israelites were given a king by God in his wrath."[77] Indeed, this
concluding passage constitutes good evidence that Milton was familiar
with sections of the Midrash *not* excerpted by Schickard. The verse
from Isaiah to which he refers appears as part of the "song" that will
greet the dawn of the Messianic age and simply reads: "O LORD our
God, other lords beside thee have had dominion over us: but by thee
only will we make mention of thy name" (Isa. 26:13). There is nothing at
all in this verse to suggest that the Israelites came to recognize that they
had made an egregious error in asking for a king in I Sam. 8—Isaiah is
plainly talking about something completely different. Milton's analysis
does, however, precisely mirror the reading offered in the last paragraph
of the Midrash: "When Israel saw what befell them on account of their
kings they all began to cry out: "We do not desire a king, we desire our
first king [*malkenu ha-rishon*]," [as it is said], For the Lord is our
Judge, the Lord is our Lawgiver, the Lord is our King; He will save us
(Isa. 33:22)." The Midrash attaches its reading to a different verse from
Isaiah, but was almost certainly responsible for suggesting to Milton the
notion that, at a certain point, the Israelites "came to their senses" and
regretted their request for a mortal king.[78] They now recognized that

they had sinned by turning to idolatrous kingship and had been punished with the curse of monarchy.

To be sure, Milton had been interested in the relationship between
monarchy and idolatry for some time before he wrote the *Defensio*. As
early as 1639, he had reflected in his Commonplace Book on the manner
in which kingship distorts the mortality of rulers:

> Kings scarcely recognize themselves as mortals, scarcely under-
> stand that which pertains to man, except on the day they are made
> king or on the day they die. On the former day they feign humanity
> and gentleness, in the hope of capturing the voice of the people. On
> the latter, having death before their eyes and in the knowledge of
> their evil deeds, they confess what is a fact, namely, that they are
> wretched mortals.[79]

Milton developed this idea further in *Eikonoklastes,* his 1649 polemic
against the *Eikon Basilike*—an account of Charles I's life and last days
then thought to have been written by the king himself. Milton begins his
assault by announcing that he takes the title of the King's book very
seriously:

> In one thing I must commend his op'nness who gave the title to this
> Book, Εἰκὼν Βασιλική, that is to say, The Kings Image; and by
> the Shrine he dresses out for him, certainly would have the people
> come and worship him. For which reason this answer also is intitl'd
> Iconoclastes, the famous Surname of many Greek Emperors, who in
> their zeal to the command of God, after a long tradition of Idolatry
> in the Church, took courage, and broke all superstitious Images to
> peeces. But the People, exorbitant and excessive in all thir motions,
> are prone ofttimes not to a religious onely, but to a civil kinde of
> Idolatry in idolizing thir Kings; though never more mistak'n in the
> object of thir worship.[80]

Milton argues here that monarchies lend themselves to a "civil kinde of
Idolatry," but he does not yet make the argument that kingship per se is
idolatry.[81] That case would wait for the 1651 *Defensio* and would then be

amplified in Milton's 1660 pamphlet, *The Readie and Easie Way,* written on the eve of the Restoration.*

In the latter text Milton casts I Sam. 8 as an intimation of a verse from the Gospel,[82] but the Midrash once again makes its presence strongly felt:

> God in much displeasure gave a king to the Israelites, and imputed it a sin to them that they sought one: but Christ apparently forbids his disciples to admit of any such heathenish government: *the kings of the gentiles,* saith he, *exercise lordship over them; and they that exercise autoritie upon them, are call'd benefactors. But ye shall not be so: but he that is greatest among you, let him be as the younger; and he that is chief, as he that serveth* [Luke 22:25-26]. . . . And what government comes neerer to this precept of Christ, then a free Commonwealth; wherein they who are greatest, are perpetual servants and drudges to the publicke at thir own cost and charges, live soberly in thir families, walk the streets as other men, may be spoken to freely, familiarly, friendly, without adoration. Whereas a king must be ador'd like a Demigod, with a dissolute and haughtie court about him, of vast expence and luxurie, masks and revels, to the debaushing of our prime gentry both male and female; nor at his own cost, but on publick revenue; and all this to do nothing but . . . pageant himself up and down in progress among the perpetual bowings and cringings of an abject people, on either side deifying and adoring him.[83]

---

* It was also a theme in Milton's *Second Defence of the English People* (1654). At the very beginning of the tract, Milton fumes that "the Indians indeed worship as gods malevolent demons whom they cannot exorcize, but this mob of ours, to avoid driving out its tyrants, even when it could, has set up as gods over it the most impotent of mortals, and to its own destruction has consecrated the enemies of mankind" (Milton, *Complete Prose Works of John Milton,* ed. Don Wolfe, trans. Donald Mackenzie [New Haven, CT, 1966], vol. 4:1, p. 551). See also Milton's admonition in the same text to Cromwell that if he were to accept the title of king he "would be doing almost the same thing as if, when you had subjugated some tribe of idolators with the help of the true God, you were to worship the gods you had conquered" (p. 672).

Milton looks forward "to the coming of our true and rightfull and only to be expected King, only worthy as he is our only Saviour, the Messiah, the Christ, the only heir of his father."[84] In the meantime, he warns his countrymen that if

> after all this light among us, the same reason shall pass for current to put our necks again under kingship, as was made use of by the Jews to return back to Egypt and to the worship of thir idol queen, because they falsly imagind that they then livd in more plenty and prosperitie, our condition is not sound but rotten, both in religion and all civil prudence.[85]

The union of monarchy and idolatry could not be more explicit; human kingship is always illegitimate because it is sin.

After the Restoration, as Milton turned from prose to poetry, he placed this theme at the very center of his project in *Paradise Lost* (1667).* It is, to begin with, an unmistakable fact about the poem that Satan and his demon followers base their opposition to God's rulership on precisely the same arguments that Milton himself had invoked in attacking the Stuart monarchy in the 1640s and 1650s—one of the facts that famously lead William Blake to declare that Milton had been "of the Devil's party without knowing it." In the Parliament of Hell in Book II, Mammon rejects all thought of reconciliation with the hosts of heaven by suggesting that ignominious servitude would be the result:

> Suppose he [God] should relent
> And publish grace to all, on promise made
> Of new subjection; with what eyes could we
> Stand in his presence humble, and receive
> Strict laws imposed, to celebrate his throne
> With warbled hymns, and to his godhead sing
> Forced hallelujahs; while he lordly sits

---

* This is not, of course, to suggest that Milton wrote no poetry before the Restoration (indeed, he was already at work on *Paradise Lost* itself in the 1650s). It is simply to acknowledge that the Restoration marked the end of his career as a prose polemicist.

> Our envied sovereign, and his altar breathes
> Ambrosial odours and ambrosial flowers,
> Our servile offerings? This must be our task
> In heaven, this our delight; how wearisome
> Eternity so spent in worship paid
> To whom we hate. Let us not then pursue
> By force impossible, by leave obtained
> Unacceptable, though in heaven, our state
> Of splendid vassalage. . . . (II. 237-252)[86]

On Mammon's account, submitting to God's will would render the demons fawning servants of a flattered lord—one very much like the king described in Milton's *Readie and Easie Way,* who (as we have seen) "pageant[s] himself up and down in progress among the perpetual bowings and cringings of an abject people, on either side deifying and adoring him." Mammon, like Milton, urges the assembly to reject such "splendid vassalage" and to choose instead to live "Free, and to none accountable, preferring/ Hard liberty before the easy yoke/ Of servile pomp" (II.252-256).[87] Likewise, in Book VI of the poem, Satan himself derides the subservience of the loyal angels by sneering that "At first I thought that liberty and heaven/ To heavenly souls had been all one; but now/ I see that most through sloth had rather serve,/ Ministering spirits, trained up in feast and song" (VI.164-167). Again, in the language of the rebel angels, submission to God's monarchy is submission to precisely the same yoke of "court-flatteries and prostrations" that Milton himself had so thoroughly stigmatized in his political prose.[88]

Yet Milton's intention here is not to vindicate the arguments of the demons, but rather to teach his readers that God's is the only monarchy against which they fail.[89] Abdiel answers Satan directly:

> Apostate, still thou err'st, nor end wilt find
> Of erring, from the path of truth remote:
> Unjustly thou deprav'st it with the name
> Of servitude to serve whom God ordains,
> Or nature; God and nature bid the same,
> When he who rules is worthiest, and excels

> Them whom he governs. This is servitude,
> To serve the unwise, or him who hath rebelled
> Against his worthier. . . . (VI.172–180)

Abdiel explains Satan's error, which is to suppose that being subject to God is equivalent to being the slave of an earthly monarch.[90] God is the only being whose nature entitles him to preeminence, and Abdiel wishes only to "serve/ In heaven God ever blessed, and his divine/ Behests obey, worthiest to be obeyed" (VI.183–185). It is not God himself but rather those who falsely pretend to His unique stature who threaten servitude. To acknowledge God's kingship is to be free; those who rebel against it necessarily enslave themselves to an idol. The first and most important of these idol kings is Satan himself. Book II famously opens with a description of Satan as an Asiatic despot in Hell:

> High on the throne of royal state, which far
> Outshone the wealth of Ormuz and of Ind,
> Or where the gorgeous East with richest hand
> Showers on her kings barbaric pearl and gold,
> Satan exalted sat. . . . (II.1–5)

Having rebelled against God's kingdom, the demons find themselves subjects to a different sort of king: "Towards him they bend/ With awful reverence prone; and as a god/ Extol him equal to the highest in heaven" (II.466–479). The demons mistake Satan for a god, and they bow down to him slavishly. Indeed, Milton makes the idolatrous character of Satan's kingship even more explicit in the account of the War in Heaven. Here we read that "the banded powers of Satan" wish "To win the mount of God, and on his throne/ To set the envier of his state, the proud/ Aspirer" (VI.88–90). As for Satan himself: "High in the midst exalted as a god/ The apostate in his sun-bright chariot sat/Idol of majesty divine" (VI.99–101). To rebel against God's kingship, Milton wants to suggest, is invariably to bow down to an idol—one who claims to be a god, but is not.[91]

Yet if Satan is the most prominent idol king in *Paradise Lost,* he is by no means the only one. We meet another at the end of the poem, when

Michael reveals to Adam the future course of human history. After the flood, he explains, human beings will dwell in peace and equality, until a fateful moment arrives:

> . . . one shall rise
> Of proud ambitious heart, who not content
> With fair equality, fraternal state,
> Will arrogate dominion undeserved
> Over his brethren, and quite dispossess
> Concord and law of nature from the earth,
> Hunting (and men not beasts shall be his game)
> With war and hostile snare such as refuse
> Subjection to his empire tyrannous:
> A mighty hunter thence he shall be styled
> Before the Lord, as in despite of heaven,
> Or from heaven claiming a second sovereignty;
> And from rebellion shall derive his name,
> Though of rebellion others he accuse. (XII.23–37)

This figure (whom Milton does not directly name here) is Nimrod. Milton represents him as the first human king[92] and insists that he acquires his "empire tyrannous" in "despite of heaven." His dominion is "undeserved" because he is not, like God, ontologically superior to his fellow human beings. Milton had made this precise argument about human kingship in the first *Defence:* there he reasoned that "it is neither fitting nor proper for a man to be king unless he be far superior to all the rest," and since men are in fact equal, it follows that Christ's kingship alone is just, "for he is worthy, and there is none like him or resembling him."[93] It is, indeed, of great importance that Milton adopts a rabbinic etymology of the name Nimrod, according to which it is derived from the Hebrew word *marad* (rebel). Here Milton is invoking a major strand of rabbinic exegesis which holds that it was Nimrod who built the Tower of Babel to depose (and then replace) God as king, even though there is no Biblical warrant for this view.[94] In the poem, Milton likewise identifies Nimrod as the one who tried to "build/ A city and tower, whose top may reach to heaven" in order to challenge God's sovereignty (XII.43–44).

This is particularly important because the rabbinic texts understand this moment as the birth of idolatry, casting Nimrod himself as the embodiment of idolatrous practices (in perennial contrast to Abraham, who embodies monotheism).[95] Milton clearly wishes to stress the degree to which monarchy and idolatry are fundamentally connected: in becoming the first king, Nimrod also becomes the first idol.[96] Accordingly, having heard this prophecy from Michael, Adam proceeds to express horror and shock:

> O execrable son so to aspire
> Above his brethren, to himself assuming
> Authority usurped, from God not given:
> He gave us only over beast, fish, fowl
> Dominion absolute; that right we hold
> By his donation; but man over men
> He made not lord; such title to himself
> Reserving, human left from human free.

The authority that a human king claims over his fellow men is "usurped"; the title of king is "reserved" to God alone, and the act of bowing down to a mortal king is rebellion against His just kingship. It is inherently and always to make a man into an idol.

IV

Milton's derivation of an exclusivist commitment to republican government from a set of rabbinic materials would have profound and longlasting consequences. Indeed, perhaps the most extraordinary fact about this story is the degree to which Milton's own contemporaries were aware of its contours. James Harrington, writing in 1658 in *The Stumbling-Block of Disobedience and Rebellion,* offers the following commentary on Biblical kingship, and the manner in which its status had recently been contested:

> [Hosea says] "O Israel, thou hast destroyed thyself, but in me is thine help; I will be thy king (which foretells the restitution of the commonwealth, for) where is any other that may save thee in all thy

cities? and thy judges of whom thou saidst, give me a king and princes? I gave thee a king in mine anger (that is in Saul) and I took him away in my wrath." That is in the captivity, so at least saith Rabbi Bechai, with whom agree Nahmoni, Gerschom, and others. Kimchi, it is true, and Maimonides are of opinion that the people, making a king, displeased God not in the matter but in the form only, as if the root of a tree, the balance of a government, were form only and not matter: nor do our divines yet, who are divided into like parties, see more than the rabbis. Both the royalists and the commonwealthsmen of each sort, that is whether divines or Talmudists, appeal unto the letter of the law, which the royalists (as the translators of our Bible) render thus: "When thou shalt say," the commonwealthsmen, as Diodati [i.e., Giovanni Diodati, Swiss Calvinist who translated the Bible into Italian],[97] thus: "If thou come to say, I will set a king over me, like all the nations that are about me, thou shalt in any wise set him king over thee, whom the Lord thy God shall choose." The one party will have the law to be positive, the other contingent and with a mark of detestation upon it; for so, where God speaketh of his people's doing anything like "the nations that were about them," it is everywhere else understood.[98]

This is a remarkably revealing passage. To begin with, it reminds us once again of the astonishing impact of Schickard's *Jus regium Hebraeorum*. The two rabbinical camps—Bahya ben Asher, the misnamed Rabba bar Nahmoni, and Gersonides *(Ralbag)* on one side, and David Kimchi *(Radak)* and Maimonides on the other—are lifted directly from Schickard's presentation of the dispute (Harrington refers to him by name on the next page). But it does a great deal more than that. Harrington here exhibits an astute understanding of the way in which the debate over monarchy had developed in the 1650s. It had become a controversy over whether Deut. 17:14 and I Sam. 8 placed a "mark of detestation" on kingship—that is, characterized it as inherently wicked—or treated it as a "positive" commandment. For many of Harrington's contemporaries, monarchy was now either required or forbidden; there was increasingly little middle ground.[99] Harrington was also aware of the startling degree to which this debate had been shaped and radicalized by the

Christian encounter with "Talmudists." These Talmudists could of course be either "royalists" or "commonwealthsmen," but Harrington left no doubt as to which side he himself came down on. He glosses I Sam. 8:7 as follows:

> "They have not rejected thee, but they have rejected me that I should not reign over them." The government of the senate and the people is that only which is or can be the government of laws and not of men, and the government of laws and not of men is the government of God and not of men. "He that is for the government of laws is for the government of God, and he that is for the government of a man is for the government of a beast."[100]

His "Talmudical commonwealthsmen" could hardly have put it better.

The Miltonic position with which Harrington engages, according to which monarchy is always and everywhere illicit because it constitutes the sin of idolatry, would continue to capture the republican imagination. Algernon Sidney, writing in 1664 in his *Court Maxims,* concludes that "monarchy is in itself an irrational, evil government, unless over those who are naturally beasts and slaves."[101] His defense of this proposition is straightforward:

> The Israelites sinned in desiring a king, let us be deterred by it. God foretold the misery that would follow if they persisted in their wickedness and guilt, and brought upon themselves the deserved punishment thereof. Let their guilt and punishment deter us, let us take warning though they would not. And if we have no communication with satan, let us have none with those thrones which uphold that which he endeavors to set up against God.[102]

Sidney elaborates on this point later in his *Discourses Concerning Government,* interpreting I Sam. 8 to teach that monarchy "was purely the peoples' creature, the production of their own fancy, conceived in wickedness, and brought forth in iniquity, an idol set up by themselves to their own destruction, in imitation of their accursed neighbours."[103] Another pamphlet makes the very same point:

Government by kings was first introduced into the world by the Heathens, from whom the children of Israel copied the custom. It was the most prosperous invention the Devil ever set on foot for the promotion of idolatry. The Heathens paid divine honors to their deceased kings, and the christian world hath improved on the plan by doing the same to their living ones. How impious is the title of sacred majesty applied to a worm, who in the midst of his splendor is crumbling into dust. . . . Near three thousand years passed away from the Mosaic account of the creation, till the Jews under a national delusion requested a king. Till then their form of government (except in extraordinary cases, where the Almighty interposed) was a kind of republic administered by a judge and the elders of the tribes. Kings they had none, and it was held sinful to acknowledge any being under that title but the Lord of Hosts. And when a man seriously reflects on the idolatrous homage which is paid to the persons of Kings, he need not wonder, that the Almighty, ever jealous of his honor, should disapprove of a form of government which so impiously invades the prerogative of heaven.

Of course, this pamphlet was written more than 100 years after the contributions of Milton, Harrington, and Sidney. Its author was an English émigré named Thomas Paine, and he called his reflections *Common Sense*.[104]

This is not, however, to suggest that constitutional pluralism disappeared from the republican tradition after the 1650s. Montesquieu defended it in his *De l'ésprit des lois* (1748), and some version of it animated both Rousseau and Kant.[105] Yet it cannot be denied that the "exclusivist" alternative to humanistic pluralism became a powerful force by the end of the seventeenth century and ultimately emerged victorious in the West after the great eighteenth-century revolutions.[106] If this is so—and if, as I have suggested, there is something to the idea that the rise of a recognizably *modern* kind of political thought should be related to the demise of constitutional pluralism—then our traditional picture of the early-modern intellectual landscape will have to be revised substantially. It is quite common, for example, to regard Thomas Hobbes as a precociously modern political philosopher or, indeed, as the very first political philosopher of the modern period. It is equally common to regard John Milton as a classicizing throwback to an earlier age, as anything but modern.[107] Yet, seen from this point of view, the picture becomes rather more complicated. It is, indeed, a remarkable fact about Hobbes that he remained, throughout his life, a committed constitutional pluralist. In the "Preface to the Readers" in *De cive* (1642), Hobbes insists that he does not wish "to seem of opinion, that there is a lesse proportion of obedience due to an Aristocraty or Democracy, then a Monarchy."[108] He concedes that he has given arguments in favor of the proposition that monarchy is "the most commodious government," but this, he immediately adds, is the "one thing alone I confesse in this whole book not to be demonstrated, but only probably stated"[109]—that is, the only claim that is, strictly speaking, not part of his demonstrative political science. He later reiterates this commitment quite prominently in *Leviathan* (1651).[110]

It seems to me that scholars have not focused sufficiently on the oddity and importance of this claim.* Why is it that Hobbes does not simply declare that the law of nature demands the establishment of monarchy? The laws of nature, we should recall, are prudential maxims of reason; they tell us how to go about the business of securing our preservation. It is, for example, a law of nature "that all men that mediate Peace, be allowed safe conduct," because "the Law that commandeth Peace, as the *End*, commandeth Intercession, as the *Means*; and to Intercession the Means is safe Conduct."[111] In other words, if our preservation requires peace, and if peace in turn requires safe conduct for mediators, then reason commits us to the latter just as it commits us to the former. The case is similar with more mundane requirements of Hobbes's theory. It is, Hobbes tells us, contrary to reason to set aside public lands and wealth in order to fund the operations of the commonwealth, since "it tendeth to the dissolution of Government, and to the condition of meere Nature

---

* Hobbes's contemporaries, in contrast, fully appreciated it. John Hall, for example, writes that establishing "the intrinsical value and expediency of this Government [i.e., monarchy]" is "a businesse so ticklish, that even Mr. Hobs in his *de Cive,* though he assured himself that the rest of his Book (which is principally erected to the assertion of Monarchy) is demonstrated, yet he doubts whether the Arguments which he brings to this businesse be so firm or no." See Hall, *The grounds and reasons of monarchy considered* (London, 1649), pp. 49–50.

and War, assoon as ever the Soveraign Power falleth into the hands of a Monarch, or of an Assembly, that are either too negligent of mony, or too hazardous in engaging the publique stock, into a long and costly war."[112] That is, a commonwealth should not rely on these finite funds, because, if they happen to become exhausted, it will find itself in dire straights. Again, this is forbidden by Hobbes's civil science because it tends to the disturbance of the commonwealth.

But, if that is the case, then why is the admonition to choose a monarch of a different status? Hobbes, after all, spends a great deal of time telling us about the grave dangers of nonmonarchical governments. It is only in a monarchy, he insists, that the interests of the sovereign and the interests of the public are united in a stable fashion; in other regimes, in contrast, "the publique prosperity conferres not so much to the private fortune of one that is corrupt, or ambitious, as doth many times a perfidious advice, a treacherous action, or a Civill warre."[113] Moreover, while a "Monarch cannot disagree with himselfe, out of envy, or interest," an "Assembly may; and that to such a height, as may produce a Civill Warre."[114] Given the evident dangers to the commonwealth arising from a nonunitary sovereign, why is it that the law of nature does not forbid aristocracy and democracy, just as it appears to forbid particular structures of state finance? One might suppose that the reason is purely pragmatic: in 1651, Hobbes could not very well argue as a monarchical exclusivist and have any hope of being welcomed back to the England of the Long Parliament. This makes a certain degree of sense, but it clearly does not apply to the context in which Hobbes wrote *De cive* in 1642. Living in French exile among committed royalists, Hobbes would only have been applauded for taking a strident monarchist line.[115] The pragmatic explanation, then, is not particularly satisfactory.

There is, however, another explanation—one which fits very well with the story I have just been telling. Hobbes was trained as a humanist and composed works of humanist scholarship throughout his life, beginning with his 1629 translation of Thucydides[116] and ending with his complete translations of the Homeric poems (1677).[117] Perhaps his refusal to part with constitutional pluralism should be regarded, not as a failure of nerve, but rather as a deeply significant legacy of his humanist formation. Perhaps, indeed, the man who declared that Aristotle was

"the worst Teacher that ever was, the worst Politician and Ethick"[118] remained in one very important respect a thoroughly Aristotelian political
scientist. The surprising conclusion is that while we moderns usually
take ourselves to be living in the age of Hobbes, there is a sense in which
we live rather in the age of Milton.[119]

CHAPTER 2

"For the Land Is Mine":
The Hebrew Commonwealth
and the Rise of Redistribution

IT IS ONE of the great ironies in the history of European political thought that republicanism has come to be associated with the redistribution of wealth. For contemporary political theorists—particularly those in the Anglophone tradition, but increasingly those on the Continent as well—a chief attraction of the republican perspective has been the belief that, unlike liberalisms of various sorts, republicanism incorporates a robust critique of economic inequality, as well as a commitment to its rectification. Thus, in Philip Pettit's influential recent account, the republican view of freedom as "non-domination," unlike the liberal view of freedom as the absence of interference or impediment, is to be preferred in large part because it validates the intuition that economic dependence (for example, that of a worker on his employer or that of society in general on a large corporation) is a form of *unfreedom* with important civic consequences.[1] The thought, as a recent critic points out, is that republicanism carries with it "an ambivalence about property and commerce," which can serve as the "basis of a postsocialist critique of market society."[2] In a similar vein, communitarian writers have become interested in the republican alternative because of their conviction that "a good society must constrain extreme inequalities," and that "redistributive measures are necessary to maintain moral equality, to express compassion for fellow citizens, and to reflect the broader prudential interdependencies that are part of any genuine civil association."[3] The republican critique of contemporary liberalism, then, consists to a significant degree in the claim that the state should redistribute wealth in order to guarantee the sort of rough equality that makes civic self-government sustainable.

Before pointing out the irony of this account, it is important to acknowledge its force. It is, after all, not implausible to argue that the "priority of liberty" in present-day liberal political philosophy significantly constrains the range of responses it can offer to the problem of economic inequality. Even John Rawls, however strongly he might reject the perspective of his more libertarian critics, nonetheless insists that inequality per se is not inconsistent with the principles of justice. On his view, as long as the position of the least well-off social group is improved under a particular economic arrangement, it does not matter that the arrangement in question might improve the situation of the most fortunate to a greater degree.[4] The only relevant question is whether some rival scheme might be envisioned that would make the least advantaged even better off; if so, the latter would be preferred even if it would result in greater inequality. So the notion that contemporary liberalism is, to some extent, indifferent to the demands of equality, while certainly debatable, does not seem far-fetched. It is also the case that, beginning in the middle of the seventeenth century, an important strand of republican political theory developed that did indeed advocate the imposition of a rough equality in holdings—and to that degree can certainly be recruited to challenge the liberal perspective. What is not appreciated, however, is that this seventeenth-century development represented the most dramatic possible break with the earlier tradition of republican thought, which had accorded enormous respect to private property rights and had exhibited a particular horror of coercive attempts to redistribute wealth. It was this earlier brand of republican politics, not its redistributive rival, that defended the idea of freedom as "non-domination"—a fact which suggests that contemporary republicans are engaged in the somewhat dubious enterprise of reviving a tradition of thought that never existed. The purpose of this chapter is to explain how and why redistribution entered the mainstream of republican political theory and to highlight the ways in which this redistributive republicanism is incompatible with the commitments of the contemporary writers who claim it for their own. My suggestion is that here again the Hebrew revival emerges as a transformative force. It was the meditation on Biblical land law—seen through the prism of rabbinic commentaries—that convinced a new generation of republican writers to reexamine the antipathy toward redistribution they had inherited from their forebears.

I

To a truly remarkable degree, early-modern debates over what we now call "distributive justice" took the form of debates about the Roman agrarian laws.[5] This in itself is a somewhat surprising fact, since these laws did not, strictly speaking, affect private property. Under Roman law, lands captured in war or bequeathed to Rome by foreign princes were designated *ager publicus* (public land). The uncultivated portions of this public territory were, in theory, meant to be distributed in small parcels among Roman citizens, who would then farm the land and pay a tithe to the republic. In reality, however, patricians quickly acquired vast tracts of the uncultivated *ager publicus,* often by means of fraud and violence, and then neglected to pay the required tax—a practice that provoked the ire of even some of the most rabidly antiplebeian Roman authors. However, by the time of the Gracchan laws (133 and 122 BCE) these large estates had been in private hands for generations and had acquired the aura of private property. As a result, the debate over the *ager publicus*—both in ancient Rome and in early-modern Europe— came to be regarded as much more than a simple controversy over the distribution of Roman public land. It emerged instead as a debate over the question of whether the commonwealth ought to impose limits on private landholding.

Beginning in the fifth century BCE, tribunes periodically proposed laws designed to redivide the *ager publicus* and distribute it among the plebs; such laws became known as *leges agrariae* (agrarian laws).[6] It is an article of faith in the surviving Latin sources (almost all of them sympathetic to the patrician cause) that these agrarian laws constituted unjust expropriations of private property, and that the controversy surrounding their proposal and passage ultimately brought about the fall of the republic. Livy, speaking of the land law put forward by the tribune Spurius Cassius in 486 BCE, observes pointedly that "this was the first proposal for agrarian legislation, and from that day to within living memory it has never been brought up without occasioning the greatest instability" (II.41).[7] Livy's Roman successors were even more emphatic on this subject, but they directed their animus chiefly toward the agrarian program of Tiberius and Caius Gracchus. In Lucan's *Pharsalia,* the Gracchi, "who dared to bring about immoderate things" *(ausosque ingentia Gracchos)* appear in the underworld alongside other famous Roman traitors in the "criminal crowd" *(turba nocens),* which rejoices at Rome's civil war while the blessed dead weep (VI.794).[8] Velleius Paterculus likewise insists that the Gracchi, having been "infected by pernicious theories," had "turned the state upside down, and brought it into a position of critical and extreme danger" by proposing agrarian laws;[9] and Florus observes that, while the Gracchan laws may have had "the appearance of equity" *(species aequitatis),* in that they claimed to give the plebs their due *(ius),* in fact they brought the state to "ruin" *(perniciem).* For "how could the plebs be restored to the land," Florus asks, "without dispossessing those who possessed it, who were themselves part of the people and held estates left to them by their forefathers by a kind of right [*ius*]?"[10]

The most forceful Roman opponent of the agrarian movement was, however, Marcus Tullius Cicero.[11] Cicero lays the groundwork for his view in the first book of the *De officiis.* "Property becomes private," he writes, in part "through long occupancy" *(vetere occupatione),* and "each one should retain possession of that which has fallen to his lot; and if anyone appropriates to himself anything beyond that, he will be violating the laws of human society" (I.21).[12] In Book II, he makes clear that the agrarian laws should be regarded as precisely such a violation. "The man in administrative office," he explains, "must make it his first care that everyone shall have what belongs to him and that private citizens suffer no invasion of their property rights by act of the state" (II.73).[13] As his example of this kind of "invasion," he submits that "ruinous policy" *(perniciose)* called the *lex agraria.* This policy, he continues, favored an "equal distribution of property." "What plague could be worse?" *(qua peste quae potest esse maior),* he asks, especially since it negates the basic purpose for which people enter civil association—namely, the preservation of their private property *(custodia rerum suarum)*. In *De legibus*, Cicero adds that the strife over the Gracchan laws in particular brought about "a complete revolution in the State" (III.20).[14] In short, Cicero characterizes the agrarian movement as seditious, dangerous, and violently unjust. For what is an agrarian law, he asks in *De officiis*, but an initiative "to rob one man of what belongs to him and to give to another man what does not belong to him?" (II.83).[15]

For Cicero, as for so many other Roman writers, agrarian laws driven by plebeian envy had disrupted the *concordia* of the Roman republic, given rise to factions, and ultimately dismembered the body politic. This conviction had profound consequences for the shape of early-modern political theory. The influence of the Roman sources (and of Cicero in particular) was so pervasive among civic humanists that the rejection of agrarian laws (or *leveling*, as the English had it) became a powerful republican orthodoxy. This commonplace is on display as early as Boccaccio's *De mulieribus claris* (1362). Alerting the reader that he intends to discuss several women who were famous but wicked, Boccaccio defends this decision by remarking that he has often read accounts of famous men that included even "the treacherous Iugurtha" and "the most seditious Gracchi" *(seditiosissimos Graccos)*.[16] Leonardo Bruni takes a similar view in the *Cicero novus* (1415), praising his hero for beating back the great "threat to the republic" *(hanc rei publice turbationem)* posed by the agrarian law of 64 BCE. On Bruni's account, "the Agrarian Law (first introduced by Tiberius Gracchus, and subsequently agitated for by raving tribunes with the greatest confrontations almost every year) that was drawing senators and plebs into endless conflict, was easily laid to rest by Cicero's prudence and eloquence."[17] Bartolomeo Sacchi (better known as Platina) agrees in the *De optimo cive* (composed between 1457 and 1461) that the Gracchi are to be classed with Saturninus, Drusus, and Spurius Melius, all rabble-rousers "whose entire lives were based on vain display."[18] Writing later in the *Dialogus de falso et vero bono*, Platina compares the schemes of the Gracchi to the "savageness, wantonness, and avarice" of Rome's other famous traitors, even going so far as to liken the agrarian laws to the rape of Virginia by Appius Claudius.[19] Francesco Patrizi of Siena, whose works became perhaps the most widely read civic humanist writings of the Cinquecento, summed up this tradition of thought in the *De institutione, statu, ac regimine reipublicae* (c. 1460) by observing that, while the Gracchi were sons of a venerable father, they themselves "turned out to be the most factious and seditious men" *(turbulentissimi, et seditiosissimi).*[20] One of them, he continues, "was overcome by Scipio Nasica in the Capitol for the preservation of the republic, and the other was forced to take his own life."[21]

The remarkable hegemony of this account within republican circles is reflected in the fact that even Renaissance writers who thoroughly rejected the Roman defense of private property rights nonetheless retained a visceral distrust of the agrarian remedy.[22] Thus Thomas More, whose *Utopia* embraces a theory of justice requiring the elimination of wealth and poverty, has Raphael Hythloday go out of his way to denounce one specific strategy for its implementation. There are some, Raphael tells us, who suppose that "laws might be made that no one should own more than a certain amount of land or receive more than a certain income."[23] But, he insists at the end of Book I, "laws of this sort may have as much effect as poultices continually applied to sick bodies that are past cure."[24] The only plausible remedy is the outright abolition of private property; redistribution is not a viable option. A similarly conflicted posture is on display in Machiavelli's *Discourses on Livy.* Although Machiavelli certainly has no patience for the Roman notion of property rights and takes the position that "well-ordered republics have to keep the public rich and the citizens poor" (I.37),[25] he nonetheless feels obliged to follow Cicero in describing the agrarian laws as a "plague" *(morbo),* which "in the end was the cause of the destruction of the republic" *(in fine fu causa della distruzione della Republica).*[26] Rome, for Machiavelli, may indeed have had a problem in respect of its distribution of wealth, but agrarian laws had only made the problem worse.

Nor was this ritualized condemnation any less ubiquitous in seventeenth-century England. When James Harrington wrote in 1656 that "agrarian laws of all others have ever been the greatest bugbears," he was not exaggerating.[27] In 1601, William Fulbecke's *Historicall Collection of the Continuall Factions, Tumults, and Massacres of the Romans* announced that the Gracchi, through their "sinister" agrarian program, had unforgivably "mingled lawes with lust, and brought the common-weale into an headlong and hideous danger."[28] Sir Walter Raleigh later insisted in his *Discourse of the Original and Fundamental Causes of . . . War* that the Roman republic had fallen victim to the "state-phrensy of sedition . . . occasioned by the reviving of the Agrarian Law."[29] "The contentions about this law," Raleigh argued, "kindled such a hatred between the people and the senate, that it never ended but with the loss of the liberty of Rome, and the dissolution of that republic."[30] Likewise, in the 1633 poem *The Reigne of King Henry the Second,* Thomas May attributed the Roman agrarian laws to the personified figure of Sedition, about whose "denn" we read: "storyes carved there/ Of his atchievements numberlesse were seene,/ Such as the Gracchis factious stirres had beene/ In ancient Rome" (I.532–535).[31] Such sentiments were not confined to writings of poets and essayists. In 1641, Edmund Waller gave a speech in the House of Commons in which he worried that an assault on episcopal prerogatives might mean that the "next demand might be *Lex Agraria,* the like equality of things Temporall."[32] And as late as 1650, the supremely malleable Marchamont Nedham could write in *The Case of the Commonwealth of England, Stated* that the masses are principally to be feared because "they fly out ever and anon into violence; and from plundering they proceed to the flat leveling of estates as is evident by those Licinian and agrarian laws made by the populacy of Rome whereby it was provided that no man should grow too rich nor be master of above fifty acres of land."[33] From here, Nedham writes, the next expression of plebeian degeneracy is "to introduce an absolute community," although he adds that "neither the Athenian nor Roman levelers ever arrived to this high pitch of madness."

We see, then, that the rejection of redistribution was a remarkably consistent feature of early-modern political discourse, particularly among republicans. By the time of the Restoration, however, this was no longer the case. A powerful new perspective on republican politics developed during the 1650s in England that placed the previously derided agrarian laws at its very center. As I have explained at length elsewhere,[34] this new approach was characterized by a pronounced turn from Roman to Greek sources and ideas—to the Greek historians of Rome (Plutarch and Appian), who lionized the Gracchi and regarded the agrarian movement as a crucial effort to save the faltering republic, and to the Greek philosophers (Plato and Aristotle) who outlined a theory of justice that seemed to make moral sense of these commitments. But the question remains, why then? What caused such an abrupt reorientation of political commitments to seem suddenly plausible in the 1650s, but not before? After all, Plutarch and Appian were well known during the Renaissance, even if less ubiqui-tous than Livy and Cicero;[35] yet their rival view of the agrarian laws was never considered a serious alternative to the Roman orthodoxy until the middle years of the Interregnum. My explanation centers on a seemingly innocuous semantic move, first made by the Dutch Hebraist Peter Cu-naeus in his path-breaking study of "the republic of the Hebrews" (1617). When Cunaeus, a professor of jurisprudence at the University of Leiden, came to reflect on the equal division of land mandated by God among Is-raelite families and tribes—and on the institution of the jubilee, which secured it against time and contingency—it seemed immediately obvious to him that this should be called an "agrarian law" *(lex agraria),* just like the one proposed by Licinius Stolo among the Romans. With one small gesture of analogy, Cunaeus rendered the agrarian laws not only respect-able but also divinely sanctioned. If God had ordained agrarian laws in his own commonwealth, then Cicero had to be wrong.[36] It now became a matter of the utmost urgency to understand in detail the character and operation of the "Hebrew agrarian law," and for this task, Cunaeus and those who followed him turned to the rabbinic tradition.

II

Rabbinic commentators and their early-modern readers found in the Hebrew Bible a distinctive theory of property, applied with considerable precision to a range of concrete cases. Perhaps the most dramatic charac-terization of this theory was offered by the great Medieval exegete Rashi (Rabbi Solomon ben Isaac of Troyes, fl. 1040–1105) at the beginning of his commentary on the Pentateuch. In his gloss on the first verse of Gen-esis, he poses a perfectly reasonable question: If the Torah is a law book for the Israelites, why does it not simply begin with the first com-mandment given to them as a nation, namely, to treat the lunar month of Nisan as "the first of months" (Exodus 12:1)? Why does it include Genesis and the first half of Exodus at all? He answers as follows:

> What is the reason, then, that it commences with the account of the
> creation? Because of the thought expressed in the text (Psalm 111:6)
> "He declared to his people the strength of his works (i.e. He gave an

account of the work of creation) in order that he might give them the heritage of the nations." For should the peoples of the world say to Israel, "You are robbers, because you took by force the lands of the seven nations of Canaan," Israel may reply to them, "All the earth belongs to the Holy One, blessed be He; He created it and gave it to whom he pleased. When he willed He gave it to them, and when He willed He took it from them and gave it to us."[37]

For Rashi, the whole purpose of the first book and a half of the Pentateuch is to establish a set of propositions about the nature of property in order to vindicate the Israelite claim to the land of Canaan. It must be demonstrated that (1) God is the creator of the earth, and therefore its owner; (2) God gives possession of his land to certain peoples under certain conditions; (3) when those conditions are violated, he may transfer possession to others;[38] (4) in this specific case, land was initially given to the Canaanite nations, who then violated the terms of their occupancy; and (5) accordingly, God transferred possession to the Israelites. Modern commentators would no doubt find it hyperbolic to claim that the defense of these propositions is the sole purpose (or even the most important purpose) of Genesis and the first half of Exodus, but Rashi's insight is nonetheless worth taking seriously. The vision of property rights that he articulates is indeed at the very center of the Biblical text, and it explains the distinctive land laws to be found within it.

The vision in question is epitomized by a striking semantic fact about the Hebrew language, well-known to Biblical scholars, but worth repeating in this context. Those of us whose languages use terms derived from Greek and Latin are used to marking a key lexical distinction between "justice" *(diké/iustitia)* and "charity" *(cháris/charitas)*. What distinguishes them is the element of personal discretion. If I give you a $5 bill to which you have a legal claim, this is an instance of justice, not charity; if, however, I give you a $5 bill to which you have no legal claim, this is an instance of charity, not justice. Hebrew recognizes no such dichotomy. The same Hebrew word *(tzedek/tzedakah)* refers both to the fulfillment of what we would regard as conventional legal obligations *and* to the performance of what we would regard as charitable acts.[39] The reason is straightforward. In the Biblical worldview, God is regarded as the owner of all things and is therefore empowered to impose whatever conditions he wishes on the use of his property by human beings. Many of these conditions involve, for example, care for the poor and indigent, but precisely because these are legal obligations imposed by a rightful owner on his tenants, they are no more *discretionary* than, say, the payment of debts.[40] The Hebrew Bible develops a theory of property according to which there is only one owner. As God says to Moses in chapter 25 of Leviticus, "the land is mine" (Lev. 25:23).[41]

This idiosyncratic theory underpins a remarkable array of Biblical statutes, far too numerous to canvass here.[42] For our purposes, we simply have to understand its relation to a particular set of laws governing the use and division of the land of Israel. To begin with, it is essential to recognize that the God of the Hebrew Bible does not seem to have any a priori objection to the unequal distribution of land. In the famous case of the Egyptian famine (Genesis 47), for instance, God is not at all unhappy with the fact that Joseph "bought all the land of Egypt for Pharaoh; for the Egyptians sold every man his field, because the famine prevailed over them: so the land became Pharaoh's" (Gen. 47:20). God does, however, have pronounced objections to any such arrangement in the specific case of the Israelites. The rationale for this distinction is to be found in a seemingly unremarkable verse from the Joseph story. The Biblical text explains that, for the Egyptians, selling their lands to Pharaoh was equivalent to declaring that "we will be Pharaoh's servants." But God makes clear that the Israelites "are my servants, which I brought forth out of the land of Egypt; they may not give themselves over into servitude" (Lev. 25:42). The Hebrew Bible uses this dictum primarily to explain the prohibition against Israelite slavery, but it clearly grounds the land laws as well (they appear in the very same chapter). One needs one's own patrimony in order not to be a slave, and since the Israelites must be servants of God alone, every Israelite must have land. The various Biblical land laws are best understood as reflections of this fundamental commitment.

In the first instance, God requires a specific sort of initial distribution once the Israelites enter the land: "And ye shall divide the land by lot for an inheritance among your families: and to the more ye shall give the more inheritance, and to the fewer ye shall give the less inheritance: every man's inheritance shall be in the place where his lot falleth; according to the tribes of your fathers ye shall inherit" (Num. 33:54). The land is to be divided in equal parcels by lot, with a greater number of parcels going to larger tribes (it is left to Joshua to perform this bureaucratic task once the Israelites have crossed the Jordan) (Josh. 11–13). A series of discrete laws is then introduced to preserve this initial distribution. First, since God had decreed that land should pass to a daughter in the absence of a male heir (Num. 27:8), it was specified that

> every daughter, that possesseth an inheritance in any tribe of the children of Israel, shall be wife unto one of the family of the tribe of her father, that the children of Israel may enjoy every man the inheritance of his fathers. Neither shall the inheritance remove from one tribe to another tribe; but every one of the tribes of the children of Israel shall keep himself to his own inheritance. (Num. 36:8–9)

That is, to prevent the tribal balance from being disturbed by the routine incorporation of a female heir's portion into the estate of her husband, such heiresses were required to marry a man from their own tribe.[43] A closely related law is the remission of debts during the sabbatical year. God describes the requirement as follows:

> At the end of every seventh year you must make a remission of debts. This is how it is to be made: everyone who holds a pledge shall return the pledge of the person indebted to him. He must not press a fellow-countryman for repayment, for the Lord's year of remission has been declared. You may press foreigners; but if it is a fellow-countryman that holds anything of yours, you must renounce all claim on it. (Deut. 15:1–3)[44]

This too is clearly designed in part to preserve the initial distribution. If a debt remains unpaid, there is no option to seize the debtor's land as collateral (or to enslave him); the debt must simply be forgiven. Indeed, the rabbis of the Talmud made the connection between the two measures explicit when they ruled that, as a matter of Biblical law, if the initial distribution of land is allowed to lapse, the cancellation of debts in the sabbatical year is likewise no longer to be observed.[45]

Without question, however, the most significant of the land laws is the jubilee. After delineating the proper observance of the seventh year, God attaches special importance to the seventh sabbatical:

Thou shalt number seven sabbaths of years unto thee, seven times seven years; and the space of the seven sabbaths of years shall be unto thee forty and nine years. Then shalt thou cause the trumpet of the jubile to sound on the tenth day of the seventh month, in the day of atonement shall ye make the trumpet sound throughout all your land. And ye shall hallow the fiftieth year, and proclaim liberty throughout all the land unto all the inhabitants thereof: it shall be a jubile unto you; and ye shall return every man unto his possession, and ye shall return every man unto his family. . . . In the year of this jubile ye shall return every man unto his possession. (Lev. 25:8–13)

The Hebrew word translated as "liberty" in the King James version *(dror)*, is better rendered as "release." What is being proclaimed throughout the land is the return of all patrimonies to their initial holders, as well as the release of slaves. No land sale, according to the Hebrew Bible, should be regarded as anything more than a lease extending to the next jubilee (and should be valued based on the number of years remaining). The text specifies a further set of observances (for instance, as in any sabbatical year, the land is to lie fallow), but the central feature of the jubilee is the release. "The land shall not be sold for ever," God explains, "for the land is mine; for ye are strangers and sojourners with me. And in all the land of your possession ye shall grant a redemption for the land" (Lev. 25:23–24).[46]

The later Biblical books suggest that this practice remained a central feature of Israelite law and self-understanding.* When Samuel warns the people against the perils of monarchy, one of his primary concerns is

---

* There is, however, considerable scholarly debate as to whether (or when) the jubilee was actually observed in ancient Israel. To the extent that any consensus has emerged, it appears to be that Lev. 25 dates to no earlier than the eighth century BCE and perhaps to as late as the period of Persian rule after the Babylonian Captivity—and, accordingly, that it does not reliably describe Israelite practice during the tribal period. That said, most scholars grant that the jubilee has *some* roots in the tribal period. Two recent studies are Jean-François Lefebvre, *Le jubilé biblique: Lev 25—exégèse et théologie* (Göttingen, Germany, 2003); and John S. Bergsma, *The Jubilee from Leviticus to Qumran: A History of Interpretation* (Leiden, 2007). The classic work remains Robert North, S.J., *Sociology of the Biblical Jubilee* (Rome, 1954).

that a king "will take your fields, and your vineyards, and your olive-yards, even the best of them, and give them to his servants" (I Sam. 8:14). And, indeed, one of the most infamous episodes in I Kings concerns precisely this disregard for the integrity of tribal inheritances. King Ahab covets the vineyard of Naboth, one of his subjects, and asks to purchase it. Naboth replies, "the lord forbid that I should surrender to you land which has always been in my family" (I Kings 21:3)[47]—that is, Naboth claims to be acting in defense of the Biblically mandated division of land. Samuel's prophecy is then promptly confirmed when Ahab's wife, Jezebel, conspires to have Naboth falsely accused of blasphemy and then executed, so that his land can safely be confiscated. Ahab, evidently content with the results, then seizes his murdered subject's patrimony, only to be famously rebuked by Elijah: "Thus sayeth the Lord, hast thou killed, and also taken possession?" (I Kings 21:19). The land laws, in short, retained enough prestige and authority during this period that the violation of them could be held up as a grave indictment of Israelite kingship.[48]

Although scholars disagree as to whether the jubilee was ever in fact scrupulously observed in pre-exilic Israel, it is clear that it was *not* observed during the Second Temple period. The Talmud offers a rationale for this adjustment in BT 'Arakin 32b:

> When the tribe of Reuben, the tribe of Gad, and the half-tribe of Manasseh went into exile, the Jubilees were abolished as it is said: *And ye shall proclaim liberty throughout the land unto all the inhabitants thereof,* i.e. [only] at the time when all the inhabitants thereof dwell upon it, but not at the time when some of them are exiled.

That is, the rabbis concluded that, since the jubilee was instituted to maintain a particular tribal distribution, it made little sense to observe it now that several of the tribes in question no longer inhabited the land.* The issue of debt relief during the sabbatical year, however, proved rather more

---

* In fact, the three tribes in question disappeared well before the destruction of the First Temple (587 BCE), so the rabbinic notion is that the jubilee requirement ceased to apply even before the exile.

complicated from the rabbinic perspective. Did this requirement remain in force? As a matter of Biblical law, the rabbis declared (as we have seen) that it did not. In BT Gittin 36a, the Talmud quotes an explanation of this ruling offered by Judah HaNasi (c. 170–200 CE), the redactor of the Mishnah:

> Rabbi says: [It is written], *Now this is the matter of the release;* [every creditor] *shall release* [Deut. 15:2]. The text indicates here two kinds of release,* one the release of land, and the other the release of money. When the release of land is in operation the release of money is to be operative, and when the release of land is not operative the release of money is not to be operative.

The rabbis conditioned debt relief on the observance of the jubilee—and since the latter had lapsed, the former was no longer in force. But the Talmud promptly adds that "the Rabbis ordained that it [debt relief] should be operative [i.e., even in the absence of the jubilee], in order to keep alive the memory of the sabbatical year." Here the Talmud invokes a key distinction in rabbinic thought between Biblical commandments *(mitzvot mi-d'oraita)* and rabbinic injunctions *(mitzvot d'rabbanan).* The former have greater authority than the latter, but rabbinic rulings still carry legal force. In this case, the rabbis declared that, even though the Torah only requires debt relief when the jubilee is observed, the practice should nonetheless be maintained (purely on rabbinic authority), lest the Jewish people forget the land laws. Accordingly, the cancellation of debts in the seventh year remained part of Jewish law until well into the first century CE.

This remnant of the Biblical land laws would, however, likewise be allowed to lapse during the rabbinic period. The Talmud records that the great sage Hillel the Elder (c. 30 BCE–10 CE) became concerned when "he saw that that people were unwilling to lend money to one another and disregarded the precept laid down in the Torah. *Beware that there be not a base thought in thine heart saying,* etc. [Deut. 15:9]" (BT Gittin 36a). That is, he noticed that, despite the Biblical injunction that one should not refuse to lend money to those in need simply because the

---

* That is, because the text uses two forms of the verb: "release" (שמיטה) and "shall release" (שמוט).

sabbatical year is approaching, his countrymen were doing precisely that. In response, he formalized a procedure known as a *prosbul*,[49] according to which a creditor could appear in front of a rabbinic court and claim the right to collect a debt even after the year of release—in effect nullifying the purely rabbinic commandment for the continued observance of the sabbatical year. As a result, the cancellation of debts joined the jubilee in obsolescence.[50]

Nonetheless, concern with the precise requirements of the Biblical land laws remained a preoccupation of rabbinic commentators even after the destruction of Jerusalem by the Romans in 70 CE—a reflection of their hope that the exile would one day come to an end, and that all of the Biblical commandments would once again be observed in the land of Israel. The canonical redaction of their various opinions appears in book seven of Maimonides's great code, the *Mishneh Torah,* under the rubric *Hilkhot shemittah ve-yovel* (Laws on the Sabbatical Year and the Jubilee). In this massively influential summa, Maimonides identifies twenty-one positive commandments (of the form "thou shalt") and twenty-two negative commandments (of the form "thou shalt not") pertaining to the observance of the land laws—and he proceeds to analyze each one in great detail. Early-modern Christian readers would find in this text a meticulous account of these distant practices, describing everything from the precise character of the horn *(shofar)* that was to be sounded on the jubilee to the legal penalties imposed for violating certain provisions of the sabbatical year.[51] It was, in short, Maimonides who offered Cunaeus and those who came after him the authoritative description of what became known as the "Hebrew agrarian law."

III

Beginning in the late sixteenth century, authors writing about the Hebrew republic began to give sustained consideration to the Biblical land laws. Whereas Bonaventure Cornelius Bertram had paid no attention whatsoever to this aspect of Israelite law in his *De politia iudaica* (1574), the Italian historian and antiquarian Carlo Sigonio discusses it extensively in his *De republica Hebraeorum* of 1582.[52] In part, this development reflects the increasingly prominent role played by the Biblical jubilee in late humanist attempts to establish an ancient chronology. The precise intervals marked by the jubilee (were they forty-nine years or fifty?), as well as the succession of sabbatical years, became a crucially important subject of study for those, like Joseph Scaliger, who wished to establish the precise dates of central Biblical events (the Flood, the Exodus, the erection and destruction of Solomon's Temple, etc.).[53] Sigonio was very much part of this humanist milieu and fully shared its obsession with chronology.[54] It is, therefore, unsurprising that in Book III of his *De republica Hebraeorum,* a summary of the "sacred days" of the Jews, he dedicates Chapter XIV to an analysis of "the seventh year" *(de septimo anno).*[55] Noting that the Hebrew Bible calls the seventh year a "sabbatical" *(Sabbatarius)* because the land is given relief from cultivation, Sigonio then dutifully reports that in the Israelite commonwealth, "a remission of debts was also to be made in the seventh year, as is next taught in Deuteronomy XV with these words: *In the seventh year you shall make a remission of debts.*"[56] In the very next chapter, Sigonio moves on to a discussion of "the fiftieth year." He tells us that "the fiftieth year was a Sabbatical, because remission was given to slaves from their servile work." But he then offers a second explanation, namely, that "alienated land returned to its former possessor: indeed, concerning this it is written in Leviticus XXV: *You shall number for yourself seven sevens of years.*"[57] He explains that this fiftieth year "is called the Jubilee because the Levites announced it with trumpets of ram's horn, which among the Hebrews are called *iovelim.*"[58] Sigonio then recounts the details of Numbers 27:8 and 36:8, in which the daughters of Zelophehad are given the right to inherit their father's land, so long as they marry someone from within their own tribe. He correctly relates this latter measure to the jubilee; both, he recognizes, were designed to preserve the initial distribution of tribal land.

Following Sigonio, authors in the *respublica Hebraeorum* tradition increasingly tried to reach a more sophisticated and detailed understanding of the land laws, and the theory of property underlying them. The center of such scholarship was in the Netherlands, thanks to its large Jewish community and the easy access it afforded to printed versions of rabbinic materials.[59] The Huguenot scholar Franciscus Junius (François du Jon), for example, was appointed to the theology chair at Leiden in 1592 and promptly took the opportunity to pen his *De politiae Mosis observatione,* published the following year. Discussing the institution of the jubilee in Leviticus 25, he first argues that, although this law might at first appear to be purely "civil" in character, it should in fact be understood to issue "from a ceremonial grounding or principle" *(ex principio sive fundamento ceremoniali).* Junius's reason is that "God wanted to show by means of a ceremonial observance that he himself was the owner of this land, and that this land or region belonged to him by the excellent law of landholding, and not to any other."[60] Accordingly, "he commanded the Israelites by this measure to acknowledge the proprietorship of God most constantly, just as lords are accustomed to impose a law of fealty, or some such thing, upon their vassals, whom they call serfs, or even upon *emphyteutae,* and always to vindicate their plenary power."[61] Here Junius is attempting to relate Israelite practice not only to European villeinage but also to the Roman law of Emphyteusis—according to which a tenant was given a perpetual right to possess and farm a piece of land, provided that he paid a required tithe to the owner at fixed times.[62] On Junius's account, God intended the jubilee "to show that he is the owner of the territory, and that the Israelites are *emphyteutae,* or perpetual tenants (as the jurisconsults call them) out of the kindness of God their lord."[63] Junius, in short, attempts to find an analog to the jubilee in classical antiquity; his method is one of comparative constitutional analysis. In this he is quite different from Sigonio, who, despite having produced learned compendia of both ancient Roman and Athenian law "in his youth" *(olim iuvenis),*[64] made no attempt to apply their insights to this aspect of Israelite practice.

Junius's successors would frequently adopt his strategy of employing classical paradigms to understand the Hebrew land laws. His disciple Johannes Althusius, writing in the *Politica methodice digesta* of 1603, compared the jubilee to the Athenian *seisachtheia*—or "release of burdens"—instituted by Solon in the sixth century BCE, on the grounds that one of its provisions required that all lands confiscated from *hektemoroi* (or "serfs") as collateral should be returned to their initial owners.[65] Hugo Grotius offered precisely the same comparison in his gloss on Lev. 25:10.[66] What distinguishes Junius's successors is, rather, the prominent role of rabbinic materials in their analyses of the land laws. While Junius neglects the rabbis entirely in his account, by the beginning of the seventeenth century the use of such sources had come to be regarded as indispensable. A good example in this regard is the English Hebraist and separatist minister Henry Ainsworth, who settled in Amsterdam in the mid-1590s and lived there until his death in 1622. Ainsworth begins his *Annotations Upon the Five Bookes of Moses, the Booke of Psalmes, and the Song of Songs, Or Canticles* (written c. 1611–1622),[67] by insisting that it is necessary to consult "Hebrew doctors of the ancienter sort, and some later of best esteeme for learning, as *Maimony,* or Rabbi Moses ben Maimon, (who abridged the Talmuds,) & others" if one wishes "to give light to the ordinances of Moses touching the externall practice of them in the commonwealth of Israel, which the Rabbines did record, and without whose helpe, many of those legall rites (especially in Exodus and Leviticus) will not easily be understood."[68] When it comes to the Hebrew land laws, Ainsworth scrupulously follows his own advice. Maimonides is the primary source for his commentary on Leviticus 25. "*The trompet of the Iubilee, and of the beginning of the yeer,*" Ainsworth tells us, "*is one in every respect,*" and for this detail he credits "*Maimon Iobel,* ch. 10, sect. 11. and Talmud in *Rosh Hasshanah,* chap. 3." On the requirement in Leviticus 25:8 to count seven sets of seven years, Ainsworth explains that "the Hebrewes hold, that this comandement of numbring seven times seven yeeres, and the commandement of sanctifying the fiftieth yeere, vers. 10. was given to the *high Synedrion* (or great Senate of Israel) *onely*: unto whom the care of proclaiming the Iubile and liberties of the same did belong. *Maim.* treat [*sic*] of the *Intermission and Iubile,* ch. 10, sect. 1." These passages, and many others like them, faithfully report Maimonides's codification of the relevant laws in book seven of the *Mishneh Torah.*[69]

We see, then, that by the turn of the seventeenth century it was far from unprecedented for Dutch Hebraists to relate the Hebrew land laws to various Greek and Roman institutions and to use Maimonides and other rabbinic sources to explicate them. Nonetheless, when Cunaeus published his *De republica Hebraeorum* in 1617, he was offering a truly remarkable intervention.[70] He begins the treatise by defending his decision to study the commonwealth of the Hebrews, assuring his readers (in the 1653 English translation of Clement Barksdale) that this republic is "the most holy, and the most exemplary in the whole World. The Rise and Advance whereof, it well becomes you perfectly to understand, because it had not any mortall man for its Author and Founder, but the immortall God; that God, whose pure veneration and worship, You have undertaken, and do maintain."[71] Because Israel had God for its lawgiver, "that people had Rules of Government, excelling the precepts of all wise men that ever were; Which Rules, we have shewed, may in good part be collected out of the holy Bible."[72] For Cunaeus, Israel is the ultimate constitutional model, and, in the second chapter of Book I, he addresses what he takes to be its very foundation. The title of this chapter reads as follows: "On the agrarian law, and its inestimable usefulness; the redemption of lands; the benefit of the jubilee; the free restitution of lands; the requirements of Talmudic law concerning it; on Maimonides and his splendid commentary."[73] Not only does Cunaeus announce his intention to use rabbinic sources (and Maimonides above all)[74] in his analysis of the land laws, but he also insists that these measures should be called *leges agrariae,* equating them with the infamous agrarian laws of Roman antiquity. This he does with no fanfare at all, as if it were the most natural and obvious analogy one could possibly draw. But he was the very first to draw it, and in doing so he knew full well that he was forcing a dramatic reconsideration of the republican inheritance.[75]

Cunaeus begins his account of the Hebrew agrarian by summarizing the principles of the initial distribution. He first establishes the size of the land of Israel, noting that "*Flavius Josephus* often cites *Hecataeus* of *Abdera,* an Author of great Faith and integrity," who in turn reports that "the Jews inhabited a very good Country, and most fruitful, conteining three million Acres."[76] Cunaeus then explains that

> so soon as the holy people had by force of Arms possessed themselves of the promised Land, the chief Captain *Iosua* presently put in execution the commands of *Moses.* The whole Country was divided into twelve portions, and gave it to be inhabited by the twelve Tribes. Then, he numbred the families in every Tribe, and according to the number of persons gave to every family a certain proportion of Lands, and prescrib'd their bounds.[77]

The utility of this initial scheme, on Cunaeus's account, was twofold. First, it ensured that "all were equally provided for; which is the prime care of good Governours in every Common-wealth."[78] Second, it had the effect of securing peace and good order, in that "had every one made that his own upon which he first set his foot, quarels and commotions among the people must needs have followed: for so it usually comes to pass; whilst every one seeks to get and appropriate to himself what was common, Peace is lost."[79]

Having provided his account and defense of the tribal distribution, Cunaeus then turns—like Sigonio and Junius before him—to an analysis of the mechanisms put in place to assure its continuity. His treatment of this topic is, however, markedly different from those of his predecessors:

> Moreover *Moses,* as it became a wise Man, not only to order things at present, but for the future ages too, brought in a certain Law providing that the wealth of some might not tend to the oppression of the rest; nor the people change their course, and turn their minds from their innocent labours to any new and strange employment. This was the *Agrarian Law;* a Law, whereby all possessors of Land were kept from transferring the full right and dominion of it unto any other person, by sale or other contract whatsoever: For, both they that on constraint of poverty had sold their Land, had a right granted them to redeem it at any time; and they that did not redeem it, receiv'd it freely again, by this Law, at the solemn feast of Jubily.[80]

On this view, the jubilee ought to be seen as the archetypal "agrarian law." And Cunaeus goes on to make clear which source we ought to consult for the details of its operation, namely, the "great writer, *Rabbi Moses Ben Maimon,* he that in his divine work entitled *Mishneh Torah* hath happily collected all the Talmudicall doctrine except the trifles, an Author above our highest commendation."[81] This divine author, he goes on to insist, "is much upon the benefit of the Jubily, consisting (saith he) herein, that all Lands returned to their antient Lords, although they had passed through the Hands of a hundred buyers. Neither are excepted by this most learned writer, the Lands which came to any one by donation."[82] Agrarian laws are now divinely sanctioned, and their authoritative expositor is a twelfth-century rabbi.

The next step in Cunaeus's argument should hardly come as a surprise, given what we have said about the character of early-modern republican thought. Once Cunaeus had convinced himself that the jubilee was a *lex agraria,* instituted by God in his own perfect commonwealth, he next had to revisit the conventional account of the Roman agrarian laws. That is, having established that Cicero, Livy, and the other Roman authorities must have had it wrong when they condemned the agrarian movement (because God trumps even Cicero), Cunaeus needed to retell the story of Roman decline in such a way as to vindicate the Gracchi and their acolytes. He turns to this task in the next chapter, observing at the outset that "we have more to say of the utility intended by *Moses* in the *Agrarian* Law" *(de legis agrariae utilitate).* "Certainly," he writes, "it was of great concernment to the Common-wealth, as before we noted, that the avarice of a few should not invade the possessions distributed with so fair equality. It is not unusuall with rich men to thrust the poor out of his inheritance, and deprive him of necessaries, whilst they enlarge their own estate superfluously."[83] But Cunaeus now offers an additional consideration. A second problem about inequality, he maintains, is that "this produceth often a change of Government: For, the truth is, That Common-wealth is full of enemies, wherein the people, many of them having lost their antient possessions, with restless desires aspire to a better fortune. These men, weary of the present, study alterations, and stay no longer, than they needs must, in an unpleasing condition."[84] As Cunaeus goes on to make clear, the particular case he has in mind is that of ancient Rome.

He defends this characterization by offering a remarkable synopsis of the Roman agrarian movement, which deserves to be quoted at length:

> Time was, when at Rome the principall men (drawing all unto themselves, insomuch that one Citizen possessed Land enough for three hundred) were confined by *Stolo*'s Law to five hundred Acres a Man. But that good order, by fraud, was quickly broken. *Stolo* himself was the first to violate his own Sanction, and was found guilty for holding a thousand Acres, making use of his Sons name, whom to that

end he had emancipated. And after, by other arts, many others eluded the sentence of the Law, themselves possessing what was purchased by their Agents. This abuse being perceiv'd by the wise *Lelius,* friend to *Scipio Africanus,* he endeavour'd to reinforce the Law, but overborn by the adverse faction, to prevent contention and discord, he desisted. So the way was open for licence, and possessions were enlarged out of all measure; till at last all Italy and the next provinces fell into a few Hands, as their proper patrimony.[85]

It is worth underlining the drama of this passage. The conventional narrative, as we have seen, had blamed the agrarian laws for provoking the fall of the Roman republic and the rise of the principate. Here Cunaeus turns this argument on its head; we are now being told that it was in fact the *lack* of effective agrarian laws that doomed Rome to civil war. It is indeed very revealing that, immediately following this summary, Cunaeus defensively adds that "it were very easy to allege testimonies" in support of the account he has just offered, "but here is needless."[86] That is, he recognizes that his surprised readers will instinctively bristle at this unfamiliar version of events—according to which the agrarian laws are no longer to be regarded as the engines of sedition anathematized in Cicero and Livy. As it happens, however, Cunaeus is understating things considerably when he claims that he can provide *testimonia* in support of his account. In fact, the narrative of the agrarian movement he offers is not "his" at all, but rather a straightforward paraphrase of a classical source: Plutarch's life of Tiberius Gracchus.[87] In need of a view of Roman history that could answer Cicero and vindicate God's design of the commonwealth of Israel, Cunaeus left the Roman sources behind and turned instead to the Greeks. He would not be the last to do so.

IV

The first English republican to reject the conventional understanding of agrarian laws was James Harrington.[88] Not only did Harrington attack "the Roman writers"[89] for misleading their readers about the character of the agrarian movement, but he also placed what he called an "agrarian law" at the very center of his model constitution, *The Com-monwealth of Oceana* (1656). According to this law, the largest lawful estate should yield no more than £2,000 per annum; no citizen is allowed to purchase additional land if doing so would raise his annual revenue above that threshold. Large fortunes are to be broken up by requiring the relatively equal division of estates among children, and dowries are restricted to the value of £1500. All those found to have acquired properties exceeding the legal limit must forfeit the excess to the state.[90] Harrington fully recognized that this feature of his theory would be widely criticized (we have already noted his observation that "agrarian laws of all others have ever been the greatest bugbears"), and he accordingly took great pains to explain the reasoning behind it. Having summarized the principles upon which *Oceana* is to be designed, he announces in the "Preliminaries" that the test of "whether I have rightly transcribed these principles of a commonwealth out of nature" involves an "appeal unto God and to the world. Unto God in the fabric of the commonwealth of Israel, and unto the world in the universal series of ancient prudence."[91] For Harrington, the ancient Greek and Roman commonwealths were imperfectly designed, but their history exhibits several important general principles, which he calls "ancient prudence." The laws of the Israelite commonwealth, on the other hand, were all "made by an infallible legislator, even God himself,"[92] and are therefore to be regarded as perfect. Indeed, in answering a critic who claims to be unaware "of any prerogative of authority belonging to the Israelitish more than any other republic," Harrington thunders that this "is to take part with the Devil."[93]

The most important principle to be derived from the experience of the ancients, on Harrington's account, is that of the "balance." The distribution of land determines the distribution of power: if one person owns the preponderance of the land in a given territory, the result is monarchy; if a few own it, we have aristocracy; if "the whole people be landlords," it is a commonwealth.[94] When a particular territory has a government that corresponds to its distribution of land, it exists in peace; when the two are mismatched, the territory suffers calamity and civil war. No regime can long survive unless it enacts laws that "fix" the balance so as to provide a stable foundation for its future. Harrington relies in part on the historical record to demonstrate the truth of this axiom, but he makes clear that its chief support lies elsewhere: "This kind of law fixing the balance in lands is called agrarian, and was first introduced by God himself, who divided the land of Canaan unto his people by lots, and is of such virtue that, whenever it hath held, that government hath not altered, except by consent." Here Harrington shows his cards. He explicitly follows Cunaeus in identifying a "Hebrew agrarian law" and is thereby able to summon the full authority of the Biblical narrative in support of the claim that all republics must similarly fix their balance. He is also able to defend the further claim that all governments should be republics, since "God, in ordaining this balance, intended popular government." "The balance of Oceana," Harrington tells us, "is exactly calculated unto the most approved way, and the clearest footsteps of God in the whole history of the Bible; and whereas the jubilee was a law instituted for preservation of the popular balance from alteration, so is the agrarian of Oceana."[95]

Harrington develops this argument in a series of works from the late 1650s, culminating in the second book of his *The Art of Lawgiving* (1659), which is, in effect, his own contribution to the *respublica Hebraeorum* genre. Throughout these writings, Harrington makes clear that he is deeply familiar with previous works on the subject, and with "the whole stream of Jewish writers and Talmudists (who should have had some knowledge in their own commonwealth)."[96] His most explicit acknowledgment of indebtedness to these earlier writers appears in the short essay "Pian Piano," his reply to the royalist divine Henry Ferne. Noting that Ferne seems to take issue with his use of the phrase "commonwealth of the Hebrews," Harrington offers a somewhat peevish response:

> In my book I call the government whereupon we are disputing the commonwealth of Israel; but though I think I did not much amiss, I am the first that ever called it so, and you make no difficulty in your first letter to speak after me. But when I come to call it as all they do that have written upon it then you begin to doubt, and it is "the commonwealth (as I call it) of the Hebrews," whence you will be more than suspected not to have read any of these authors.[97]

Harrington argues, in short, that Ferne reveals his ignorance of the subject matter at hand by choosing the wrong issue to fret about. The innovative piece of nomenclature in *Oceana* is the phrase "commonwealth of Israel"; yet Ferne apparently has no problem with this. He chooses instead to quibble over the phrase "commonwealth of the Hebrews," which had been current throughout the republic of letters for at least two generations. Harrington then lists the "authors" whom Ferne appears to neglect, those who had written before him on the *respublica Hebraeorum:* "Carolus Sigonius, Buxtorfius, Cornelius Bertramus, Hugo Grotius, Selden and Cunaeus."

The last of these authors is the most important for Harrington, as he promptly makes clear when he turns to answer a second and much more significant criticism offered by Ferne. If, as Harrington argues, a popular balance of land yields popular government, then *ex hypothesi* Israel could not have had one, since it was in fact governed by kings. Harrington took this challenge very seriously and offered the following response:

> And for the monarchy of the Hebrews, you say "that you cannot apprehend it to have been upon a popular balance." But the land of Canaan, as it is computed by Hecataeus Abderites in Josephus against Apion [I.195], contained three million of acres; and they among whom it was divided, as appears (Numbers 1:46) at the cense of them taken by Moses in Mount Sinai, amount unto 603,550. Now if you allow them but four acres a man, it comes unto two millions four hundred thousand acres and upwards, by which means there could remain for Joshua's lot, Caleb's portion, with the princes of the tribes, and the patriarchs or princes of families, but a matter of five hundred thousand acres, which holdeth not above a sixth part in the balance with the people; and yet you will not apprehend that this was a popular balance.[98]

Here Harrington attempts to vindicate Cunaeus's claim that the Hebrew agrarian law maintained the equality of tribal patrimonies and did not allow excessive wealth to kings or magistrates. The arithmetic is straightforward: he begins (as Cunaeus had in the *De republica Hebraeorum*)[99] by taking Josephus's estimate of the total available land and calculates that even if the patrimonies were a mere four acres each, they would consume all but 500,000 acres of that total. The remaining land, while sizable, would not be sufficient to produce a monarchical balance. Fair enough, Ferne might counter, but Israel *did* actually have kings. Harrington's reply to this objection is somewhat slippery: "the monarchies of the Hebrews, being the only governments of this kind that ever were erected upon a popular balance, were the most infirm and troubled of all others."[100] That is, the reason we know that Israel had a popular balance is because its monarchy was so disastrous! Harrington had made precisely this argument in *Oceana* itself:

> For if the Israelites, though their democraticall balance, being fixed by their agrarian, stood firm, be yet found to have elected kings, it was because, their territory lying open, they were perpetually invaded, and being perpetually invaded turned themselves to anything which, through the want of experience, they thought might be a remedy; whence their mistake in election of their kings (under whom they gained nothing but to the contrary lost all they had acquired by their commonwealth, both estates and liberties) is not only apparent, but without parallel.[101]

The government did not match the balance, which explains why the Davidic monarchy disintegrated and Israel was given over into captivity.

Returning to this theme in *The Art of Lawgiving*, Harrington offers his most sweeping defense of the proposition that the Hebrew Bible grounds his notion of "balance":

> The over-balance of land, three to one or thereabouts, in one man against the whole people, createth absolute monarchy, as when Joseph had purchased all the lands of the Egyptians for Pharaoh. The constitution of a people in which, and like cases, is capable of entire servitude. *Buy us and our land for bread, and we and our land will be servants unto Pharaoh.* The over-balance of land, unto the like proportion, in the few against the whole people createth aristocracy, or regulated monarchy, as of late in England; and hereupon saith Samuel unto the people of Israel when they would have a king: *He will*

take your fields, even the best of them, and give them unto his ser-
vants. Nec totam libertatem nec totam servitutem pati possunt. The
constitution of a people in this and in like cases is neither capable of
entire liberty, nor of entire servitude. The over-balance of land unto
the like proportion in the people, or where neither one nor the few
over-balance the whole people, createth popular government; as in
the division of the land of Canaan unto the whole people of Israel by
lot. The constitution of a people in which, and like cases, is capable
of entire freedom, nay, not capable of any other settlement.[102]

In order for a commonwealth to endure, it must rest upon an appropriately
wide distribution of property. Such a distribution, in turn, can only be
preserved through the institution of agrarian laws. This, for Harrington,
is the basic lesson of the *respublica Hebraeorum:* "The whole people of Israel, through a popular distribution of the land of Canaan among themselves by lot, and a fixation of such popular balance, by their agrarian law,
or jubilee, entailing the inheritance of each proprietor upon his heirs for-
ever, was locally divided into twelve tribes."[103] The equal agrarian had
now found its way to the heart of republican politics.

Like Cunaeus before him, however, Harrington recognized that his
defense of agrarian laws would remain fundamentally incomplete until
he could offer a revisionist history of Roman decline—one that could
answer the Ciceronian orthodoxy that blamed agrarian rabble-rousers
for the collapse of the republic. Also like Cunaeus, he found such a narrative in the Greek historians of Rome.[104] In the Preliminaries to *Oceana,*
Harrington turns to discuss "this example of the Romans who, through
a negligence committed in their agrarian laws, let in the sink of luxury
and forfeited the inestimable treasure of liberty for themselves and pos-
terity."[105] Having aligned himself firmly with Cunaeus's revisionist commitments, Harrington proceeds to offer his own synopsis of the Roman
agrarian movement:

> Their agrarian laws were such whereby their lands ought to have been
> divided among the people, either without mention of a colony, in
> which case they were not obliged to change their abode; or with the
> mention and upon condition of a colony, in which case they were to

change their abode, and leaving the city, to plant themselves upon the lands so assigned. The lands assigned, or that ought to have been assigned, in either of these ways, were of three kinds: such as were taken from the enemy and distributed to the people; or such as were taken from the enemy, and, under color of being reserved to the public use, were through stealth possessed by the nobility; or such as were bought with the public money to be distributed. Of the laws offered in these cases . . . such as drove at dispossessing the nobility of their usurpations, and dividing the common purchase of the sword among the people, were never touched but they caused earthquakes, nor could they ever be obtained by the people; or being obtained, be observed by the nobility, who not only preserved their prey, but growing vastly rich upon it, bought the people by degrees quite out of those shares that had been conferred upon them. This the Gracchi coming too late to perceive, found the balance of the commonwealth to be lost.[106]

The Gracchi perhaps "did ill" in trying so "vehemently" to correct the travesty that had occurred, but Harrington excuses their zeal on the grounds that "if a cure be necessary, it excuseth not the patient, his disease being otherwise desperate, that it is dangerous; which was the case of Rome."[107] Rome fell, on this account, not because agrarian laws were proposed, but because they were never enacted.

This narrative clearly does not derive from a Roman source. A marginal note in the first edition refers the reader to Sigonio's *De antiquo iure civium Romanorum* (1560); and Sigonio, in turn, attributes his own analysis of the Roman *ager publicus* to the Greek historians Appian and Plutarch.[108] Writing elsewhere, Harrington is more explicit about his sources. In *The Art of Lawgiving*, he insists that "he who, considering the whole story or only that of the Gracchi in Plutarch, shall judge aright, must confess that, had Rome preserved a good agrarian but in Italy, the riches of her provinces could not have torn up the roots of her liberty."[109] Elsewhere in the same text, Harrington likewise exclaims, "Let a man read Plutarch in the lives of Agis and of the Gracchi; there can be no plainer demonstration of the Lacedaemonian or Roman balance."[110] Here Harrington is alluding to the fact that in Plutarch's parallel lives of famous Greeks and Romans, the brothers Gracchus are paired with the Spartan kings Agis and Cleomenes, who similarly tried to re-distribute land. The lesson of these works, Harrington announces, is that "as the people that live about the cataracts of Nilus are said not to hear the noise, so neither the Roman writers . . . seem among so many tribunician storms to hear their natural voice."[111] In attributing Rome's tumultuous decline to strife "about the agrarian," these Roman writers were mistaking "the remedy for the disease." For the truth about the Roman agrarian laws—and a vindication God's own constitutional design in the *respublica Hebraeorum*—one had to turn instead to the Greeks.

This turn, however, came with serious consequences. After all, Plutarch had his own reasons for embracing the Gracchi and rejecting the standard Roman view of the agrarian movement. He was a committed Platonist who defended what he called "the unwritten laws concerning balance and the equality of property" (*Comp.* II.2) on the grounds that such measures were needed to ensure the rule of reason, in the persons of the best men (this he equated with "justice"). As a result, Harrington found in Plutarch not only a defense of the Biblical scheme but also a particular *theorization* of it. Cunaeus, in contrast, did not seem to provide one. The Dutchman had certainly taught Harrington that since God's blueprint for the ideal republic had included agrarian laws, such laws ought to be incorporated into any well-constituted commonwealth. But he had not explained precisely *why* God had instituted the land laws, apart from stressing the purely prudential point that they maintain stability. Harrington, armed with his Plutarch, went much further. God ordained agrarian laws in his perfect commonwealth, Harrington was now prepared to argue, because only a republican balance allows the rule of "justice and right reason."[112] There is, on this account, a "natural aristocracy diffused by God throughout the whole body of mankind," and the people have "not only a natural but a positive obligation to make use of their guides." These chosen few are allowed to rule in well-regulated republics because "the eminence acquired by suffrage of the people in a commonwealth, especially if it be popular and equal, can be ascended by no other steps than the universal acknowledgment of virtue."[113] But in unequal commonwealths it is the corrupt rich, and not the natural aristocrats, who end up ruling. The result is that such common-wealths are governed by passion instead of reason. But, on Harrington's

Platonizing view, "where, by the lusts or passions of men, a power is set above that of the law, deriving from reason which is the dictate of God, God is in that sense rejected or deposed."[114] The rule of God is the government of reason; and the government of reason is the rule of the best men. God's commonwealth had become Plato's Republic.*

V

It is a measure of Harrington's extraordinary influence that, from 1660 onwards, agrarian laws would remain permanently at the center of republican political thought. Writers from Montesquieu to Rousseau, and from Jefferson to Tocqueville, would regard it as axiomatic that republics ought to legislate limits on private ownership in order to realize a particular vision of civic life. Before Cunaeus and Harrington, European political theory had been dominated by the unequal contest between two views of property: one that saw the protection of private property as the central obligation of the state and another that saw the abolition of private property as the ultimate salvation of mankind. Cunaeus's innocuous semantic move in 1617 had opened up a "third way"— one that remains central to modern political thought and practice. A significant strand of republican political theory would now embrace neither the protection nor the abolition of private property, but rather its redistribution. The coercive power of the state would be used to impose limits on private wealth and to generate a roughly egalitarian diffusion of property throughout the commonwealth. Many republican thinkers

---

* This was a comparison that later seventeenth-century authors took very seriously. Claude Fleury, for example, writes in his *Moeurs des Israelites* (1681; trans. 1683) that "*Plato* studied several years in *Egypt,* and he makes *Socrates* speak so many excellent things, founded upon the Principles, which *Moses* taught, that we may conjecture, he had a knowledge of them. The *Jews* really did practice, what he proposes best in his *Common-wealth* [i.e., the *Republic*] and in his Laws; every one to live by his own Labour without Luxury and Ambition, without being liable to be ruined, and growing too Rich, Counting Justice for the greatest good, avoiding all change and novelty. In the Persons of *Moses, David,* and *Solomon* we find examples of that Wise-man, whom he wished for the Government of a State, and the rendering it happy." See Claude Fleury, *The Manners of the Israelites in Three Parts* (London, 1683), p. 212. Fleury's work, in turn, inspired Fénelon's portrayal of the Utopia "Bétique" in Book VII of his massively influential *Les aventures de Télemaque, fils d'Ulysse* (1699).

continued to invoke the example of the Biblical land laws to defend this approach—from Harrington's close friend Henry Neville, who praised Moses for having "divided the lands equally,"[115] to the eighteenth-century Anglican divine Thomas Allen, who argued for limits to the rights of landowners by invoking the "wisdom of *God*" embodied in the Jubilee, and observing that "nothing but such a law as this, well practised, according to *Cunaeus de Repub. Hebraica*, can secure even the temporal peace of the world."[116] Nor were such voices lacking on the other side of the Atlantic. The Boston Patriot Perez Fobes, for example, declared in a 1795 sermon that

> we feel also, and revere the wisdom of GOD in the appointment of a jubilee, as an essential article in the Jewish policy. This, it is probable, was the great palladium of liberty to that people. A similar institution perhaps may be the only method in which liberty can be perpetuated among selfish, degenerate beings in every government under heaven.[117]

But for most, the Biblical warrant for agrarian laws disappeared from view, leaving only the Platonizing rationale that Harrington had developed alongside it. Redistribution in the eighteenth and nineteenth centuries would find a home in republican political theory (and in its socialist variant),* not because it had been authorized by the divine landlord of the earth, but because it was thought to secure the rule of a naturally superior elite. For contemporary republicans, this must seem a somewhat unsettling provenance.

---

* I have in mind here what Marx would later call "utopian socialism"—for example, the programs of Mably and Saint-Simon. For Mably's hierarchical defense of redistribution, see Eric Nelson, *The Greek Tradition in Republican Thought* (Cambridge, 2004), pp. 176–183. Saint-Simon, for his part, was simply parroting Harrington when he wrote that "only when property is allied with enlightenment can the government be solidly based on it." (See Saint-Simon, "De la Réorganisation de la Société Européenne," in *The Political Thought of Saint-Simon*, ed. Ghita Ionescu [Oxford, 1976], p. 90; cf. Saint-Simon, "Catéchisme des Industriels," in *The Political Thought of Saint-Simon*, p. 188). I argue, in short, that it is a great mistake to distinguish "republicanism" from "socialism" during this period. The early socialists should rather be seen as republicans in the Greek, rather than the Roman tradition. Their central commitment is to the rule of experts.

CHAPTER 3

Hebrew Theocracy and the
Rise of Toleration

W HEN PRESSED TO identify the salient and distinguishing features
of political thought in the modern West, many of us would begin
with the principle of religious toleration. Indeed, the notion that the
state should be barred from using its coercive power to compel religious
conformity stands at the very center of modernity's self-understanding.
Yet how well do we really understand the character and history of this
crucial feature of our common world? Despite the recent proliferation of
scholarship on the development of toleration in early-modern Europe,
two serious misconceptions about it remain particularly widespread.
The first is that toleration depends upon, and emerged out of, a process
of *secularization*. That is, as one recent author puts it, religious toleration "could be established only once the questions that inspire political
theology were put to rest";[1] once it had been accepted that "for the purposes of political philosophy and political argument, all appeals to a
higher revelation would be considered illegitimate."[2] The second mis-
conception is that toleration depends upon, and emerged out of, a conviction that church and state should remain fundamentally separate,
neither encroaching upon the prerogatives and responsibilities of the
other. Thus another recent author regards it as a "paradox" that one such
as Hugo Grotius could have embraced broad toleration even though he

"never departed from the conviction that the church was subject to the sovereignty of the state."[3]

Each of these misconceptions, it must be said, contains within it a kernel of truth. There were indeed political writers in the sixteenth and seventeenth centuries who adopted a so-called *politique* defense of toleration, endorsing the practice for purely prudential, secular reasons.[4] And there certainly were sectarian writers (anti-Trinitarians, Anabaptists, Quakers, etc.) who defended toleration while arguing for the radical separation of church and state.[5] I argue, however, that the scholarly focus on these authors has obscured what is the most important and influential tradition of early-modern tolerationist thought—one inextricably linked to the Hebrew revival. Indeed, it is Hebraism, perhaps more than any other cultural force, that explains two vital though counterintuitive facts about the turn toward toleration in Western Europe: that it was primarily inspired by the religious conviction of the "Biblical Century," not by creeping secularization; and that it emerged to a very great extent out of the Erastian effort to unify church and state, not out of the desire to keep them separate.

At the center of this story stands the figure of Josephus, a wealthy Jew of the priestly class who defected to Rome during the Jewish War (66 to 73 CE), and then, as a favored member of the Flavian imperial household, attempted in a series of works to explain his own people to the Hellenized world.[6] It was Josephus who first suggested to Europeans that Israelite society could be regarded as a *politeia*—a political constitution of the sort familiar to Greek philosophy—and that Moses could be understood as its lawgiver *(nomothetes)*.[7] But if Israel had a politeia, of what sort was it? Greek constitutional analysis had identified a limited set of possibilities: the rule of one, the few, or the many, each having correct and deviant forms. Did the Israelite constitution fit one of these paradigms? Josephus's answer, offered in the second book of his *Against Apion,* was revolutionary:

> There is endless variety in the details of the customs and laws which prevail in the world at large. To give but a summary enumeration: some peoples have entrusted the supreme political power to monarchies, others to oligarchies, yet others to the masses. Our lawgiver, however, was attracted by none of these forms of polity, but gave to his

constitution the form of what—if a forced expression be permitted—
may be termed a "theocracy," placing all sovereignty and authority in
the hands of God. To him he persuaded all to look, as the author of all
blessings, both those which are common to all mankind, and those
which they had won for themselves by prayer in the crises of their
history.[8]

For Josephus, Israel had a unique politeia, one in which God himself
was the civil sovereign. As we saw in Chapter 1, Josephus further develops this view in Book Six of the *Jewish Antiquities,* where he narrates
the rise of Israelite kingship. Josephus's Samuel reproaches the people
for having "deposed God from his kingly office"[9] in requesting a mortal
king. The Israelites of the time were

> unaware that it was their highest interest to have the best of all rulers
> at their head and that the best of all was God; nay they chose to have
> a man for their king, who would treat his subjects as chattels at his
> will . . . one who, not being the author and creator of the human
> race, would not lovingly study to preserve it.[10]

God had been their civil sovereign, but, in their folly, they had ejected
him from his throne.[11]

What has this to do with toleration? The connection must at first appear strange. After all, Josephus himself highlights the "unity and identity of religious belief" and the "perfect uniformity in habits and customs" that characterized Israelite theocracy.[12] Why for early-modern
thinkers would such a model have suggested that religious nonconformity should be tolerated? The answer comes when we reflect on what it
means to say that God was the civil sovereign of the Israelite politeia. As
Josephus is anxious to point out, the law code that God gave to his people through Moses contained legislation pertaining to every facet of life,
from the punishment of crime to the regulation of temple cult and the
observance of the Sabbath. That is, the Mosaic law regulated both what
we would regard as civil matters and what we would regard as religious
affairs. No distinction between them was recognized. Yet God gave all of
these laws as *civil* sovereign and entrusted the administration of both

sets of laws to his highest civil magistrate, namely, Moses (and later to Joshua, the judges, kings, and Sanhedrin).[13] Israelite religious laws, in short, were *part* of the Hebrew politeia; they were, on this account, only law in virtue of having been promulgated by the civil sovereign. But this, as Josephus goes on to insist, is not simply or exclusively a fact about ancient Israel—the practice of a defunct republic, without any wider potential application. Rather it stands as a central feature of God's own authoritative constitutional design and, as such, commands universal deference and emulation. "The original institution of the Law," Josephus writes, "was in accordance with the will of God."[14] As a result, "what could one alter in it? What more beautiful one could have been discovered? What improvement imported from elsewhere? Would you change the entire character of the constitution? Could there be a finer or more equitable polity?"[15] The structure of the Israelite commonwealth is perfect, because God is its architect. In this commonwealth there is only one source of law (the civil sovereign) and only one jurisdiction (that of the civil magistrate).[16] God therefore endorses this arrangement and commends it to those who would pursue a godly politics.

For a great many early-modern Hebraists—who used Josephus's analysis as a prism through which to view the full range of Hebrew sources (from the Talmud itself to midrashic works and later rabbinic commentaries)—the notion that God instructs the faithful to lodge plenary power to make all laws, both civil and religious, in the hands of the civil sovereign would serve as a royal road to toleration.[17] For why, they asked, would a civil sovereign make religious law in the first place? Why would such laws be part of a politeia? Their answer: for *civic* reasons. But what sorts of religious practice and observance have important civic consequences? Which were truly vital to the commonwealth, and which were actually incompatible with its goals? These became the only relevant questions, and as early-modern authors scrutinized the records of the Hebrew republic in order to answer them, the set of religious matters deemed worthy of civil legislation grew steadily smaller—until at last it was virtually empty.[18] The emptying of this set did not, however, reflect an emerging conviction that religion ought to have no role in political argument. On the contrary, it proceeded under the fervent belief that God himself required the emptying.[19]

I

Erastianism is usually defined as the conviction that the state ought to have jurisdiction over ecclesiastical matters, but since those we call *Erastians* disagreed sharply among themselves concerning the degree to which the state should in fact regulate religious observance, it would be better to say simply that Erastians regarded the civil magistrate as the only potential source of valid religious law.[20] That is, they insisted that for a religious practice or observance to become law, it must be promulgated as such by the civil sovereign. The central role of the Hebrew revival in the articulation of this Erastian case is evident in its very origins. The Swiss theologian Thomas Lüber (Erastus), who gave his name to the position with which we are concerned, authored the 1568 *Explicatio gravissimae quaestionis utrum excommunicatio . . . mandato nitatur divino, an excogitata sit ab hominibus,* published posthumously in 1589, and later translated into English in 1659.[21] A Zwinglian who opposed the effort to establish Calvinist church discipline in Heidelberg, Erastus wished to vindicate the claim that the church lacks any independent power of excommunication.[22] He begins his 75 *Theses* by announcing that, in considering the question of the relative power of church and state, "I returned to the holy Scriptures: and in my reading I diligently noted, according to my understanding, what was consonant or dissonant to the received opinion."[23] In particular, he continues,

> the consideration of the Jewish Republick and Church did not a little help me. For I thought thus with my self: The Lord himself doth testifie, *Deut.* 4. that his people hath Statutes and Laws so just and wise, that the Institutes of no people, that the Sanctions of no Republick, that no Ordinances, however, wisely constitute, were able to compare with them.[24]

Erastus turns to the commonwealth of the Hebrews for guidance on this crucial matter because he regards it as the authoritative expression of God's own political preferences. Accordingly, he announces that "that Church is most worthily and wisely ordered, which cometh nearest to the constitution of the Jewish Church."[25]

But how should we understand the relationship between civil and ecclesiastical authority in ancient Israel? Here is where the Josephan story comes in. Erastus insists that "in this the matters were so ordered by God, that we find not any where two divers Judicatories concerning manners, the one Politick, and the other Ecclesiastick . . . we did not find either under *Moses,* or under the Judges, or Kings, or under the Government of these that were called Rulers, such two discrepant Judicators."[26] Of particular importance to Erastus is the claim that the Jewish Sanhedrin ("the *Jewish* Magistracy or Senate") had jurisdiction over religious matters as well as civil affairs. To defend this claim, Erastus argues, one need only point out that the Sanhedrin retained religious jurisdiction even under Roman rule. "The *Romanes,*" he writes, "permitted all people but namely the *Jews* living within and, without *Judea,* to use their own Laws in matters belonging to Religion, as so freely according to the Law and rites and manners as *Josephus* witnesseth."[27] Thus, while we should "not doubt but that the Romans had taken to themselves either all or most part" of the Sanhedrin's power in "politick matters, and in cases of wrong" *(in politicis rebus & causis iniuriarum),* we find that the council retained the right to punish crimes "against their Religion" *(contra religionem).*[28] After all, as Erastus argues, in the case of Jesus (who "did not innovate the forme of Judicatories, and government which were administered according to the Laws"),[29] the Sanhedrin sent "armed men to apprehend [him]; it examineth witnesses against him, as it would have it so seem, commandeth Christ to be brought before it," and so on.[30] In short, from the time of the Mosaic revelation through to the final collapse of Jewish sovereignty, God's people observed no distinction between civil and religious law.

But if that is so, Erastus reasons, "I see not why the Christian Magistrate ought not to do the same [as] at this time in the *Jewish* Commonwealth, he was commanded by God to do. Do we think that we can constitute a better form of Church and Common-wealth?"[31] After all, "in the 4. Chapter of *Deuteronomy,* we read that for the judgment and statutes which God had given to the people of *Israel,* that all Nations should admire and praise their wisdome and understanding."[32] If we take this imperative seriously, we will replicate the Israelite system, according to which "the power of restraining unclean and criminall persons was in the Magistrate, whose duty it was not only to punish these men according to the Law of God, but likewise to constitute all the externall Religion, for not *Aaron* but *Moses* did this: God so commanding."[33] The last sentence, in turn, reveals the extent to which Erastianism found itself linked to toleration, even at this foundational moment. Here Erastus reminds his readers that the whole point of his discourse had been to argue that ancient Israel "wanted [i.e., lacked] this Excommunication" *(illi caruerunt hac Excommunicatione)*. Although the Israelites could of course punish those who had committed civil offences, there was no *spiritual* sanction for errors in doctrine or belief: "verily we do not read that any Person at any time amongst the *Jews*, was for the aforesaid cause [impiety], forbid by the Priests, Levites, Prophets, Scribes, or Pharisees to come to the Sacrifices, Ceremonies, or Sacraments."[34] In a politeia where the only binding law is civil law, intrusions of this sort upon the private conscience will not occur. While "externall Religion" falls within the purview of the magistrate (because it can affect civil peace and order), internal religion does not. For, as Erastus asks, "who judgeth the heart but God?"[35]

An almost identical focus on Israelite theocracy is to be found in the next great sixteenth-century expression of Erastian piety, Richard Hooker's *Of the laws of ecclesiastical polity*. Although Hooker composed this classic defense of the Elizabethan Church settlement in the 1590s, the sections of the work dealing most specifically with the question of ecclesiastical authority (all to be found in Book 8) were not published until 1648. Here Hooker introduces his discussion by stating that "we come now to the last thing, whereof there is controversy moved, namely the *power* of *Supreme Jurisdiction*, which for distinction sake, we call the power of *Ecclesiastical Dominion*."[36] Like Erastus before him, Hooker then immediately invokes the unimpeachable authority of God's own ancient commonwealth: "It was not thought fit in the *Jews' Commonwealth* that the exercise of *Supremacy Ecclesiastical* should be denied unto him, to whom the exercise of *Chiefty Civil* did appertain, and therefore their kings were invested with both."[37] God himself had united "Chiefty Civil" with "Supremacy Ecclesiastical," making no distinction between civil and religious law.

Hooker attempts to establish this proposition by taking his reader on a brief tour of Israelite history, beginning with the Hasmonaean period and working backward. Citing I Maccabees (14:41–42), he writes that the Israelites gave plenary power to make all law, civil and religious, "unto *Simon,* when they consented that he should be their *Prince,* not only to set men over the works and over the Country, and over the weapons and over the fortresses, but also to provide for *the holy things.*"[38] Anticipating the objection that "thus much was given unto *Simon* as being both *Prince* and *High Priest,* which otherwise (being only their *Civil Governor*) he could not lawfully have enjoyed"—that is, that he only enjoyed supremacy in both civil and religious affairs because he happened to occupy two different offices—Hooker counters that "we must note that all this is no more than the ancient *Kings* of that people had being *Kings* and not *Priests.* By this power *David, Asa, Jehosephat, Hezekiah, Josiah* and the rest made those laws and orders, which the Sacred History speaketh of concerning mater of mere religion, the affairs of the *Temple* and *Service* of God."[39] The fact that Simon possessed ecclesiastical jurisdiction simply by virtue of being the civil magistrate (and not because he happened also to be high priest) is established by the Bible's attribution of such authority to the early Israelite kings, who lacked the priesthood. Adding one last argument, Hooker insists that "had it not been by the virtue of this power [i.e., the civil magistrate's power over religious affairs], how should it possibly have come to pass that the piety or impiety of the *King* did always accordingly change the public face of religion, which thing the *Priests* by themselves never did."[40] Why would the piety of Josiah, or the infamy of Uzziah, have affected Israelite religious practice, if they had lacked any authority over it?

Having established the crucial Josephan claim that the commonwealth of the Hebrews recognized no distinction between civil and ecclesiastical law or authority, Hooker follows Erastus in drawing the obvious conclusion: "If therefore with approbation from heaven the *Kings* of God's own chosen people had in the affairs of *Jewish* religion supreme power, why not *Christian Kings* the like power also in *Christian* religion?"[41] The constitutional design of ancient Israel retains authority in the Christian world because God himself was its author. Hooker's basic defense of the Elizabethan settlement is thus that it replicates this divinely

sanctioned arrangement. Against those seeking "to prove perpetual separation and independency between the *Church* and the *Commonwealth,*"
Hooker argues that "our estate is according to the pattern of God's own
ancient elect people, which people was not part of them the *Commonwealth* and part of them the *Church* of *God,* but the selfsame people whole
and entire, were both under one chief Governor, on whose supreme authority they did depend."[42] England's politics is godly to the degree that
it follows this example.

So the sixteenth century's last great statement of the Erastian case
fully embraced Erastus's own extraordinary reverence for the Hebrew
commonwealth. For Hooker, as for his predecessor, Hebrew theocracy
served a crucial role of authorization, offering a divine imprimatur for
the legal monopoly of the civil sovereign. But it is equally important to
note that Hooker also followed Erastus in appreciating the degree to
which this model might have profound implications for the question of
religious toleration. Later in Book 8, Hooker invokes his broader argument about ecclesiastical jurisdiction in order to argue for a particular
limitation on the idea of legitimate religious law. "No man doubteth," he
writes, "but that for matters of action and practice in the affairs of God,
for the manner of divine service, for order in Ecclesiastical proceedings
about the regiment of the *Church* there may be oftentimes cause very
urgent to have laws made."[43] But, Hooker continues, "the reason is not
so plain wherefore human laws should appoint men what to believe."
Having identified this distinction between the external, public practice
of religious rituals and the purely internal matter of belief or conviction,
Hooker proceeds to offer two reasons for why the second category
should not be the object of legislation. The first is purely practical: "as
opinions do cleave to the understanding and are in heart assented unto it
is not in the power of any human law to command them, because to pre-
scribe what men shall think belongeth only unto God."[44] Here Hooker invokes an argument that would become a staple of tolerationist polemic
for the next century: laws governing belief should not be made, because
such laws cannot be enforced. Yet Hooker offers a second argument that
is much more interesting for our purposes. The aspect of external religious observance that makes it a proper object of legislation is, he tells
us, its relation to civic peace: opinions in and of themselves have no civic

consequences, but "as opinions are either fit or inconvenient to be professed, so man's law hath to determine of them. It may for public unity's sake require men's professed assent or prohibit contradiction to special articles, wherein as there happily [i.e., by happenstance] hath been controversy what is true, so the same were like to continue still not without grievous detriment to a number of souls except law to remedy the evil should set down a certainty which no man is to gainsay."[45] For Hooker, as for Erastus, the *civil* character of all binding religious law argues for a narrowing of the range of cases in which religious matters should be legislated. This narrowing would become much more pronounced as the center of Erastian argument shifted to the Netherlands.

II

During the first two decades of the seventeenth century, the infant Dutch republic found itself embroiled in a fierce controversy over the creed and authority of the Calvinist Reformed Church. Orthodox Calvinists, led by the Leiden theologian Franciscus Gomarus, insisted that belief in predestination (that is, the notion that God foreordains which human beings will be granted salvation), along with a corresponding denial of any human freedom to cooperate with divine grace, was a nonnegotiable aspect of Protestant faith. They also argued that the Church possessed independent power to enforce uniformity in this and other respects. Gomarus's chief opponent was the second professor of theology at Leiden, Jacobus Arminius, who dissented from the Calvinist orthodoxy on predestination and held the Erastian view that the civil magistrate ought to be sovereign in religious affairs (Arminius had studied with Erastus). Like the sixteenth-century Erastians we have been considering, Arminius also argued for broad toleration of doctrinal differences, denying the right of magistrates to compel adherence to any particular set of credal propositions.[46] Arminius had been nominated to his Leiden chair thanks to the support of Johan van Oldenbarnevelt, the Advocate of the States of Holland (effectively chief magistrate of the United Provinces), whose own Erastianism and Arminianism would eventually lead to his fall from power and execution in 1619. Before he fell, however, Oldenbarnevelt patronized a remarkable circle of Arminian theorists (also known as

"Remonstrants," after the 1610 *Remonstrantie* drafted by one of their chief advocates, Jan Uytenbogaert),[47] whose meditations on the relationship between Erastianism and toleration would prove enormously influential in the later seventeenth century. The first and most famous of these theorists was Hugo Grotius.

As a client of Oldenbarnevelt, it is hardly surprising that Grotius should have endorsed the broad nexus between Erastianism and toleration. But Grotius is far more explicit than even most Dutch Arminians about the degree to which the example of the *respublica Hebraeorum* was responsible for producing that nexus. Grotius first broaches this subject in the *De republica emendanda,* a manuscript treatise he composed sometime between 1600 and 1610. Here Grotius offers his proposals for a much-strengthened Dutch Council of State—independent of the States-General—which could serve to unify the fractious federation of the United Provinces. As he begins his analysis, however, he pauses to consider the standard of evidence we ought to employ in political argument. Which institutions and practices should we hold up as exemplary? Which texts should we regard as authoritative? Men are fallible and, as a result, even their best efforts need not carry any normative force. Yet there is, Grotius firmly believes, a way out of this uncertainty: "If, however, there is somehow to be found a republic which could rightly point to the true God as its founder, then this must clearly be the one that all other ones should set themselves to imitate and seek to resemble as closely as they can."[48] If God himself had designed a commonwealth, then the constitution of that republic would be perfect and authoritative. And, as Grotius promptly adds, God *did* design such a commonwealth: the republic of the Hebrews.

If the Israelite example is to teach us anything, however, we must first know what sort of arrangement it embodied, what sort of politeia it was. Accordingly, Grotius next inquires, "Of what kind then, should we say, was this Hebrew state? For of course we fully appreciate the different types of government distinguished by the philosophers, and the names put to them."[49] At this point Grotius expresses a familiar reservation:

> But perhaps we had better not after all rely too much on these men
> who, to be perfectly honest, could not make head or tail of this field

of civil arts and who in fact understood just as little as the man who has decided to compete in a race without proper knowledge of the location of the starting-boxes or finishing-post. For what else are people doing who put human intelligence in the place of divine providence and merely praise the usefulness of a work instead of, as they ought to, glorifying its author?[50]

The philosophers who taught us about the different types of government (chiefly Aristotle) were laboring in the dark; they did not know God's providence, and so they could not understand the proper goal of political science: namely, to approximate as closely as possible God's own perfect constitutional design. Having rejected the civil science of Greek philosophy, Grotius turns to the obvious alternative:

I think therefore that to this matter, which was in fact unknown to these men of old, we should rather apply a new term, one which was actually coined most appropriately by Josephus, a man who was knowledgeable in the history of his native country as he was intimate with the finenesses of a foreign language. Josephus was the first to call this form of government "theocracy," to denote, no doubt, that in this state the highest and only authority belonged to God, to whose worship all other things were made subservient.[51]

The last sentence of this passage might seem to suggest that Grotius drew a deeply anti-Erastian lesson from the example of Israelite theocracy. That is, the claim that "all other things" in ancient Israel were made subservient to God's worship might seem to be an argument for giving full civil authority to priests, rather than full religious authority to kings. But Grotius promptly clarifies the Erastian direction of his thoughts. The point, once again, is that the Josephan model makes God himself a civil sovereign and demonstrates that all Israelite religious law was civil law. "The Hebrew nation," Grotius insists, "received from God laws which concerned both his worship and their secular lives."[52] The Hebrew republic offers no example of independent ecclesiastical jurisdiction—all laws were given by God as civil sovereign. Furthermore, as Grotius goes on to argue, God placed both civil and religious authority in the hands of his chief civil magistrate: first the judges, then the kings, and finally in the Sanhedrin. Grotius is particularly anxious to establish this final point. Citing the Talmudic tractate *Sanhedrin,* he notes that "the learned interpreters of the Talmud understood the powers of this council [Sanhedrin] to mean that it was authorized to interpret divine laws and enforce new laws and that it was this body that in fact exercised control over public affairs, not only in the days of kings and rulers, but also when there was no king or ruler."[53] Arguing, as many early-modern Hebraists did, that the Sanhedrin was coeval with Biblical monarchy,* Grotius insists that this supreme civil authority also possessed supreme religious jurisdiction. He defends this claim by invoking the power of the Sanhedrin to suspend various religious obligations and to offer absolution:

> That the right to pardon and administer justice against the rigidity of the highest law was also one of this council's prerogatives, I conclude from the fact that they had the right to discharge men of oaths and vows. Indeed the Jews state expressly in the explanation of the imperative prescripts of the law that the Sanhedrin could in fact allow the temporary dispensation of something prohibited if there was good reason.[54]

For Grotius, the Sanhedrin's authority to suspend religious law proves its ecclesiastical supremacy and vindicates the Erastian conviction that a well-ordered republic will assign religious jurisdiction to the civil magistrate.

Grotius expanded on these ideas considerably in his great treatise on church government, the *De imperio summarum potestatum circa sacra,* completed in 1617, but not published until 1647 (two years after his death). His thesis, once again, is that the example of the Hebrew republic teaches Christians to be Erastians, and he makes this case by surveying Israelite history and arguing that, in each of its phases, no distinc-

---

* In this they were simply following the account given in the Talmud (BT Sanhedrin 2a), according to which the seventy elders whom Moses was commanded to bring with him into the Tabernacle (see Numbers 11:16) were themselves (along with him) the first Sanhedrin.

tion was made between civil and ecclesiastical jurisdiction. To show that the early Israelite kings possessed supreme authority in religious affairs, he elaborates on a central argument of the *De republica emendanda*.

> The Hebrew kings even exempted, as it were, some actions from God's law; for although it was the law *that nobody shall eat of the sacrifice of the Lord's peace offerings while an uncleanness is on him* [Lev. 7:10 and 22], yet Hezekiah, having poured forth prayers to God, granted an indulgence to the unclean to eat from the sacrifice [2 Chron. 30:18]. It was also the law that sacrificial animals should be slain by the priests [Lev. 1:5]; and yet we read that twice under Hezekiah the Levites were brought in to perform that priestly duty, for lack of priests [2 Chron. 29:34 and 30:17]. This is not to say that the kings released anyone from the bond of God's law, for no man can do that: they gave in to equity (the best interpreter of divine and human law), and declared that by God's own intention God's law lost its obligation in such situations.[55]

While fully acknowledging God's status as civil sovereign in Israel, Grotius once again highlights the prerogative of Hebrew kings to suspend or amend various religious obligations arising out of the Mosaic law. God gave this authority to the civil magistrate, and to no one else.

Grotius then turns his attention to the Second Temple period, following the Babylonian Captivity. Here too, he wants to argue, Israelite government preserved the religious authority of the civil magistrate. In respect of "criminal jurisdiction" *(criminalis iurisdictio)*, which applies to "those who commit a crime in sacred matters as well,"[56] the authority of the Hebrew kings was transmitted first to Ezra (mediated by the authority of the Persian kings), and then to the Sanhedrin. Grotius writes, "For just as Ezra possessed all kinds of jurisdiction granted him by the Persian king, so the Sanhedrin of the Jews, by permission of the Roman people and afterwards of the emperors, kept this part of that jurisdiction together with the right of detention and flogging."[57] Perhaps the most important aspect of this religious jurisdiction—one which, as we have seen, had always occupied a central place in Erastian argument—concerned excommunication. Grotius makes his case by offering a somewhat confused typology of the different levels of excommunication discussed in the Talmud and later rabbinic sources (chiefly Maimonides).

> The Hebrew masters [i.e., rabbis] teach us that there were three degrees of expulsion from the synagogue; the first of these is called *nidduy*: this punishment meant that the man in question had to stand in the synagogue, on his own and in a humiliating place; the second was the *herem*: it was unlawful for someone notified of this to appear in the synagogue; the others did not use his services for anything, and he received only the bare minimum to keep him alive. The third degree is called in Aramaic *shammata*; it is applied to someone who would have been condemned to death by Mosaic law, but could not be killed since the authority of imposing capital judgment had been taken away; his company and touch were shunned by everyone.[58]

In fact, the Talmud uses the Aramaic term "shammata" as an equivalent for *nidduy* and (according to some) *herem* as well, not to identify a yet more severe form of excommunication.[59] Nonetheless, Grotius's interest in this final form is quite understandable: the fact that it stands in for a capital sentence makes clear, on his account, that excommunication in the Hebrew republic was part of criminal jurisprudence. That is, it was emphatically within the authority of the civil magistrate, and its object was the punishment of crime, not impiety.

Now Grotius is fully aware that "some men assign to it [the Sanhedrin] a double structure: one civil, the other ecclesiastical," and that "they have authorities for their view who are great but recent."[60] But Grotius insists that their arguments are "unsound" *(invalida)*. To begin with, "who are more fit to believe in a historical question regarding the Jewish state than the Jews themselves?"[61] Having argued that the testimony of Jewish sources is to be privileged when it comes to the deciphering of Israelite governance, Grotius then notes that "the Jewish rabbis, not to be despised as authorities in such matters, say that this great Sanhedrin did render judgment in all cases put before them,"[62] both civil and religious. The Sanhedrin was entrusted with "God's affairs" *(Dei res)*, and "it is more in agreement with Scripture to understand by 'God's affairs' everything which is defined by God's law and which is to be judged from God's law."[63] Grotius concludes, therefore, that "it has been proved that jurisdiction in sacred affairs belongs to the supreme powers as a part of their authority in the broad sense. . . . No jurisdiction naturally belongs to priests, that is no coercive or imperative judgement, since their whole function by its nature includes no such thing."[64]

Yet Grotius wants to place the matter beyond doubt by demonstrating that the religious supremacy of the civil magistrate was retained in the Jewish world even after the final expulsion from the land of Israel in the year 70 CE. He begins this proof by citing an observation of Maimonides: "Maimonides, the most learned of the Jews, notes that the high priest did not attain his office by right of succession, but because he was elected by the great Sanhedrin, yet from a limited number of families, and that the deputy of the high priest was chosen in a similar manner."[65] Grotius then argues, again with reference to Maimonides, that "this right of the election which the Sanhedrin possessed, seems to have been a royal prerogative in the time of the kings. Otherwise we could hardly account for the reference in Scripture to the effect that Zadok *was put in the place of Abiathar by the king,* clearly in the same terms as Benaiah is said to *be put over the army in the place of Joab.*"[66] In other words, the Sanhedrin had been entrusted with the responsibility of electing the high priest, and this right of election had originally been a royal prerogative. The next stage of Grotius's argument aims to establish that "the rulers who later attained to the royal position, the Syro-Macedonians, the Romans and the descendants of Herod laid claim to the creation of high priests by appealing to the same right, whereas in all other matters, they left the Jews their self-governing status."[67] That is, on Grotius's account, the various foreign occupiers of the land of Israel had asserted their right to designate priests on the grounds that they had inherited all of the prerogatives of the Israelite *civil* sovereign. In making this argument, they revealed their assumption that, in the Israelite politeia, the civil magistrate had possessed supreme jurisdiction over religious affairs. In this respect, the postexilic Jews then merely aped the practices of their conquerors:

> The following may well be mentioned too: as once the Jews in Babylonian captivity had a leader who was called Ras Galiuth, so after

> the destruction of Jerusalem the Jews were led by different patri-
> archs in different parts of the world; the Jews believed that these
> were the offspring of David, and therefore obeyed them as their law-
> ful rulers. . . . These patriarchs did everything as if by royal right,
> and they also appointed rulers of the synagogues and priests in
> charge of the synagogues.[68]

The Jewish *resh galuta,* or "exilarch" (*rosh ha-golah* in Hebrew), who
claimed descent from the Davidic monarchy, likewise asserted an inherited right to appoint clergy.[69] All of this, for Grotius, makes plain that,
throughout the history of the Israelite *politeia,* the civil magistrate had
always been granted supremacy over religious affairs.

Grotius, then, fully embraced the Erastian commitment to civil supremacy and, like his predecessors, derived his arguments for that position from the authoritative example of the *respublica Hebraeorum.* It is by
no means coincidental that he also emerged as an important defender of
religious toleration. Already in the *De imperio,* Grotius had begun to
sketch the implications of his ecclesiology for the question of religious
nonconformity. In legislating religious matters, Grotius argued, the supreme magistrate ought to be motivated by the need to foster "harmony,"
order, and civic peace,[70] not the desire to impose doctrinal uniformity
(an effort that, on his account, tends to the disturbance of common-
wealths). That is, religious laws ought to be made for civic reasons—and
God cannot intend the civil sovereign to legislate that which threatens
civic upheaval. It is, however, in the *De iure belli ac pacis* of 1625 that
Grotius makes fully explicit the direction of his thoughts. He broaches
the subject in Book II, chapter 20, in the midst of an expansive discussion of the right to punish. The question is: What sorts of religious errors are punishable by human, civil law? In formulating the question
this way, Grotius has, of course, already advertised his Erastian commitments: he clearly assumes from the beginning that religious errors cannot be punishable on earth by anything *other* than civil law. Indeed,
Grotius immediately acknowledges that, in asking whether a given religious practice or belief ought to be criminalized, he will simply be considering "its peculiar effects" on "human society."[71] Religious belief itself,
Grotius proceeds to argue, is useful for civil society, in that it encourages

private morality and the cultivation of civic virtue—and "the Usefulness of Religion is even greater in that great Society of Mankind in general, than in any particular Civil Society,"[72] because it compensates for the absence of coercive law in nature. As a result, it becomes immediately apparent that Grotius's civil sovereign will have *some* interest in religious affairs, because certain features of religious belief and observance do have important civic consequences. The question remains: which?

In venturing an answer, Grotius returns to an argument he had first developed in a short, unpublished 1611 manuscript on theological disagreement, entitled *Meletius* (named for Meletius Pagas, the late sixteenth-century patriarch of Alexandria, who had attempted to unite the various Christian denominations in common cause against the Turks).[73] He posits the existence of a "true Religion, which has been common to all Ages"— one which forms the foundation of all human religions—and argues that it rests on four "fundamental Principles":

> the first is, that there is a GOD, and but one GOD only. The second, that GOD is not any of those Things we see, but something more sublime than them. The third, that GOD takes Care of human Affairs, and judges them with the strictest Equity. The fourth, that The same GOD is the Creator of all Things but himself.[74]

These four principles, on Grotius's account, comprise the basic human religious sensibility, and they have profoundly important civic consequences. The first two establish the existence of an authoritative divinity. The third "is the Foundation of an Oath, in which we call GOD to witness what passes in our Hearts, and at the same Time submit to his Vengeance; whereby we likewise acknowledge his Justice and Power."[75] The fourth, in identifying God as the creator of the world, offers "a tacit Indication of his Goodness, and Wisdom, and Eternity and Power."[76] For Grotius, "these Truths lead to Virtue."[77] The general belief in a God who cares about human affairs is a necessary condition of effective civil society. As a result, Grotius is happy to concede that "those who first attempt to destroy these Notions, ought, on the Account of human Society in general, which they thus, without any just Grounds, injure, to be restrained, as in all well-governed Communities has been usual."[78]

When it comes to other sorts of beliefs, however, Grotius draws a very different conclusion. In addition to arguing that belief in the four foundational principles is necessary for civic life, Grotius also wants to establish that it is sufficient.[79] On his account, no additional doctrinal views are required in order for men to be good citizens; the politically necessary "Sort of Religion" can "be kept up" without them.[80] The result is clear enough: the civil sovereign will have no reason to legislate belief in these extraneous doctrines, and broad toleration will be the rule. Grotius's example is once again ancient Israel.

> The Law of GOD, tho' delivered to a Nation [Israel], which by the concurrent Proof of Prophecies and Miracles, either seen or transmitted to them by incontested Authority, was infallibly assured of the Truth of these Notions, tho' it utterly detested the Adoration of false Gods, did not sentence to Death every Offender in that Case, but such only whose Crime was attended with some particular Circumstance; as, for Instance, one who was the Ringleader and Chief in seducing others, *Deut.* xii.1, or a City that began to serve Gods unknown before, *Deut.* xiii.12, or him who paid divine Honour to any of the Host of Heaven, hereby cancelling the whole Law, and entirely relinquishing the Worship of the true GOD, *Deut.* xvii.2. . . . Nor did GOD himself think the Canaanites, and their neighbouring Nations, tho' long addicted to vile Superstitions, ripe for Punishment, till by an accumulation of other Crimes they had enhanced their Guilt, *Gen.* xv.16.[81]

Grotius's argument is straightforward. Even in the case of ancient Israel, which had received the law as a direct and unimpeachable revelation (so that there could be no question of its authenticity), heterodox beliefs about the deity were not regarded as criminal, unless they were employed to disturb the peace, or to question the politically necessary belief in the four fundamental principles. Within the Hebrew republic itself, as Grotius had pointed out in the very first chapter of *De iure,*

> there always lived some Strangers . . . in the *Hebrew, hasidei 'ummot, Righteous among the Gentiles;* as it is read in the *Talmud, Title of the*

King [*sic*]. . . . These, as the *Hebrew Rabbins* say, were obliged to
keep the Precepts given to *Adam* and *Noah,* to abstain from Idols and
Blood, and from other Things, which shall be mentioned hereafter in
their proper Place; but not the Laws peculiar to the *Israelites.*[82]

Those who did not abide by the Mosaic law were allowed to live among
the Israelites unmolested, provided that they observed a minimal standard of general morality.[83] The Canaanites, for their part, had been
punished by God, not for holding false beliefs about the divine, but on
account of manifest crimes. Grotius concludes from all of this that one
may not make war on non-Christian peoples as a punishment for their
denial of Christ, and that it is illicit to punish Christians (like Arminius
and his followers) "because they are doubtful, or erroneous as to some
Points either not delivered in Sacred Writ, or not so clearly but to be capable of various Acceptations, and which have been differently interpreted by the primitive Christians."[84] This latter point, like the entirety
of Grotius's Erastian politics, is established "from the standing Practice
of the Jews."[85]

A second Dutch Remonstrant, Peter Cunaeus, elaborated on Grotius's arguments in the *De republica Hebraeorum libri III* of 1617.[86] Cunaeus's friendship with Grotius seems to have begun in 1608–1609 and
continued throughout the latter's long exile. Apart from sharing important political and theological commitments, the two men had several
close mutual friends (among them Johannes Boreel, who introduced
Cunaeus to Maimonides's *Mishneh Torah*), and both had strong roots
in the Dutch province of Zeeland (the birthplace of Cunaeus and the
home of Grotius's wife, Maria van Reigersbergh).[87] Cunaeus makes clear
at the very outset of the text that he will be arguing the Erastian line.[88]
The epigraph to Book I is taken from Josephus's *Against Apion,* and Cunaeus underlines its implications in the opening chapter. He first insists
(in Clement Barksdale's 1653 English translation),[89] addressing the States
of Holland, that the commonwealth of the Hebrews should be regarded
as "the most holy, and most exemplary in the whole World. The Rise and
Advance whereof, it well becomes you perfectly to understand, because
it had not any mortall man for its Author and Founder, but the immortall God; that God, whose pure veneration and worship, You have

undertaken, and do maintain."[90] Having posited the peculiarly authoritative character of Israelite governance, Cunaeus then turns to an analysis of its form. Speaking of Moses, he writes that

> In his institution of that Common-wealth [Israel], the most holy
> upon earth, he assigned the Supreme Power to God; and when
> others find other names (as the matter requires) calling the Government Monarchy, Oligarchy, or Democracy, he conceived none
> of these appellations suitable to the nature of so great an Empire:
> Wherefore he ordained such a kind of Government, which *Flavius* [Josephus] saith may very significantly be stil'd *Theocracy,*
> that is, a Commonwealth whose Ruler and President is God alone;
> for he provided all affairs were managed by divine judgement and
> Authority.[91]

Citing the familiar Erastian *locus classicus* from Josephus, Cunaeus announces his conviction that, in ancient Israel, "all affairs," both civil and religious, were placed under the jurisdiction of the civil magistrate. Cunaeus returns to this theme in Book I, chapter 14, during his discussion of Israelite kingship. "We said above," he writes, that "the Jews had such a Common-wealth, which in the Scripture is called a Priestly Kingdom. Whence it follows, that their Kings did not only govern in civill affairs, and military, but were Presidents of Religion and holy Ceremonies."[92] Kings in the Israelite commonwealth were "sacred persons, to whom Gods Commission and the voice of a Prophet gave Empire, honour and authority."[93] The Levites certainly had particular duties with respect to the Temple, but "the Over-sight of Sacred things, the Soveraign power and judgment pertained unto them [the kings]."[94] Cunaeus amplifies his point by turning to Maimonides:

> The Talmudicall writers well observe how much the King excelled
> all, both Priests and Prophets: which we will relate out of Maimonides. The words are to this effect [MT, *Melakhim* 2]: *It was a*
> *Statute, that the chief Priest should reverence the King, and yield his*
> *place to sit in, and himself stand, when the King came to him. But the*
> *King standeth not in the presence of the Priest.*[95]

By telling us that the high priest was required to yield his place to the king, and not the other way around, Cunaeus's Maimonides establishes the supremacy of the civil magistrate in ancient Israel. Furthermore, Cunaeus (like Grotius before him) insists on the prerogative of the Sanhedrin—appointed by the monarch—to judge in religious matters. He writes, turning once again to Maimonides, that "the Talmudic tractate called Middot records that the power and judicial authority of the senators who belonged to the great council lay above all in the fact that they held court (in the part of the Temple called Gazith) over the cases of priests whose membership in their family or clan was disputed."[96] He adds that "in the second chapter of this Talmudic tractate, it is written that these senators also made decisions about the physical flaws and illnesses that (as though they were evil omens) made any priests they afflicted legally unfit to serve."[97] Indeed, as Cunaeus goes on to explain, it was the departure from this divinely instituted Erastian regime that doomed the republic of the Hebrews. After the Babylonian captivity, the "injustices of the age" gave birth to a "new scheme of government":[98] "the High Priests ruled all, without assuming the Title of Prince or King."[99] These corrupt, unrestrained priests "enjoyed themselves, or disposed of to others, all favour, wealth, and power: the rest were Plebeians without honour, without authority."[100] The result of their depravities was such that, by the time of the Maccabees, "nothing of the sound and the ancient customs remained."[101]

Cunaeus highlights one particular feature of this depraved and degenerate Second Temple commonwealth. It was, according to Cunaeus, only after the erosion of ancient Israel's divinely instituted Erastian constitution that the Jews "fought one another over their conflicting interpretations of the Holy Book, and their disagreements about doctrine and matters of ritual."[102] This was the birth of "sects and heresies" *(sectae haeresesque)*. Cunaeus, following Grotius, spends a great deal of energy illuminating the folly and danger of these divisions.

> Men whose religion was excessively zealous split themselves into opposing factions, and once divided by a single mistake they disagreed on everything and came to be entirely at odds with one another. Now, for the first time, a great many people embraced the

Sadducees' insane idea that the soul like the body is mortal, and that after this life good and evil men receive neither rewards nor punishments. At the same time, the Pharisees (who were far too argumentative) used their imaginations to broaden the scope of divine law far beyond anything Moses had intended. After these two sects a third emerged, the Essenes; they scrutinized every aspect of religious purity with somewhat more care than the others, in accordance with anxious superstitions of their own.[103]

Robbed of both kings and prophets, the Jews "wasted no time in applying their mental energies to burrowing into every area of knowledge, and their dull human minds wrapped themselves up in their own obscure thoughts."[104] The result is that "it became the sickness of an inferior age to dig up controversies and questions from sacred texts."[105] Cunaeus's aim in this discussion is abundantly clear. He wishes to show that in the true, pristine Hebrew commonwealth, there had been no attempt to generate an orthodox, dogmatic religious creed or to establish divisive metaphysical propositions. The health of the politeia did not depend in any way on the assertion of such views or on the suppression of dissenting opinions. Quite the contrary, it was understood that any attempt to establish uniformity concerning opaque matters of doctrine would create unnecessary dissension and disturb the commonwealth.[106] The godly politics of the Hebrew commonwealth embraced toleration.

Cunaeus returns to this theme in Book III, offering his own account (deeply reminiscent of Grotius's) of the minimal religion that ancient Israelite law insisted upon. He writes that "the principles in which the whole community of Israelites necessarily had to believe were more or less as follows: that the power of God was able to accomplish great and remarkable things; that his promises were ironclad; that he was to be worshipped not with shallow appearances (the easiest way to put on a show of piety) but with submission of the soul."[107] Acceptance of these principles, Cunaeus suggests, is indeed necessary for the establishment of effective civil society and may therefore be legislated by the civil sovereign. These essential articles of faith, with their important civic role, are to be sharply distinguished from the "ridiculous superstition" *(ridic-*

ula superstitio) that makes a fetish out of "definitions" *(de definitionibus)* and precise "formulas" *(formulas)*.[108] The adoption of these dogmatic assertions, and the accompanying endorsement of legal coercion against dissenters, lead only to "strife, anger, and a total free-for-all."[109] Cunaeus makes clear at this point that he is thinking not only of ancient Israel after the Babylonian Captivity but also about the quarrel between Remonstrants and their orthodox adversaries in the contemporary Netherlands. "If the Apostles and the writers of the gospels were to enjoy a brief stay on earth and return to the company of men, they would be astonished at how many different analyses and approaches were being used to interpret their books, and how many bizarre constructions had been assembled from the trivial notions of the sophists."[110] Alas, in "this world grown old,"[111] we have lost sight of God's plan. Such theological minutiae were never given the force of law in God's own *politeia*. In Israelite theocracy, God gave all religious law as civil sovereign, and no civil sovereign (least of all God) would ever legislate that which is inimical to civic life. A godly, Erastian regime will therefore tolerate disagreement over inessential points of religious doctrine.

III

The troika of Hebraism, Erastianism, and toleration, forged so powerfully in the Dutch Remonstrant controversy, would resurface almost identically in the ecclesiological debates surrounding the English Revolution.[112] When the Westminster Assembly of Divines convened in July of 1643 (in defiance of Charles I) to debate the proper form of the Church of England, the three most prominent Erastian spokesmen were all eminent Hebraists—Thomas Coleman (nicknamed "Rabbi Coleman"),[113] John Lightfoot, and John Selden.[114] Indeed, in the English context, one can say without much exaggeration that to be a Hebraist was to be an Erastian, and vice versa.[115] Debate within the assembly quickly focused on the question of the relationship between civil and ecclesiastical jurisdiction, and discussion turned predictably to the Hebrew commonwealth. As one of the first historians of the Assembly, John Strype, put it in 1700, "these Divines in their Enquiries into the Primitive Constitution of the Christian Church, and Government thereof in the Apostles

Days, built much upon the Scheme of the *Jewish* Church; which the first Christians being *Jews,* and bred up in that Church, no question conformed themselves much to."[116] John Lightfoot, who took careful notes on the proceedings, reports that one of the Presbyterian ministers, Joshua Hoyle of Dublin, "fell to speak of the layelders among the Jews in their Sanhedrim [*sic*]: to which I answered they were their highest civil magistrates; and that the Houses of Parliament judge in ecclesiastical matters, and yet were never yet held lay-elders."[117] That is, in response to the claim that the Sanhedrin was itself a kind of independent ecclesiastical authority, Lightfoot reminded the Assembly of the Sanhedrin's civil role in ancient Israel, likening it to Parliament. The ensuing debate was so fierce that it occupied an entire day of deliberation, December 11, 1643: Lightfoot summarizes the day's discussion by announcing that "our business was upon the elders in the Jewish church"[118]—and notes that when one of the discussants, Sir Benjamin Rudyerd, complained that "it would prove but weak ground" to build the Church of England "upon the Jewish," no one came to his defense.[119]

The first sustained intervention of the day was by Thomas Coleman, who undertook to brief the Assembly on the function of "elders" in the Hebrew republic.

> 1. Elders were not chosen purposely for ecclesiastical business. There were four sorts of officers in Israel: 1. *zekenim* 2. *rashei 'avot* 3. *shofetim* 4. *shoterim.* The *zekenim* [elders] were the gravest and wisest men in country, city, or calling; and they were not assistant to the priest, for there is mention of *ziknei kohanim* [priestly elders] Jer. xix. 1, 2 Kings xix.
> 2. Their election by the people, Num. i. 16.3. They were the representative body of the whole congregation for all business ecclesiastical or civil. Lev. xiv. 15, Ezra x.14.
> 3. They were messengers of state, Judges xi.1.
> 4. They were messengers of any public contract.
> 5. They were to be present at the public courts of judicature.
>
> The lxx senators in the Sanhedrim were civil officers, Deut. 1. assisters to Moses, not to the priests: "Regibus assidere soliti" ["they were accustomed to sitting with the kings"] Philo. Jud.[120]

Coleman's intention, of course, was to establish the civil jurisdiction of the Sanhedrin and deny the existence of any independent ecclesiastical authority in God's commonwealth.[121] When a Presbyterian critic, George Gillespie, attempted to answer Coleman by arguing that the Jews "had two sorts of consistories in every city, one in the gates, and the other in the synagogue"—and, accordingly, that "elders [read: church governors] are distinct from rulers"—Lightfoot himself rose to the challenge: "Here I spake, That the two sanhedrims and the two consistories in every city are not owned by the Jewish authors:—and for that I alleged Maimonides at large, and proved three courts in Jerusalem, and yet no difference of one ecclesiastical and the other civil; and that there was but one court or consistory in every city."[122] The elders in the Sanhedrin were, he insisted, "civil magistrates, as our Parliament," and yet they had jurisdiction over "blasphemy, idolatry, false doctrine, &c.," for which "the censure was civil, being capital."

The other primary defender of the Erastian case at Westminster was, as Lightfoot makes clear, "Mr. Selden," who introduced an extended discussion of the Jewish law of excommunication in order to establish the civil character of the punishment (Selden would later describe Erastus as "another Copernicus").[123] Selden was, of course, the most famous English Hebraist of the seventeenth century and had been deeply influenced by Grotius (he owned two manuscript copies of the latter's *De imperio*).[124] Already in his 1617 *History of Tithes* (for which he was excoriated by clerical opponents), Selden had insisted that the *respublica Hebraeorum* bestowed supreme jurisdiction over ecclesiastical matters on the civil magistrate. The payment of tithes, Selden argued, was a *civil* obligation in ancient Israel, regulated and supervised by the civil magistrate. Early in the text, he offers an example:

> How the payment of these Tenths was either obserued or discontinued partly appeares in holy Writ, partly in their institution of more trustie Ouer-seers (whom they called *ne'emanim*) for the true payment of them. For after the new dedication of the Temple by Iudas Machabaeus, untill his fourth successor Ioannes Hyrcanus (being neer thirtie yeers) all duly paid their first fruits and Therumahs, but the first or second Tithe few or none iustly; and that through the

corruption of those Ouerseers. Whereupon their great Sanhedrin, or Court of seuentie Elders (that is, the *bet din ha-gadol*, that is, the greatest Court, that determined also, as a Parliament, of matters of State) enacted, that the Ouerseers should be chosen of honester men.[125]

In other words, the fact that the selection of overseers was left to the Sanhedrin (the "Parliament") demonstrates that this crucial religious practice was firmly within the purview of the civil magistrate in the Hebrew republic.

Selden would return to this theme throughout his life, culminating in his massive study of ancient Jewish jurisprudence, the *De synedriis et praefecturis iuridicis veterum Ebraeorum* (1650–1655), which likewise aimed to vindicate the authority of the civil magistrate over religious affairs.[126] But it was in a different, earlier work that Selden, like Grotius and Cunaeus before him, explored the consequences of his Hebraic Erastianism for the question of toleration. This work, the *De jure naturali et gentium iuxta disciplinam Ebraeorum* (1640), was published three years before the convening of the Westminster Assembly and contained Selden's derivation of a universal morality from a set of commandments putatively given to Noah and his children after the flood— the so-called *praecepta Noachidarum,* the Noachide laws *(Mitzvot B'nei Noach).* These laws included a prohibition of idolatry and blasphemy; a commandment to establish courts and laws; and a ban on murder, theft, sexual immorality, and the cutting of meat from live animals (the first six were, on the rabbinic account, also given to Adam).[127] The enumeration of these seven laws does not appear in the Bible itself, nor does the idea that they constitute a minimal standard of sufficient moral behavior for non-Jews. Selden owes all of this to rabbinic literature—specifically, to the canonical account in BT Sanhedrin 56a–b and its elaboration in Maimonides's *Mishneh Torah.* As we have seen, Grotius had made some use of the *praecepta Noachidarum,* but Selden went much further than his teacher in suggesting that these laws were *themselves* to be understood as the laws of nature: that is, Selden rejected the notion that natural law was accessible to the unaided reason of human beings and argued instead that it was the result of divine legislation.

For Selden, the fact that the Hebrew commonwealth regarded observance of these Noachide laws as morally and religiously sufficient for
non-Israelites demonstrated God's embrace of broad toleration. The
Mosaic law, Selden explains, allowed non-Jews of various sorts to reside
among the Israelites and did not require all such persons to observe the
full array of Biblical commandments. The rabbis explained this state of
affairs by invoking the post-Biblical conceit of the Noachide laws: the
"sons of Noah" (the rabbinic idiom for non-Jews) were to be judged in
ancient Israel solely on the basis of their degree of fidelity to these universal commandments given by God to all men. Selden elaborates as
follows:

> There were two classes of men from the Noachide peoples or Gen-
> tiles who were permitted to reside in Israelite territory. The first of
> these comprised those who completely converted to the rite of the
> Hebrews, or who, having been admitted in the manner shortly to be
> indicated, openly acknowledged the authority of the body of Mosaic
> law. The second of these classes included those who were permitted
> to reside there without any profession of Judaism.[128]

Following the rabbis, Selden refers to the first class as "proselytes of justice" *(proselyti iustitiae;* Heb. *gerei tzedek),*[129] and the second as "proselytes of the dwelling-place" *(proselyti domicilii;* Heb. *gerei toshav).*[130] The
existence of the second category—sojourners who were allowed to live
within the Hebrew republic even though they did not acknowledge or
abide by the full Mosaic law—proves, for Selden, that Israelite theocracy
practiced toleration.[131]

Selden gives two broad explanations for this state of affairs. The first
is to be found in the rabbinic maxim that "the righteous among the gentiles will have a share in the world to come" (BT Sanhedrin 105a).[132]
Once again following the rabbis, Selden insists that the Biblical God
looked with favor on those "sons of Noah" who observed the seven post-
diluvian laws. It was not necessary to their salvation to abide by any additional strictures or to hold any additional beliefs (although it was necessary to observe the Noachide laws for the right *reason,* namely, out of a
belief that God had commanded them). Accordingly, one explanation

for Israelite toleration is to be found in the rabbinic conviction that there was no theological reason to compel the "sons of Noah" to observe the Mosaic law.

The second explanation is far more familiar, in that it closely approximates the one offered by Grotius. The general observance of these precepts, for Selden, is sufficient to ensure civil peace—and the Erastian framework of Israelite theocracy will not allow additional religious laws that serve no civic purpose. Indeed, Selden goes a good deal further than Grotius by insisting that even the demands of the Noachide laws themselves were less exacting than usually supposed. Turning once again to the rabbis, Selden points out that the "blasphemy" criminalized in the Noachide laws was to be understood quite narrowly: it referred only to the act of publicly and brazenly defaming or denying "the holiness, power, truth, or unity of the Divinity," and transgressors were not to be put to death unless they had actually cursed God's name.[133] Moreover, the view of previous Christian Hebraists—Schickard among them—that the second Noachide law (forbidding blasphemy) constituted a requirement for "sons of Noah" to join in the public worship of God was simply erroneous: these scholars had misconstrued the law *('al birkat ha-Shem)* as a command to "bless God," whereas in fact it is an injunction not to "curse God" (the Hebrew root בָּרָךְ , as Selden explains, can carry both meanings).[134]

Even in the case of idolatry, Selden is anxious to inform us (again echoing Grotius) that the Israelites were only required to remove all traces of pagan religion from within their borders—they were not required to eliminate idolatry elsewhere.[135] As Selden's energetic disciple Henry Stubbe would put it in 1659, the requirement to banish idolatry "was not ever extended to the *Gentiles* living separate from the *Jews:* for the *Israelites* were not hereby obliged to destroy all their Neighbours that were Idolators, they never practiced such a thing."[136] The requirement was, rather, to be understood as "part of the *Political* Law of *Moses.*"[137] And while the Israelites did indeed understand the Noachide ban on idolatry to require veneration of the true God, Selden eagerly points out that even those proselytes who lived among them were not punishable by civil law if they refused to join in public worship—their punishment, rather, was expected to come "from the hand of heaven" *(mi-yad shammaim)*, since their nonparticipation posed no civic threat.[138] On Selden's Erastian reading of Israelite theocracy, God only endorses compulsion in matters of religion when it is necessary to secure the health of the politeia.*

Selden's Hebraic scholarship inspired an entire generation of political writing, culminating in the work of England's two most prominent Interregnum Erastians, James Harrington and Thomas Hobbes. Harrington, for one, announces his Hebraic Erastianism at the very outset of *Oceana* (1656). In the Hebrew republic, "the government of the national religion appertained not unto the priests and Levites, otherwise than as they happened to be of the Sanhedrim or senate, to which they had no right at all but by election . . . in Israel the law ecclesiastical and civil was the same; therefore the Sanhedrim [*sic*], having the power of one, had the power of both."[139] Hebrew theocracy recognized no distinction between civil and religious law; both had a common source in the will of the civil sovereign (God), and both fell within the jurisdiction of the civil magistrate. This was certainly true in the case of Moses, "nor, after the institution of the Sanhedrim, was the high priest other than subordinate unto it, whether in matters of religion or state. Nay, if he had given them just cause, he might be whipped by the law, as is affirmed by the Talmudists."[140] As Harrington would put it later in *The Art of Lawgiving* (1659), "between the law and the religion of this government there was no difference; whence all ecclesiastical persons were political persons, of which the Levites were an entire tribe, set more peculiarly apart unto God, the king of this commonwealth, from all other cares than that only of his government."[141] One can therefore say without hesitation that the sort of "civil power" that "cometh nearest unto God's own pattern, regards as well religion as government."[142]

In his later works, Harrington attempted to advance this argument by wading into a deeply fraught controversy over the history of the primitive church. The question was whether the early, apostolic church had

---

* It should be noted in this connection that Selden explicitly argued in favor of toleration for Catholics during the Westminster Assembly, and he denied that they should be regarded as idolators. See Gerald Toomer, *John Selden: A Life in Scholarship*, 2 vols. (Oxford, 2009), vol. 2, pp. 574–575.

ordained officers using *chirotonia* (balloting by the showing of hands) or *chirothesia* (anointing by the imposition of hands). The stakes in this seemingly abstruse debate were actually quite high. If one could show that apostolic church officials were in fact designated by a process of general balloting, that would imply that they were civil appointees—and would accordingly suggest an acknowledgment of civil supremacy over ecclesiastical affairs. If, however, church officials were ordained through the imposition of hands (i.e., by other church officials), that would suggest the existence of an independent ecclesiastical authority. Since it was generally agreed that the practice of the primitive church in this respect must have derived from Jewish practice, the debate quickly came to focus on the manner in which religious officials were ordained in the Hebrew republic. Harrington's argument on this point is predictable: "Ordination in the commonwealth of Israel, being primarily nothing else but election of magistrates, was performed by the suffrage of the people" (recall that, for the republican Harrington, the people were collectively the highest civil authority).[143] He elaborates in a crucial section of *The Prerogative of Popular Government* (1658): "All ordination of magistrats, or of the senators or elders of the sanhedrim, of the judges or elders of inferior courts, of the judge or *suffes* of Israel, of the king, of the priests, of the Levites, whether with the ballot or viva voce, was perform'd by the *chirotonia* or suffrage of the people."[144] In the Hebrew republic, church officials were selected by ballot because they were not qualitatively different from civil officials. Harrington justifies this claim by invoking "the authority of the Jewish lawyers, and divines call'd the Talmudists," and proceeds to offer a list of those upon whom he relies: "the Gemara Babylonia, Midbar Rabba, Sepher Siphri, Sepher Tanchuma, Solomon Jarchius [Rashi], Chiskuny, Abarbanel, Ajin Israel, Pesiktha Zotertha."[145] Harrington makes clear that he himself has little direct familiarity with these sources. "The truth is," he admits, that "in all that is talmudical I am assisted by Selden, Grotius, and their quotations out of the rabbys, having in this learning so little skill, that if I miscall'd none of them, I shew'd a good part of my acquaintance with them." J. G. A. Pocock wryly (and correctly) observed some time ago that, in this respect, "Harrington was not indulging in false modesty."[146] Although Harrington writes of Selden and Grotius that he "makes use of their learning, but of my own reason," his debt to his Hebraic Erastian teachers is profound.

What Harrington adds to the account of his predecessors is a particular narrative of decline, locating the rise of "priestcraft" (the usurpation of political power by clerics) in a particular moment of Israelite history.[147] In this respect, he echoes Cunaeus's earlier account, while adding his own idiosyncratic touch. He agrees with Cunaeus that the rise of priestcraft should be traced to the untrammeled rule of the high priests after the Babylonian captivity, but his focus is on a shift from divinely ordained *chirotonia* to the corrupt practice of *chirothesia*. All Israelite officers were chosen by ballot "till the sanhedrim got a whim of their own, without any precept of God, to ordain their successors by the *chirothesia* or imposition of hands, and the parties being so ordained called Presbyters, became capable of being elected into the judicatories, whereby cheating the people of the right of electing their magistrates, the sanhedrim instituted the first Presbyterian government."[148] Even at this stage, however, the process of degeneration was not yet complete, in that "the senate, if not every senator, by this innovation had right to ordain"—the priests were not yet firmly in control. Soon, however,

> by Hilel high priest and prince of the sanhedrim, who liv'd some three hundred years before Christ, means was found to get the whole power into his hand, which being of such consequence, that no magistrate could thenceforth be made but by the high priest, it changed this same first presbytery, the high priests becoming afterwards monarchs, as I may say, into the first Papacy.[149]

Harrington argues that "this track was exactly trodden over again by the Christians." "First," he writes, came "the presbytery [i.e., lay-elders], from thence to the bishop, and that by means of the same chirothesia or imposition of hands taken up from the Jews, and out of this bishop stept up the Pope, and his seventy cardinals, anciently the presbytery, or seventy elders of Rome, in imitation of those of Israel." The descent from *chirotonia* to *chirothesia,* first in the Hebrew commonwealth and then in Christ's church, epitomizes the degeneration of godly Erastianism into corrupt priestcraft.

For Harrington, this story of priestly usurpation maps on to a narrative about the decline of toleration. He adopts from Grotius and Selden a firm conviction that the pristine Hebrew republic broadly tolerated diverse religious practices and commitments. Also like his predecessors, he grounds this conviction in an interpretation of the Noachide laws:

> It is a tradition with the Rabbins, that there were seven precepts delivered to the children of Noah: 1. concerning judicatories: 2. concerning blasphemy: 3. concerning perverse worship: 4. concerning uncovering of nakedness: 5. concerning the shedding of man's blood: 6. concerning rapine or theft: 7. concerning eating of things strangled, or of a member torn from a living creature. This tradition throughout the Jewish government is undoubted: for to such as held these precepts, and no more, they gave not only (as I may say) toleration, but allowed them to come so near unto the temple as the gates, and called them "proselytes of the gates."[150]

Like Grotius and Selden, Harrington uses this aspect of the rabbinic tradition to assert that, in God's commonwealth, observance of a minimal standard of universal religious and moral behavior was regarded as politically sufficient. No further coercive religious law was promulgated because there was no civil reason for it—and in the Hebrew republic, religious law was a matter for the civil magistrate alone. It is precisely this model of toleration that Harrington recommends for Oceana. There will be a national religion, just as there was in ancient Israel (Harrington defends this as a means of securing "liberty of conscience" for the nation as a collective whole).[151] But there will also be liberty of conscience for individuals, constrained only by the need to secure the politeia. His proposal is as follows:

> That no religion being contrary unto or destructive of Christianity, nor the public exercise of any religion being grounded upon or incorporated into a foreign interest, be protected by or tolerated in this state. That all other religions, with the public exercise of the same, be both tolerated and protected by the council of religion; and that all professors of any such religion be equally capable of all elec-

tions, magistracies, preferments and offices in this commonwealth, according unto the orders of the same.[152]

The phrase "contrary unto or destructive of Christianity" is interesting in this context. By "contrary unto," Harrington clearly does not mean "in disagreement with," since he is on record stating that "not everyone in the Christian commonwealth should be any more a Christian indeed, than everyone in the Israelite commonwealth was an Israelite indeed"— and, as we have seen, he himself referenced the rabbinic view that non-Israelites were allowed to live in the Hebrew republic, so long as they observed the Noachide laws.[153] Rather, he evidently uses the term to mean "set in opposition to"—that is, dedicated to undermining Christianity in some public and ostentatious manner. This would fit well with other contemporary uses of the phrase "destructive of Christianity."[154] Only religions hostile to the "well settled peace of the kingdom,"[155] or those requiring extranational loyalties (i.e., Catholicism) are to be excluded. The goal, as Harrington makes clear, is that "decency and order, with the liberty of conscience, would still flourish together."[156]

Harrington does not simply argue, however, that toleration should be adopted because it does no civic harm: he also insists that it confers a great civic benefit. It alone makes republican government possible. As an empirical matter, one cannot have true civil liberty without liberty of conscience: "The power that can invade the liberty of conscience can usurp civil liberty, and where there is a power that can usurp civil liberty, there is no commonwealth."[157] Moreover, "men who have the means to assert liberty of conscience have the means to assert civil liberty; and will do it if they are oppressed in their consciences."[158] The two liberties are intertwined; they are mutually supporting, and the denial of one threatens a rejection of the other. The existence of a power capable of compelling the conscience beyond what it necessary for civic peace is incompatible with republican government—and only republican government allows human beings to live as citizens in a godly commonwealth. This, on Harrington's account, explains the decline of the Hebrew republic: ancient Israel protected the liberty of conscience "till the civil liberty of the same was lost, as under Herod, Pilate, and Tiberius, a three-piled tyranny."[159] But Harrington believes that it is within the reach of any human community to restore the pristine Hebrew theocracy. To be ruled by republican laws is to be ruled by reason, rather than by the passions of men. But, on Harrington's account, to be ruled by reason is to be ruled by God. The rule of reason cannot survive the creation of a power strong enough to deny the liberty of conscience, which means that theocracy forbids religious coercion. Once again, Hebraism, Erastianisn, and toleration go together.

When the Anglican divine Henry Ferne penned his critique of Harrington's *Oceana,* he declared that "what is said in relation to the church, or religion in the point of government, ordination, excommunication, had better beseemed Leviathan and is below the parts of this gentleman."[160] At first glance, this will appear to be a remarkably perverse claim. Harrington and Hobbes, one might suppose, could not have been more different: the former, after all, was a republican Platonist who hailed from the gentry, while the latter was a materialist defender of absolute monarchy whose father had been a drunken curate. But Harrington himself was happy to admit that, when it came to questions of ecclesiology, he was an ally of "Mr Hobbes."[161] The reason is that Harrington found in Hobbes's works a thoroughgoing defense of precisely his own brand of Hebraic Erastianism (the more remarkable, given that Hobbes seems to have known no Hebrew at all).[162] Harrington also recognized, as did several acute seventeenth-century readers, that Hobbes's political science offered a surprisingly sweeping endorsement of toleration—and that these two facts were closely related. Although it has become commonplace to suggest that Hobbes's Erastianism was rather tepid in *De cive* (1642) and only emerged fully in *Leviathan* (1651), the former text in fact contains an explicit derivation of Erastian politics from the model of Josephan theocracy.[163] Hobbes begins this discussion by distinguishing, very much as Grotius had, between two types of divine law: "*naturall* (or *morall*) and *positive.*" Natural law "is that which God hath declared to all men by his *eternall word* borne with them, to wit, their *naturall Reason.*"[164] These laws are universally binding on men as such. Divine positive law, on the other hand, refers to "the Lawes which he [God] gave to the Jewes concerning their government, and divine worship, and they may be termed the *Divine civill Lawes,* because they were peculiar to the civill government of the Jewes, his peculiar people."[165] This second category includes only the laws that God gave the Israelites as their civil sovereign. The covenant at Sinai, Hobbes reminds us, transformed Israel into the "Kingdom of God" *(regnum Dei)* a fact established, on Hobbes's Josephan account, by the fact that I Samuel 8 describes the election of Saul as a rejection of God's kingship.[166] For further support, Hobbes turns explicitly to Josephus: the character of Israelite theocracy is demonstrated by

> the doctrine also of *Judas Galilaeus*, where mention is made in *Ioseph. Antiq. of the Iewes, 18. Book, 2. Chap.* in these words: *But* Judas Galilaeus *was the first authour of this fourth way of those who followed the study of wisdome. These agree in all the rest with the Pharisees, excepting that they burn with a most constant desire of liberty, beleeving God alone to be held for their Lord and Prince, and will sooner endure even the most exquisite kinds of torments, together with their kinsfolks, and dearest friends, then call any mortall man their Lord.*[167]

The God of Israel, as civil sovereign, gave laws concerning both "government" and "divine worship," both civil and ecclesiastical affairs. From this authoritative example, we should learn that the civil magistrate is the only legitimate source of law; that "all *humane law* is *civill*" and that "*civill Lawes* may be divided according to the diversity of their subject matter, into *sacred*, or *secular*."[168]

Hobbes maintains course nine years later in *Leviathan*, while intensifying his polemical assault on independent Episcopal authority. The chief ground of the argument is, once again, "the Kingdome of God, (administered by *Moses*,) over the Jewes, his peculiar people by Covenant."[169] Indeed, Hobbes's meditation on Israelite theocracy occupies such a large proportion of Part III ("Of a Christian Common-wealth") that it would not be unreasonable to describe this section of *Leviathan* as Hobbes's own contribution to the *respublica Hebraeorum* genre. Hobbes repeats his conviction that

> by the *Kingdome of God,* is properly meant a Commonwealth, instituted (by the consent of those which were to be subject thereto) for their Civill Government and the regulating of their behaviour,

not only towards God their King, but also towards one another in point of justice, and towards other Nations both in peace and warre; which properly was a Kingdome, wherein God was King, and the High priest was to be (after the death of Moses) his sole Viceroy, or Lieutenant.[170]

God as civil sovereign handed down both civil and ecclesiastical laws and instituted as subordinate magistrates first Moses and then the high priest.[171] While Moses held this office, "neither Aaron, nor the People, nor any Aristocracy of the chief Princes of the People, but Moses alone had next under God the Soveraignty over the Israelites: And that not onely in causes of Civill Policy, but also of Religion."[172] Moreover, "from the first institution of God's Kingdome, to the Captivity, the Supremacy of Religion, was in the same hand with that of the Civill Sovereignty; and the Priests office after the election of Saul, was not Magisteriall, but Ministeriall."[173]

Having offered this analysis of God's politeia, Hobbes is quick to draw the standard Erastian conclusion. Because Moses enjoyed both civil and ecclesiastical jurisdiction, "we may conclude that whosoever in Christian Commonwealth holdeth the place of Moses is the sole messenger of God and interpreter of His commandments."[174] The Christian commonwealth should model itself on the Hebrew republic, assigning complete jurisdiction over religious affairs to the civil magistrate. There can be no independent ecclesiastical authority. Like Selden (whom he seems to have befriended at around the time he published *Leviathan*),[175] Hobbes insists that contemporary clerics make a grave mistake in supposing that they have an independent "divine right" to tithes; such offerings were simply "Publique Revenue" in "the Kingdom of the Jewes, during the Sacerdotall Reigne of God,"[176] and as such were collected under the authority of the civil sovereign. Hobbes likewise follows his Erastian predecessors in arguing (again based on Israelite practice) that excommunication is "without effect" when "it wanteth the assistance of the Civill Power."[177] Legitimate coercion can only arise from the civil law. Hobbes writes,

A Church, such a one as is capable to Command, to Judge, Absolve, Condemn, or do any other act, is the same thing with a Civil

Common-wealth, consisting of Christian men; and is called a *Civill State,* for that the subjects of it are *Men;* and a *Church,* for that the subjects thereof are *Christians. Temporall* and *Spirituall* Government, are but two words brought into the world, to make men see double, and mistake their *Lawfull Soveraign.*"[178]

There is, as Hobbes delights in arguing,

no other Government in this life, neither of State, nor Religion, but Temporall; nor teaching of any doctrine, lawfull to any Subject, which the Governour both of the State, and of the Religion, forbiddeth to be taught: And that Governor must be one; or else there must needs follow Faction, and Civil war in the Common-wealth between the *Church* and *State;* between *Spiritualists* and *Temporalists;* between the *Sword of Justice,* and the *Shield of Faith.*[179]

Here the law of nature joins the law of the Hebrew republic in proclaiming the ecclesiastical supremacy of the civil magistrate—which is hardly surprising since, according to Hobbes, God is the author of both.

Given the force of these arguments, Hobbes's Erastian credentials have never been in doubt. It is only recently, however, that scholars have begun to take seriously the seventeenth-century view that Hobbes should also be regarded as an advocate for toleration. This revisionist account of the Hobbesian project initially invites a degree of understandable skepticism. It is undeniable, after all, that Hobbes gives his sovereign extremely broad powers to shape religious life in the commonwealth: the Hobbesian sovereign has the right to establish the ceremonials of public religious worship,[180] determine which Biblical books are to be regarded as canonical,[181] interpret scripture on behalf of the commonwealth as a whole,[182] excommunicate subjects,[183] regulate which books may be printed and which opinions publicly uttered,[184] and compel subjects to perform even those actions that they regard as contrary to the dictates of their conscience.[185] But, as several scholars have pointed out, Hobbes was equally explicit about the *limits* placed by his political science on the right of sovereigns to dictate doctrine and belief.[186] The more cynical may observe that Hobbes's most extensive attacks on the criminalization of doctrinal nonconformity (the *Historical Narration Concerning Heresy,* the *Dialogue between a Philosopher and a Student of the Common Laws of England,* and the *Historia Ecclesiastica*) all date to the period in the late 1660s during which he himself was under investigation for heresy. Yet Hobbes had already insisted in *Leviathan* that the rights of the sovereign flow from the laws of nature, and that the laws of nature aim at peace. The sovereign should therefore stand ready to make all laws necessary for the preservation of peace, but none besides.[187] And like Grotius and Selden before him, Hobbes argued that most religious laws will be excluded by this reasoning.

Hobbes begins by accepting the fundamental tolerationist piety that, although subjects "ought to obey the laws of their own Soveraign, in the externall acts and profession of Religion," when it comes to "the inward *thought* and *beleef* of men, which human Governours can take no notice of, (for God onely knoweth the heart) they are not voluntary, nor the effect of the laws, but of the unrevealed will, and of the power of God, and consequently fall not under obligation."[188] But Hobbes goes very much further than this, and the vehicle for his argument is once again the example of the Hebrew republic. His strategy is to exploit an opening left by Selden's analysis of the Israelite prohibition on idolatry: recall that Selden had been anxious to use rabbinic sources to demonstrate that, even in the case of idolatry (a behavior prohibited under the universally binding Noachide laws), the Mosaic law did not require Israelites to enforce conformity beyond their borders. Hobbes, for the first time, supplies a *reason* for this forebearance: in God's own commonwealth (and only there), idolatry counts as an act of treason:

> For God being King of the Jews, and his Lieutenant being first Moses, and afterward the High Priest; if the people had been permitted to worship, and pray to Images, (which are Representations of their own Fancies,) they had had no farther dependence on the true God, of whom there can be no similitude; nor on his prime Ministers, Moses, and the High Priests; but every man had governed himself according to his own appetite, to the utter eversion of the Commonwealth, and their own destruction for want of Union. And therefore the first Law of God was, *They should not take for Gods,* ALIENOS

DEOS, that is, *the Gods of other nations, but that only true God, who vouchsafed to commune with Moses, and by him to give them laws and directions, for their peace, and for their salvation from their enemies.* And the second was, that *they should not make to themselves any Image to Worship, of their own Invention.* For it is the same deposing of a King, to submit to another King, whether he be set up by a neighbour nation, or by our selves.[189]

On this revolutionary line of argument, idolatry is criminalized within the Hebrew republic, ᴁnd not outside of it, because the practice only takes on *civic* significance when God himself is the civil sovereign.[190]

Hobbes places this claim about idolatry at the center of a broad reconsideration of religious laws in the Hebrew republic. His basic argument is that the large number of these statutes in ancient Israel is to be explained by the unique character of that politeia. Where God is the civil sovereign, a substantially greater number of religious matters will acquire civic significance. What follows, of course, is that very few religious matters will take on such significance when God is *not* civil sovereign. Hobbes is perhaps most explicit on this point in his discussion of the Decalogue. While the second table of the law (containing the prohibitions on theft, murder, adultery, etc.) specifies the "duty of one man towards another" under the law of nature, the first is a very different matter:

Of these two Tables, the first containeth the law of Soveraignty: 1. That they should not obey, nor honour the Gods of other Nations, in these words, *Non habebis Deos alienos coram me;* that is, *Thou shalt not have for Gods the Gods that other Nations worship, but only me:* whereby they were forbidden to obey, or honor, as their King and Governour, any other God, than him that spake unto them by Moses, and afterwards by the High Priest. 2. That they *should not make any Image to represent him;* that is to say, they were not to choose to themselves, neither in heaven, nor in earth, any Representative of their own fancying, but obey Moses and Aaron, whom he had appointed to that office. 3. That *they should not take the Name of God in vain;* that is, they should not speak rashly of their King, nor dispute his Right, nor the commissions of Moses and Aaron, his

Lieutenants. 4. That *they should every Seventh day abstain from their ordinary labour*, and employ that time in doing him Publique Honor.[191]

Hobbes was not, of course, the first to distinguish the first table from the second or to suggest that while the latter summarized universal laws of nature, the former contained positive laws given only to the Israelites. But Hobbes is saying a good deal more than this. He is arguing that the laws against idolatry, blasphemy, and Sabbath violation are themselves to be understood as *political* laws that only make sense in a common-wealth governed by God as civil sovereign.[192] In God's commonwealth, idolatry is treason, and blasphemy is sedition. In all other common-wealths, however, the case is fundamentally different. The laws of the Hebrew republic do not bind Christians, and Jesus "hath not subjected us to other Laws than those of the Common-wealth; that is, the Jews to the Law of Moses, (which he saith (*Mat.* 5) he came not to destroy, but to fulfill,); and other Nations to the Laws of their severall Soveraigns, and all men to the Laws of Nature."[193] The result, as Hobbes makes clear, is that very few religious laws will be required in his Christian Common-wealth. At the end of *Leviathan,* he famously praises the "Independency of the Primitive Christians to follow Paul, or Cephas, or Apollos, every man as he liketh best," because "there ought to be no Power over the Consciences of men, but of the Word it selfe, working Faith in every one, not alwayes according to the purpose of them that Plant and Water, but of God himself, that giveth the Increase."[194]

IV

The case of Hobbes might, however, appear to present a major difficulty for the broader argument I have been making in this chapter. After all, I have not only insisted that the Hebrew revival largely explains the con-junction of Erastianism and toleration, I have also suggested that this explanation argues against the view that toleration emerged out of a pro-cess of *secularization*. That is, I have made the case that Hebraist Eras-tians defended toleration out of the deeply held *religious* conviction that God himself established the practice in his perfect commonwealth.

When it comes to Hobbes, however, there are good reasons for supposing that this cannot be the case.[195] For while Hobbes is prepared to acknowledge the logical necessity of a "first mover" God, he is emphatic
that we cannot know anything about this putative creator (because we
only have experience, through our senses, of the material world; and
we cannot infer anything about the nature of God from the nature of the
world as we experience it). Moreover, he offers lengthy arguments denying that the Bible can be regarded as a pristine, divine revelation. The
books of the Hebrew Bible, he tells us, were for the most part written,
not by Moses himself, but rather by others (and then redacted by Ezra
after the Babylonian Captivity),[196] and even the direct revelation that
Moses may have received must have been in some important sense mediated.[197] That is, we can only have access to God's revelation *as Moses
understood it*—which is different from having access to the revelation itself. These convictions would appear to make it very difficult for Hobbes
to regard the "republic of the Hebrews" as an authoritative expression of
God's own constitutional preferences. His use of the Israelite example
might, therefore, seem fully compatible with a secularization narrative.
For Hobbes, we might suppose, the purpose of identifying ancient Israel
as a republic is not to hold it up as exemplary and authoritative, but
rather to *diminish* its grip on our imagination. The Hebrew Bible, on
this account, is to be understood simply as the political constitution of a
defunct republic—one no more or less inspired than any other ancient
republic. As such, it would have no more to teach us about how we should
structure our politics than, say, the laws of Lycurgus.

   This account, it must be said, is far from implausible, especially given
Hobbes's notoriously opaque characterization of his religious convictions. My own view, however, is that it is mistaken, and that Hobbes
does in fact regard the republic of the Hebrews as peculiarly authoritative.[198] In support of this proposition, I can offer both a negative and a
positive argument. On the negative side, Hobbes never actually makes
the deflationary argument sometimes attributed to him, and it certainly
does not *follow* from the beliefs in question (i.e., that we can have no
knowledge of God's properties, and that all revelation is mediated) that
the Bible is not an authoritative revelation of God's will. The fact that we
cannot be absolutely sure that the Biblical text corresponds in every

particular to God's intended message does not necessarily mean that it carries no authority—on the contrary, it might still be regarded as the closest approximation of that message and therefore as highly authoritative (if often ambiguous). Indeed, my positive argument is that Hobbes takes precisely this view. Although he argues that much of the Biblical text was composed long after Moses's death, he nonetheless insists that Moses did indeed write all of those sections directly attributed to him (including the law codes).[199] As for the remaining sections, Hobbes affirms that he sees no "reason to doubt, but that the Old, and New Testament, as we have them now, are the true Registers of those things, which were done and said by the Prophets, and Apostles."[200] He also expresses his belief that God instructed the Israelites "by a Voice, as one man speaketh to another";[201] that "God himself hath revealed" his word to his prophets and apostles;[202] and that, for modern men, the Biblical books "supply the place" of direct revelation,[203] comprising "all rules and precepts necessary to the knowledge of our duty both to God and man."[204] These comments appear to suggest that Hobbes's understanding of the Hebrew commonwealth was far more complicated than the secularizing view supposes.

Yet, however ambiguous and contentious the case of Hobbes may be, there certainly were other important thinkers who did indeed use the topos of the Hebrew republic to advance this deflationary agenda—to undermine the authority of Scripture, in the service of a secularizing political science. In many ways the father of this approach was Machiavelli, who notoriously presented Moses as "just another lawgiver," alongside Romulus, Theseus, and Cyrus.[205] But, without question, the most influential exponent of this view was Baruch Spinoza. This fact is all the more important to appreciate since, on first inspection, Spinoza's use of the Israelite example in his *Tractatus theologico-politicus* (1670) bears remarkable similarities to that of Grotius, Selden, and Harrington. Like his predecessors, he treats the Hebrew constitution as an embodiment of the Erastian ideal. Reason teaches us, on Spinoza's account, that the "sovereign power" *(summa potestas)* should "have supreme authority for making any laws about religion which it thinks fit."[206] Moreover, "religion acquires its force as law solely from the decrees of the sovereign."[207] It is therefore both a necessary and sufficient condition of valid religious

law that it be promulgated by the civil sovereign. Spinoza has nothing
but contempt for those who attempt to prove the contrary from the example of the Hebrew republic:

> I do not pause to consider the arguments of those who wish to sepa-
> rate secular rights from spiritual rights, placing the former under the
> control of the sovereign, and the latter under the control of the uni-
> versal Church; such pretensions are too frivolous to merit refuta-
> tion. I cannot, however, pass over in silence the fact that such per-
> sons are woefully deceived when they seek to support their seditious
> opinions (I ask pardon for the somewhat harsh epithet) by the ex-
> ample of the Jewish high priest, who, in ancient times, had the right
> of administering the sacred offices. Did not the high priests receive
> their right by the decree of Moses (who, as I have shown, retained
> the sole right to rule), and could they not by the same means be de-
> prived of it? . . . This right was retained by the high priests after-
> wards, but none the less were they delegates of Moses—that is, of the
> sovereign power.[208]

For Spinoza, as for the other Hebraist Erastians, the Mosaic constitution
placed full religious authority in the hands of the civil magistrate. Also
like them, he emphasizes the point that God himself was regarded as the
civil sovereign of Israel, and, as such, gave both civil and religious law.
"For this reason," he notes, "the government could be called a Theocracy, inasmuch as the citizens were not bound by anything save the rev-
elations of God."[209]

Spinoza is equally conventional in developing his Erastian commitment into a defense of toleration.[210] If all valid religious law is civil law—
and if all legitimate civil law aims at civil peace and prosperity—then,
Spinoza tells us, we can identify two familiar limitations on the category
of permissible religious law. The first states that, while "the rites of religion and the outward observances of piety should be in accordance with
the public peace and well-being, and should therefore be determined by
the sovereign power alone,"[211] personal religious beliefs are quite another matter. As Spinoza puts it, "inasmuch as [personal religious con-
viction] consists not so much in outward actions as in simplicity and

truth of character, it stands outside the sphere of law and public author-ity."[212] He offers two reasons for this exclusion. The first is that "simplic-ity and truth of character are not produced by the constraint of laws, nor by the authority of the state, no one the whole world over can be forced or legislated into a state of blessedness."[213] Here we have the familiar view that private belief should not be legislated because it cannot be co-erced. But, like his Erastian predecessors, Spinoza then offers a second consideration: "The only reason for vesting the supreme authority in the interpretation of law, and judgment on public affairs in the hands of the magistrates, is that it concerns questions of public right."[214] Private be-lief per se has no important civic consequences and therefore ought to stand outside the sphere of public law.

This last point leads straightforwardly to Spinoza's second Erastian proviso, which states that laws regulating outward religious observance should themselves only be adopted if they serve an important civic pur-pose. Spinoza makes this point by invoking the example of the Hebrew republic once again. "In the law," he tells us, "no other reward is offered for obedience than the continual happiness of an independent common-wealth and other goods of this life; while, on the other hand, against contumacy and the breaking of the covenant is threatened the downfall of the commonwealth and great hardships."[215] Accordingly, "the only reward which could be promised to the Hebrews for continued obedi-ence to the law was security and its attendant advantages, while no surer punishment could be threatened for disobedience, than the ruin of the state and the evils which generally follow therefrom."[216] Like his Eras-tian predecessors, Spinoza then has to confront the question of why so many religious laws existed in ancient Israel—many of which bear no obvious relation to civic peace. Here Spinoza straightforwardly repro-duces Hobbes's distinctive argument:[217]

> God alone . . . held dominion over the Hebrews, whose state was in virtue of the covenant called God's kingdom, and God was said to be their king; consequently the enemies of the Jews were said to be the enemies of God, and the citizens who tried to seize the dominion were guilty of treason against God; and, lastly, the laws of the state were called the laws and commandments of God. Thus in the

Hebrew state the civil and religious authority, each consisting solely of obedience to God, were one and the same. The dogmas of religion were not precepts, but laws and ordinances; piety was regarded as the same as justice, impiety as the same as crime and injustice. Everyone who fell away from religion ceased to be a citizen, and was, on that ground alone, accounted an enemy: those who died for the sake of religion, were held to have died for their country; in fact, between civil and religious law and right there was no distinction whatever.[218]

Spinoza, in short, follows Hobbes in arguing that the Hebrew republic had so many religious laws because God was regarded as its civil sovereign. Accordingly, actions that would ordinarily have no civic import took on a very different character in that particular state. Where God is king, idolatry is treason, and religious martyrdom a kind of patriotic virtue. The strong implication, once again, is that in all other commonwealths the legal regulation of such matters has no place.

Yet, however consistent Spinoza's deployment of the Hebrew example may be with the standard presentation of Hebraic Erastianism and toleration, his distinctive, radical vision of the Hebrew Bible places him outside this tradition. For Spinoza, the God of the Hebrew Bible simply does not exist. To be sure, Spinoza acknowledges the existence of something called "God," but he makes clear in the *Ethics* (1677) that this thing is identical with the underlying order of the natural world (which he calls "substance").[219] Such a God does not "talk" to anyone, nor can he (or, better, "it") have constitutional preferences (except in the remote, metaphorical sense that he/it can be said to "recommend" those policies which reflect a correct understanding of how the world in fact works). The result is that Spinoza cannot endorse the form and practices of the *respublica Hebraeorum* on the grounds that they express the divine will. Quite to the contrary, he makes clear that they have no special authority of any kind:[220]

We must say of Moses that from revelation, from the basis of what was revealed to him, he perceived the method by which the Israelitish nation could best be united in a particular territory, and could form a body politic or state, and further that he perceived the method by which that nation could best be constrained to obedience; but he did not perceive, nor was it revealed to him, that this method was absolutely the best, nor that the obedience of the people in a certain strip of territory would necessarily imply the end he had in view. Wherefore he perceived these things not as eternal truths, but as precepts and ordinances, and he ordained them as laws of God, and thus it came to be that he conceived God as a ruler, a legislator, a king, as merciful, just, &c., whereas such qualities are simply attributes of human nature, and utterly alien from the nature of the Deity.[221]

The laws of Moses were simply prudential maxims arising out of the particular situation of the Israelites at a crucial moment in their national history. They have no universal force, and the notion that they were "given" by God is merely an anthropomorphizing illusion. The Hebrew republic was simply one ancient politeia among others, and its distinctive laws "were only valid while that kingdom lasted."[222]

This is, indeed, a radically different approach to the Israelite example. Its intention is to remove the aura of authority that accompanies the Biblical text, in the service of an avowedly secular politics. If, as Spinoza declares, the Hebrew republic is not authoritative for moderns, and if Jesus gave no laws,[223] then religion truly has been banished from political life. The deflationary use of the Hebrew republic is, then, a real and important dimension to the story of political Hebraism.[224] But what I want very much to deny is that it characterizes the story as a whole, or even that it constitutes the most important and influential chapter of that story.[225] As we have seen, the vast majority of Hebraists who deployed the Israelite example to defend Erastianism and toleration did *not* take Spinoza's path. They regarded the Hebrew republic as an authoritative expression of God's constitutional preferences and fervently believed that, in asserting the religious supremacy of the civil magistrate and in arguing for limits on the scope of religious legislation, they were doing His will. Machiavelli's Israel may have inspired Spinoza, but it was the Israel of Grotius, Cunaeus, Selden, and Harrington that more profoundly shaped the development of what would emerge as liberal political thought in the modern West.

To see this, one need only look for a moment at the figure of John Locke. In his *Letter Concerning Toleration* (1689), Locke follows his Hebraic Erastian predecessors in analyzing the religious law of the "commonwealth of Israel." Like Grotius and Selden (as well as the Arminian Simon Episcopius, whose works he read quite carefully),[226] he stresses that the Hebrew republic practiced broad toleration, welcoming residents who did not obey the Mosaic law—and even tolerating idolatry outside its borders:

> Amongst so many captives taken, so many nations reduced under their obedience, we find not one man forced into the Jewish religion and the worship of the true God and punished for idolatry, though all of them were certainly guilty of it. If any one, indeed, becoming a proselyte, desired to be made a denizen of their commonwealth, he was obliged to submit to their laws; that is, to embrace their religion. But this he did willingly, on his own accord, not by constraint. He did not unwillingly submit, to show his obedience, but he sought and solicited for it as a privilege. And, as soon as he was admitted, he became subject to the laws of the commonwealth, by which all idolatry was forbidden within the borders of the land of Canaan. But that law (as I have said) did not reach to any of those regions, however subjected unto the Jews, that were situated without those bounds.[227]

Locke then follows Hobbes in arguing that the criminalization of idolatry *within* the Hebrew republic is to be explained by the fact that "God being in a peculiar manner the King of the Jews, He could not suffer the adoration of any other deity (which was properly an act of high treason against Himself) in the land of Canaan, which was His kingdom."[228] God's rule over his peculiar people was "perfectly political," and as a result, the "acknowledgment of another god" implied the acknowledgment of "another king." In all other republics, however, this is simply not the case.

Where God is not the civil sovereign, Locke argues, the number of religious matters worthy of legislation is vanishingly small, confined to "civil concernments" understood quite narrowly.[229] Locke's magistrate has no business establishing forms of public worship by law, and his purview does not include "the salvation of souls."[230] For this reason, it might seem strange to describe the Locke of 1689 as any kind of Erastian—indeed it has become commonplace to draw the sharpest of lines between the self-evident Erastianism of Locke's early *Two Tracts on Government* and his later commitment to broad religious liberty (reflected in the 1667 *Essay Concerning Toleration* and in the three subsequent *Letters Concerning Toleration*).[231] To be sure, this picture is not wholly false: the Locke of 1689 is anything but a traditional advocate for the ecclesiastical jurisdiction of the civil sovereign. But he does nonetheless explicitly defend the legitimacy and importance of the national church,[232] and he also retains the two most basic Erastian convictions: that all binding religious law is civil law, and that the civil sovereign should only make religious laws that are politically necessary (but *must* make those).[233] Locke certainly regards far fewer religious laws as politically necessary than many of his predecessors, but the reasoning is the same. Variety in public worship may not threaten civil order, but "that church can have no right to be tolerated, by the magistrate, which is constituted upon such a bottom, that all who enter into it, do thereby, *ipso facto,* deliver themselves up to the protection and service of another prince."[234] Likewise, "those are not at all to be tolerated who deny the being of God" because "promises, covenants, and oaths, which are the bonds of human society, can have no hold upon an atheist."[235] For Locke, atheism and (perhaps) Catholicism* endanger the state and therefore should not be

---

* While it seems clear to me that the passage quoted above does refer to Catholicism, it must be said that, elsewhere in the *Letter,* Locke seems to entertain the possibility of extending toleration to Catholics: "If a Roman Catholic believe that to be really the body of Christ, which another man calls bread, he does no injury thereby to his neighbour" (Locke, *Two Treatises of Government and A Letter Concerning Toleration,* ed. Ian Shapiro [New Haven, CT, 2003], p. 240). The problem, of course, is that Locke might well believe that this *particular* Catholic belief poses no civic threat, while still believing that other Catholic beliefs do (e.g., that the Pope has the power to absolve subjects of allegiance to their civil sovereign—the belief Locke had highlighted in his 1667 *Essay*). For the argument that Locke does wish to advocate toleration for Catholics, see Jeremy Waldron, *God, Locke, and Equality: Christian Foundations in Locke's Political Thought* (Cambridge, 2002), pp. 219–223. For an account of Locke's evolving position on the issue, see John Marshall, *John Locke, Toleration, and Enlightenment Culture* (Cambridge, 2006), pp. 686–694.

tolerated. Behind these claims lurks the shadow of Israelite theocracy, as the Erastians understood it.

Yet Locke's embrace of the Hebrew republic could not be more different from Spinoza's. While Spinoza's God is simply nature itself, and his Israel just one ancient commonwealth among many, Locke's God is the God of both testaments, and his Israel is God's kingdom. To put it another way, Spinoza's politics is secular because, for him, the Biblical God does not exist; Locke's politics is secular because, on his account, the Biblical God who sent us into the world "by his order, and about his business" wants it that way.[236] Both thinkers endorse toleration, but only Spinoza does so for secular reasons. The result is a deep ambiguity in the character of the political ideas we have inherited from this crucial period. The same institutions and practices (representative government, toleration, etc.) have historically been justified in two very different ways: as politics in the absence of God or as what Godly politics requires. The question of which predominates in the modern West must remain open, but given the force of the story we have been telling, we might well wonder whether God remains our sleeping sovereign after all.

Epilogue

THE EUROPEAN ROMANCE with Hebraica did not end suddenly in
1700. Distinguished studies of the Hebrew republic continued to be
published throughout the first half of the eighteenth century,[1] and this
corpus of writings enjoyed a significant afterlife in the debates surrounding the American Revolution at the century's end. Nonetheless, it is clear
that the authority of Biblical example declined dramatically in eighteenth-
century European political discourse. That authority had depended
upon the conviction that although the Jews later fell from grace, God had
initially chosen them from among the nations and had given them the
Hebrew Bible as a pristine revelation. Yet, for many in the European republic of letters, the intellectual upheavals of the long eighteenth century
called this belief into serious question. The new Biblical criticism (pio-
neered by Hobbes and Spinoza) undermined scholarly confidence in
Scripture's divinity, just as advancing historical investigation challenged
the reliability of the grand narrative contained within it.[2] For an increas-
ing number of the learned, the Bible ceased to be a privileged conduit to
the Almighty and became instead a fallible human document composed
in historical time. The political constitution it described was, on this account, no longer to be regarded as divine in origin and could therefore
claim no particular authority in contemporary debates.

This is not, to be sure, a simple story. We have learned that it will not do to talk about a single, unitary Enlightenment in European intellectual history, still less to assume that Enlightenment and revealed religion were invariably (or even usually) opposed.[3] Yet there is no doubt that when the *philosophes* looked at the Hebrew Bible, they rarely liked what they saw. Where so many seventeenth-century readers had found toleration, republican liberty, and a care for equality, the *gens de lettres* of the eighteenth century tended to detect only barbarity, despotic legalism, and a chauvinistic particularity. Recast as a tribal relic from the primitive past, the Pentateuch could safely be dismissed as absurd and uncivilized—in Voltaire's words, as a tiresome history of "the forgotten chiefs of an unhappy, barbarous land."[4] And rabbinic literature, now no longer a crucial, if imperfect, source of political guidance, could be ridiculed when not simply ignored.

But it was not always so, and it would be an unfortunate error to project the *philosophes'* understanding of the Hebrew Bible back onto the sixteenth and seventeenth centuries. For roughly 100 years—from the time of Bertram until the time of Spinoza—European Protestants made the Hebrew Bible the measure of their politics. They believed that the same God who thundered from Sinai, and who later sent his son into the world, had revealed to Israel the form of a perfect republic. They labored with the help of their rabbinic authorities to interpret his design and attempted in their own societies to replicate it as closely as possible. In the process, they made crucial contributions to the political thought of the modern world. Republican exclusivism, redistribution, and toleration have all been defended on different grounds in the intervening centuries; but in the beginning, all were authorized by the divine will made manifest in the constitution of the Hebrew republic. This is, perhaps, not the history that we in the twenty-first century would choose for several of our most fundamental ideals, but neither should we turn away from it.

Notes

1. The phrase is Mark Lilla's. See Lilla, *The Stillborn God: Religion, Politics, and the Modern West* (New York, 2007). His discussion of political theology is, like most, heavily indebted to Carl Schmitt. See, for example, Schmitt's 1929 Barcelona lecture, "Das Zeitalter der Neutralisierungen und Entpolitisierungen," in Schmitt, *Positionen und Begriffe im Kampf mit Weimar–Genf–Versailles, 1923–1939,* 2nd ed. (Berlin, 1988), pp. 120–132. See also Schmitt, *Politische Theologie: Vier Kapitel zur Lehre von der Souveränität* (Berlin, 1979), chap. 3.

2. This narrative has received support from a wide variety of scholarly perspectives. It is associated with the writings of such diverse figures as Hans Blumenberg, Leo Strauss, C. B. Macpherson, Michael Oakeshott, and John Rawls. The most important recent endorsements are Jonathan Israel, *Enlightenment Contested: Philosophy, Modernity, and the Emancipation of Man, 1670–1752* (Oxford, 2006); Israel, *Radical Enlightenment: Philosophy and the Making of Modernity, 1650–1750* (Oxford, 2001); and Lilla, *The Stillborn God.* Lilla writes from within the Straussian tradition, whereas Israel writes as a contextualist historian of ideas. As a result, they have different things to say about particular authors: Lilla's Locke, for example, is a crypto-atheist, while Israel's is still mired in the theologized worldview from which Spinoza liberates the West. But they both subscribe to the basic narrative I have summarized. For a subtle engagement with this narrative, see Charles Taylor, *A Secular Age* (Cambridge, MA, 2008). Note that I am using the notoriously fraught term *secularization* to refer to the banishment of religious argument from the sphere of acceptable political or public discourse—not to refer to the elimination of independent ecclesiastical jurisdiction or to the steady dwindling of instances in which the state uses its coercive power to compel or forbid various kinds of religious behavior. Much seventeenth-century political thought is indeed committed to these latter projects, but simply to assume that these are secularizing trends is to beg the very question we are trying to answer. We want to know *why* it is that seventeenth-century theorists argued for the end of independent ecclesiastical jurisdiction, and so forth. It is, as we shall see, far from obvious that the motivation for such commitments must be secular.

3. If, as Mark Lilla suggests (*The Stillborn God,* p. 3), political theology should be defined as the practice of appealing to divine revelation in order to ground political principles, then it is far from obvious that even Thomas Aquinas was a political theologian. His project, after all, was to establish that the truths of revelation are *consistent* with those arrived at by natural reason—not to *ground* the latter in the former. And though it is certainly true that theology plays a major role in Thomas's political thought, the case is very different with other important Medieval theorists, such as Ptolemy of Lucca and Marsilius of Padua.

4. For a parallel phenomenon in the realm of natural philosophy, see Ann Blair, "Mosaic Physics and the Search for a Pious Natural Philosophy in the Late Renaissance," *Isis* 91 (2000): 32–58. See also Peter Harrison, *The Bible, Protestantism, and the Rise of Natural Science* (Cambridge, 1998).

5. Other recent attempts include Eldon Eisenach, *Two Worlds of Liberalism: Religion and Politics in Hobbes, Locke, and Mill* (Chicago, 1981); Michael Allen Gillespie, *The Theological Origins of Modernity* (Chicago, 2008); Joshua Mitchell, *Not by Reason Alone: Religion, History, and Identity in Early Modern Political Thought* (Chicago, 1993); and Henning Graf Reventlow, *The Authority of the Bible and the Rise of the Modern World* (Philadelphia, 1985). These texts all follow to some degree in the tradition of Weber, Troeltsch, Tawney, and Blumenberg; the important difference is that, whereas these earlier writers argued (broadly) that Protestantism gave rise to a *secular* modernity, Eisenach et al. regard modernity itself (and liberalism in particular) as decidedly nonsecular in character. In this respect, they are closer to the view of Karl Löwith (see Löwith, *Meaning in History: The Theological Implications of the Philosophy of History* [Chicago, 1957]).

6. The use of the term *respublica* to translate the Greek term *politeia* (referring not to the idea of a constitution in general, but rather to a particular regime) derives from Leonardo Bruni's Latin translation of Aristotle's *Politics* (1437). On this, see James Hankins, "Exclusivist Republicanism and the Non-Monarchical Republic," forthcoming in *Political Theory* 38 (2010). See also David Wootton, "The True Origins of Republicanism: The Disciples of Baron and the Counterexample of Venturi," in *Il repubblicanesimo moderno: L'idea di repubblica nella riflessione storica di Franco Venturi,* ed. Manuela Albertone (Naples, 2006), pp. 271–304.

7. The classic account of this position appears in Aristotle, *Politics* (III) 1279a–b.

8. This is not to repeat the claim—familiar from the writings of Schmitt and Löwith—that modernity is structured around secularized versions of theological ideas (e.g., that the theological concept of *sovereignty* was simply transferred from God to the secular state, or that the idea of *progress* is secularized millenarianism). My claim, in contrast, is that these three crucial early-modern developments in political thought were not secular at all.

9. We still await a history of political Hebraism—indeed, I have my doubts about the feasibility of such a project. Just as political Hellenism is far too large and multifaceted a subject to allow for a coherent, comprehensive treatment, political Hebraism too might well be beyond the reach of any single study.

10. Maimonides, MT *Melakhim* 3:2. For Milton's use of this dictum, see *Complete Prose Works of John Milton,* 7 vols., ed. Merritt Hughes (New Haven, CT, 1962), vol. 4, p. 355.

11. This summary is intended for readers who are unfamiliar with the broad outlines of the story of Christian Hebraism. Scholars of the subject will of course notice significant lacunae and omissions (the inevitable cost of attempting to summarize anything as large as this). My brief account relies heavily on several excellent studies of the phenomenon, including F. L. Hoffmann, "Hebräische Grammatiken Christlicher Autoren bis Ende des XVI. Jahrh. in der Hamburger Stadtbibliothek," *Jeschurun* 6 (1868): 33–48, 145–152; Ludwig Geiger, *Das Studium der hebräischen Sprache in Deutschland vom Ende des XV. bis Mitte des XVI. Jahrhunderts* (Breslau, 1870); Moritz Steinschneider, *Christliche Hebraisten: Nachrichten über mehr als 400 Gelehrte, welche über nachbiblisches Hebräisch geschrieben haben* (Hildesheim, 1973; orig. published 1896–1901); Jerome Friedman, *The Most Ancient Testimony: Sixteenth-Century Christian Hebraica in the Age of Renaissance Nostalgia* (Athens, OH, 1983); Aaron Katchen, *Christian Hebraists and Dutch Rabbis: Seventeenth Century Apologetics and the Study of Maimonides'* Mishneh Torah, Harvard Judaic Texts and Studies 3 (Cambridge, MA, 1984); William McKane, *Selected Christian Hebraists* (Cambridge, 1989); Peter T. van Rooden, *Theology, Biblical Scholarship and Rabbinical Studies in the Seventeenth Century: Constantijn L'Empereur (1591–1648), Professor of Hebrew and Theology at Leiden* (Leiden, 1989); Frank Manuel, *The Broken Staff: Judaism through Christian Eyes* (Cambridge, MA, 1992); and Stephen G. Burnett, *From Christian Hebraism to Jewish Studies: Johannes Buxtorf (1564–1629) and Hebrew Learning in the Seventeenth Century* (Leiden, 1996).

12. "Ante annos VIII jubilaeum quoque suum Evangelicae, qua late Reformatus orbis patet, Ecclesiae celebrarunt. Gratiae actae Deo, quod ante annos centum excitasset incomparabiles Heroas, Lutherum, Melanthonem, Erasmum, Reuchlinum, &c. qui tot in Christianismo seculis grassatae barbarei intrepido animo bellum denunciavere, & felicissime gessere." See Sixtinus Amama, *Anti-Barbarus Biblicus in vi libros distributos* (Amsterdam, 1628), sig. B8ᵛ–C1ʳ. The text of this oration, the *De barbarei oratio,* runs from sig. B8ᵛ–F2ʳ.

13. "Calculum meum appono magno Calvino, qui Scholasticam Theologiam definit, diabolicam artem litigandi, nihil aliud continentem quam otiosas & ad nihil utiles speculationes, in quibus quo quis fuit doctior, eo fuit miserior." Amama, *Anti-Barbarus Biblicus,* sig. C7ʳ.

14. "Ecce enim linguarum studia paulo post collapsa sunt, & cum iis rursus negligi coepit sacer codex." Amama, *Anti-Barbarus Biblicus,* sig. D4ʳ. All translations are my own, unless otherwise indicated.

15. Amama, *Anti-Barbarus Biblicus,* sig. F1ᵛ–F2ʳ. On this oration, see van Rooden, *Theology, Biblical Scholarship and Rabbinical Studies in the Seventeenth Century,* pp. 69–70.

16. For the Hebrew scholarship of the "Carolingian Renaissance," see Avrom Saltman's introduction to Pseudo-Jerome, *Quaestiones on the Book of Samuel,* ed. Avrom Saltman (Leiden, 1975), pp. 3–62.

17. For twelfth-century Hebraism, see Michael A. Singer, "Polemic and Exegesis: The Varieties of Twelfth-Century Hebraism," in *Hebraica Veritas? Christian Hebraists and the Study of Judaism in Early Modern Europe,* ed. Allison Coudert and Jeffrey Shoulson (Philadelphia, 2004), pp. 21–32. For the Hebraism of Andrew of St. Victor, see McKane, *Selected Christian Hebraists,* pp. 42–75.

18. See Manuel, *The Broken Staff,* pp. 16–17. The translation was made, not from the Judeo-Arabic original, but from Yehuda Alharizi's Hebrew translation. For the pre-Reformation European reception of Maimonides, see Katchen, *Christian Hebraists and Dutch Rabbis,* pp. 1–14.

19. See, for example, van Rooden, *Theology, Biblical Scholarship and Rabbinical Studies in the Seventeenth Century,* pp. 174–179.

20. See Katchen, *Christian Hebraists and Dutch Rabbis,* p. 62.

21. On Nicholas of Lyra and his Hebrew studies, see Deeana Copeland Klepper, "Nicholas of Lyra and Franciscan Interest in Hebrew Scholarship," in *Nicholas of Lyra: The Senses of Scripture,* ed. Philip D. W. Krey and Lesley Smith (Leiden, 2000), pp. 289–312.

22. It seems that a Hebrew lectureship was briefly established in Oxford following the decision of the Council; it was still in existence in 1327, but after that date, there is no evidence of Hebrew instruction at Oxford (or any other English university) for the next two centuries. See Joseph L. Mihelic, "The Study of Hebrew in England," *The Journal of Bible and Religion* 14 (1946): 94–100 (esp. p. 96); Gareth Lloyd Jones, *The Discovery of Hebrew in Tudor England: A Third Language* (Manchester, U.K., 1983), esp. pp. 180–220; and Roberto Weiss, "England and the Decree of the Council of Vienne on the Teaching of Greek, Arabic, Hebrew, and Syriac," in *Medieval and Humanist Greek: Collected Essays by Roberto Weiss* (Padua, 1978), pp. 68–79. Similarly, there is evidence that a converted Jew, John Salviati of Villeneuve, was being paid by the diocese of Langres to teach Hebrew at Paris in 1320 (Weiss, "England and the Decree of the Council of Vienne," p. 70).

23. See Manuel, *The Broken Staff,* p. 69.

24. See van Rooden, *Theology, Biblical Scholarship and Rabbinical Studies in the Seventeenth Century,* p. 43. The title translates as Book of Roots.

25. See, classically, D. P. Walker, *The Ancient Theology: Studies in Christian Platonism from the Fifteenth to the Eighteenth Century* (Ithaca, NY, 1972).

26. The significant interest in Judaism (that is, in post-Biblical Hebraica) that we find in Pico and Ficino is anticipated by such early Quattrocento humanists as Ambrogio Traversari, Giannozzo Manetti, and Annio da Viterbo. See, for example, Riccardo Fubini, *Storiografia dell'Umanesimo in Italia: Da Leonardo Bruni ad Annio da Viterbo* (Rome, 2003), esp. pp. 290–333; and Daniel Stein Kokin, "The Hebrew Question in the Italian Renaissance: Linguistic, Cultural, and Mystical Perspectives," unpublished PhD dissertation, Harvard University, 2006. For Manetti in particular, see Paul Botley, *Latin Translation in the Renaissance: The Theory and Practice of Leonardo Bruni, Giannozzo Manetti, Erasmus* (Cambridge, 2007), pp. 63–99. The literature on Renaissance Italian Hebraism is now quite large and includes important contributions by Moshe Idel, Fabrizio Lelli, and Giulio Busi, among others.

27. For Ficino's interaction with this tradition, see James Hankins, *Plato in the Italian Renaissance* (Leiden, 1991), pp. 269–359. See also Moshe Idel, "Prisca Theologia in Marsilio Ficino and in Some Jewish Treatments," in *Marsilio Ficino: His Theology, His Philosophy, His Legacy,* ed. Michael J. B. Allen, Valery Rees, and Martin Davies (Leiden, 2002), pp. 137–158; and Ilana Klutstein, *Marsilio Ficino et la théologie ancienne: Oracles chaldaïques, Hymnes orphiques, Hymnes de Proclus* (Florence, 1987). Ficino's fullest statement of this position was his *Platonic Theology,* 2 vols., ed. James Hankins, trans. Michael J. B. Allen Cambridge, MA, 2001) (c. 1469–1474).

28. For Alemanno, see Fabrizio Lelli, *Yohanan Alemanno: Hay Ha-'Olamim (L'Immortale)* (Florence, 1995). For Alemanno and Pico, see B. C. Novak, "Giovanni Pico della Mirandola and Jochanan Alemanno," *Journal of the Warburg and Courtauld Institutes* 45 (1982): 125–147. For Pico and Flavius Mithridates, see Giulio Busi, "'Who Does Not Wonder at This Chameleon?' The Kabbalistic Library of Giovanni Pico della Mirandola," in *Hebrew to Latin, Latin to Hebrew: The Mirroring of Two Cultures in the Age of Humanism* (Berlin, 2006), pp. 167–196. See also Manuel, *The Broken Staff,* pp. 40–41.

29. On this, see in particular Chaim Wirszubski, *Pico della Mirandola's Encounter with Jewish Mysticism* (Cambridge, MA, 1989); Brian Copenhaver, "Number, Shape, and Meaning in Pico's Christian Cabala: The Upright *Tsade,* the Closed *Mem,* and the Gaping Jaws of Azazel," in *Natural Particulars: Nature and the Disciplines in Renaissance Europe,* ed. Anthony Grafton and Nancy Siraisi (Cambridge, MA, 1999), pp. 25–76; Copenhaver, "The Secret of Pico's Oration: Cabala and Renaissance Philosophy," *Midwest Studies in Philosophy* 26 (2002): 56–81; Moshe Idel, "Jewish Mystical Thought in the Florence of Lorenzo il Magnifico," in *La cultura ebraica all'epoca di Lorenzo il Magnifico,* ed. Dora Liscia Bemporad and Ida Zatelli (Florence, 1998), pp. 17–42; and Paola Zambelli, *L'apprendista stregone: Astrologia, cabala e arte lulliana in Pico della Mirandola e seguaci* (Venice, 1995).

30. Pico della Mirandola, *Conclusiones nongentae: Le novecento tesi dell'anno 1486,* ed. and trans. Albano Biondi (Florence, 1995), pp. 76, 84. "Si qua est lingua prima et non casualis, illam esse hebraicam multis patet coniecturis" (*Conclusiones* 5.2.80); "Qui ordinem hebraicae linguae profunde et radicaliter tenuerit atque illum proportionaliter in scientiis servare noverit, cuiuscumque scibilis perfecte inveniendi normam et regulam habebit" (*Conclusiones* 5.3.55). The translation is Copenhaver's ("Number, Shape, and Meaning," pp. 40–41).

31. This point was eloquently made by Eugenio Garin. See Garin, *Italian Humanism: Philosophy and Civic Life in the Renaissance,* trans. Peter Munz (Oxford, 1965), pp. 106–111.

32. On this, see Eric Nelson, *The Greek Tradition in Republican Thought* (Cambridge, 2004), pp. 27–28. More's text is a free translation of the biography written by Pico's nephew, Giafrancesco. It can be found in *The Complete Works of St. Thomas More,* vol. 2, ed. Anthony S. G. Edwards, Katherine Gardiner Rodgers, and Clarence H. Miller (New Haven, CT, 1997).

33. Erasmus himself regarded Hebrew as a barbaric language and regretted the degree to which Hebraism might distract Christians from the far more important business

of learning Greek. On this, see Shimon Markish, *Erasmus and the Jews* (Chicago, 1986), esp. pp. 112–141. He also held a traditionally dismissive view of the Hebrew Bible. See Reventlow, *The Authority of the Bible*, pp. 44–47.

34. Manuel, *The Broken Staff*, p. 59. Levita composed the famous *Sefer Massoreth ha-Massoreth* (1538), which argued that the vocal pointilization of the Hebrew Bible was considerably less ancient than the text itself.

35. See Erika Rummel, *The Case against Johann Reuchlin: Religious and Social Controversy in Sixteenth-Century Germany* (Toronto, 2002).

36. See Jeremy Cohen, *Living Letters of the Law: Ideas of the Jew in Medieval Christianity* (Berkeley, 1999), pp. 260–264.

37. On this, see Kenneth Stow, "The Burning of the Talmud in 1553, in the Light of Sixteenth Century Catholic Attitudes toward the Talmud," *Bibliothèque d'Humanisme et Renaissance* 34 (1972): 435–459. See also Stow, *Catholic Thought and Papal Jewry Policy, 1555–1593* (New York, 1977); and Amnon Raz-Krakotzkin, *The Censor, the Editor, and the Text: The Catholic Church and the Shaping of the Jewish Canon in the Sixteenth Century*, trans. Jackie Feldman (Philadelphia, 2007). This is not, of course, to suggest that the printing of rabbinica was uncontroversial in the Protestant world. Opinions submitted by the theology faculty at Basel and by the printer Ambrosius Froben defending the printing of the Basel edition of the Talmud in 1578–1579 made substantial use of Reuchlin's arguments. See Stephen G. Burnett, "The Regulation of Hebrew Printing in Germany, 1555–1630: Confessional Politics and the Limits of Jewish Toleration," in *Infinite Boundaries: Order, Dis-order, and Reorder in Early Modern German Culture*, ed. M. Reinhart and T. Robisheaux (Kirksville, MO, 1998), esp. pp. 339–340.

38. See Marion Kuntz, *Guillaume Postel: Prophet of the Restitution of All Things, His Life and Thought* (The Hague, 1981). Postel was expelled from the Jesuit order, flirted extensively with Lutherans, was declared mad by the Inquisition, and was imprisoned in the monastery of St. Martin des Champs for the last two decades of his life.

39. One would also want to include the various contributors to the Complutensian Polyglot Bible (1521), financed by Cardinal Francisco Ximénez de Cisneros.

40. For a recent study of sixteenth-century Catholic scholarship in Semitic languages, see Robert J. Wilkinson, *Orientalism, Aramaic and Kabbalah in the Catholic Reformation: The First Printing of the Syriac New Testament* (Leiden, 2007). Wilkinson pays due attention to Postel, but also reminds us of the importance of other Catholic scholars in his circle, including the German Johann Albrecht Widmanstetter.

41. On the Council of Trent, see McKane, *Selected Christian Hebraists*, pp. 78–79, 85; on the Sisto-Clementine Index, see Salo Wittmayer Baron, "The Council of Trent and Rabbinic Literature," in *Ancient and Medieval Jewish History* (New Brunswick, NJ, 1972), pp. 353–371. See also Adam Sutcliffe, *Judaism and Enlightenment* (New York, 2003), p. 27. Under the direction of Paul IV, the Inquisition prohibited Jews from owning Hebrew books other than the Bible itself in 1557.

42. On this, see Kalman Neuman, "Political Hebraism and the Early Modern 'Respublica Hebraeorum': On Defining the Field," *Hebraic Political Studies* 1 (2005):

57–70 (see esp. p. 61); and Reventlow, *The Authority of the Bible,* pp. 67–69, 105–109.

43. See Harrison, *The Bible, Protestantism, and the Rise of Natural Science,* pp. 107–120; Cf. Hans Frei, *The Eclipse of Biblical Narrative* (New Haven, CT, 1974), p. 40; Jaroslav Pelikan, *The Reformation of the Bible, the Bible of the Reformation* (New Haven, CT 1996). Paul Korshin offers an important qualification when he notes that a number of Protestant exegetes reinterpreted the typological tradition to understand Biblical events as *types* of contemporary occurrences. See Paul Korshin, *Typologies in England, 1650–1820* (Princeton, NJ, 1982), p. 31.

44. This milieu is discussed extensively in van Rooden, *Theology, Biblical Scholarship and Rabbinical Studies in the Seventeenth Century;* and Katchen, *Christian Hebraists and Dutch Rabbis.*

45. See Sutcliffe, *Judaism and Enlightenment,* pp. 26–27.

46. Carlo Imbonati, *Bibliotheca latino-hebraica; sive De scriptoribus latinis, qui ex diversis nationibus contra Iudaeos, vel de re hebraica utcumque scripsere* (Rome, 1694). Imbonati carried on the work of his teacher Giulio Bartolucci (professor of Hebrew at the Collegium Neophytorum in Rome—a college for Jewish converts to Christianity). Bartolucci's magnum opus (magnum in both senses) was the four-volume *Bibliotheca magna rabbinica* (1675–1693).

47. See K. H. Burmeister, *Sebastian Münster: Versuch eines biographischen Gesamtbildes* (Basel, 1963). Münster learned his Hebrew from Conrad Pellican and Elias Levita.

48. On Scaliger at Leiden, see Anthony Grafton, *Joseph Scaliger: A Study in the History of Classical Scholarship,* vol. 2: *Historical Chronology* (Oxford, 1983), pp. 361–459.

49. Drusius had also been professor of oriental languages at Oxford, beginning in 1572.

50. See Katchen, *Christian Hebraists and Dutch Rabbis,* pp. 161–169, 178–235. A Latin translation of the first chapter of the *Mishneh Torah (Hilkhot Yesode ha-Torah)* was published by G. H. Vorstius in 1638. In 1631, a Latin translation of the *Hilkhot Teshuvah* (Laws of Repentance) was published in England under the initials "G. N." The author has now been identified as William Norwich. See J. I. Dienstag, "Christian Translators of Maimonides' *Mishneh Torah* into Latin," in *Salo Wittmayer Baron Jubilee Volume,* ed. Saul Lieberman (New York, 1974), pp. 287–310 (esp. p. 299).

51. There is some debate concerning the precise degree of Grotius's knowledge of Hebrew and Hebraica. Two points, however, seem uncontroversial: (1) Grotius knew some Hebrew; and (2) he made copious use of rabbinic sources, particularly in the later part of his career. See, for example, Edwin Rabbie, "Grotius and Judaism," in *Hugo Grotius, Theologian: Essays in Honour of G. H. M. Posthumus Meyjes,* ed. Henk J. M. Nellen and Edwin Rabbie (Leiden, 1994), pp. 99–120.

52. For the early-modern revival of Aramaic, and the particular difficulties the language presented for Hebraists, see Stephen G. Burnett, "Christian Aramaism: The Birth and Growth of Aramaic Scholarship in the Sixteenth Century," in *Seeking Out the Wisdom of the Ancients: Essays Offered to Honor Michael V. Fox on the Occasion of His Sixty-Fifth Birthday,* ed. Ronald L. Troxel, Kelvin G. Friebel, and Dennis R. Magary (Winona Lake, IN, 2005), pp. 421–436.

53. Willem Surenhuis [or Surenhuys], ed., *Mischna: Sive totius Hebraeorum juris, rituum, antiquitatum, ac legum oralium systema,* 6 vols. (Amsterdam, 1698–1703).

54. Phillipe D'Aquin, *Sentenze: Parabole di Rabbini. Tradotti da Philippo Daquin* (Paris, 1620). The tractate had been translated into Latin by Paulus Fagius in 1541.

55. For one important example, see Josef Funkenstein, *Das Alte Testament im Kampf von regnum und sacerdotium zur Zeit des Investiturstreits* (Dortmund, Germany, 1938).

56. This phenomenon certainly had Medieval antecedents—most notably Ptolemy of Lucca's completion of the *De regimine principum* (c. 1300)—but the sustained attempt to systematize and then replicate the Israelite constitution can safely be dated to the early-modern period.

57. There has been a very welcome surge of interest in this phenomenon over the last two decades or so, culminating in the launch of the journal *Hebraic Political Studies* in 2005. Important contributions include Lea Campos Boralevi's Introduction to Petrus Cunaeus, *De Republica Hebraeorum,* ed. Lea Campos Boralevi (Florence, 1996); Boralevi, "Classical Foundational Myths of European Republicanism: The Jewish Commonwealth," in *Republicanism: A Shared European Heritage,* vol. 1, ed. Martin van Gelderen and Quentin Skinner (Cambridge, 2002), pp. 247–261; Vittorio Conti, *Consociatio civitatum: Le reppubliche nei testi elzeviriani (1625–1649),* Politeia: Scienza e Pensiero 4 (Florence, 1997); François Laplanche, "L'érudition Chrétienne aux XVIe et XVIIe siècles et l'état des Hebreux," in *L'écriture sainte au temps de Spinoza et dans le système Spinoziste* (Paris, 1992), pp. 133–147; Manuel, *The Broken Staff,* pp. 109–161; Neuman, "Political Hebraism"; Fania Oz-Salzberger, "The Jewish Roots of Western Freedom," *Azure* 13 (2002): 88–132; Johann Sommerville, "Hobbes, Selden, Erastianism, and the history of the Jews," in *Hobbes and History,* ed. G. A. J. Rogers and Tom Sorell (New York, 2000), pp. 160–188; Mark Somos, "The History and Implications of Secularisation: The Leiden Circle, 1575–1618," Unpublished PhD dissertation, Harvard University, 2007; Anna Strumia, *L'immaginazione repubblicana: Sparta e Israele nel dibattito filosofico-politico dell'età di Cromwell* (Turin, 1991); Sutcliffe, *Judaism and Enlightenment,* esp. pp. 42–57; and Richard Tuck, *Philosophy and Government: 1572–1651* (Cambridge, 1993). This literature is indebted to several pioneering works by earlier scholars, including S. B. Liljegren, "Harrington and the Jews," *Bulletin de la societé royale des lettres de Lund* 4 (1931–1932): 656–692; J. G. A. Pocock, "Time, History and Eschatology in the Thought of Thomas Hobbes," in *Politics, Language, and Time: Essays on Political Thought and History* (New York, 1971), pp. 148–201; and Pocock, Introduction to James Harrington, *The Political Works of James Harrington,* ed. J. G. A. Pocock (Cambridge, 1978).

58. Henry Ainsworth, *Annotations upon the five bookes of Moses, the booke of Psalmes, and the Song of Songs, or Canticles* (London, 1627), Preface.

59. Ibid. Ainsworth wrote as follows: "As for the theologicall exposition, therein the later Rabbines are for the most part blinde; but we are enlightened by the Apostles of Christ. . . . Another reason why I cite the Rabbines, is to shew how in many words, phrases, and point of doctrine, they approve the new Testament; though sometime

to the condemning of themselves: and so the testimony of the adversary against himselfe, helpeth our faith."

60. It lists only those texts which include the phrase *respublica hebraeorum* (or some variant thereof) in their titles. It therefore does not include texts such as Harrington's *The Art of Lawgiving* (1659) or Hobbes's *Leviathan* (1651), which are organized to a great degree around an analysis of the Mosaic constitution.

61. Jean Bodin, *Methodus ad facilem historiarum cognitionem* (Amsterdam, 1967), pp. 298–301. Bodin's great political treatise, *Les six livres de la république* (1576), also frequently discusses the Hebrew republic. Moreover, at the end of his life, Bodin authored the notoriously heterodox *Colloquium heptaplomeres*, a dialogue in six books among representatives of seven different religious traditions. At the end of the dialogue, it becomes clear that the author sympathizes most with the Jew and the "Deist." Bodin's authorship of this text has been disputed for some time, but the question has recently been settled in Bodin's favor by Noel Malcolm. See Noel Malcolm, "Jean Bodin and the Authorship of the *Colloquium Heptaplomeres*," *Journal of the Warburg and Courtauld Institutes* 69 (2006): 95–150. Machiavelli famously described Moses as a "lawgiver," but he did not analyze the Mosaic constitution (nor does it seem that he had any access to rabbinic materials). See, for example, Niccolò Machiavelli, *The Prince*, ed. Quentin Skinner, trans. Russell Price (Cambridge, 1988), pp. 20–21. One could also mention Martin Bucer's *Regnum Christi: Libri duo* (Paris, 1550), which characterized the political laws of the Hebrew Bible as authoritative for Christians. On this text, see Reventlow, *The Authority of the Bible*, pp. 85–87.

62. Cornelius Bertram, *Comparatio grammaticae Hebraicae et Aramaicae* (Geneva, 1574).

63. Cornelius Bertram, *La Bible: Qui est toute la saincte Escriture du Vieil & du Nouveau Testament, autrement L'Anciene & la Nouvelle Alliance. Le tout revueu & conferé sur les textes Hebrieux & Grecs par les pasteurs & Professeurs de l'Église de Geneve* (Geneva, 1588).

64. Cornelius Bertram, *Lucubrationes Frankentallenses, seu Specimen Expositionum in Difficiliora Utriusque Testamenti Loca* (Geneva, 1586).

65. For Bertram's *De politia judaica*, see Jonathan Ziskind, "Cornelius Bertram and Carlo Sigonio: Christian Hebraism's First Political Scientists," *Journal of Ecumenical Studies* 37 (2000): 381–401.

66. Van Rooden, *Theology, Biblical Scholarship and Rabbinical Studies in the Seventeenth Century*, p. 255.

67. Sigonio published his *De antiquo iure civium Romanorum, Italiae, provinciarum* in 1560 and his *De republica Atheniensium libri IV* in 1564. For Sigonio's life and career, see William McCuaig, *Carlo Sigonio: The Changing World of the Late Renaissance* (Princeton, NJ, 1989).

68. Carlo Sigonio, *De republica Hebraeorum libri VII: Ad Gregorium XIII pontificem maximum* (Bologna, 1582). The most recent study of this text is Guido Bartolucci, *La repubblica ebraica di Carlo Sigonio: Modelli politici dell'età moderna* (Florence, 2007); see also Bartolucci, "Carlo Sigonio and the Respublica Hebraeorum: A Reevaluation," *Hebraic Political Studies* 3 (2008): 19–59.

69. On this, see McCuaig, *Sigonio,* p. 76ff.

70. Another Catholic contributor to the *respublica Hebraeorum* genre was the Jesuit Giovanni Stefano Menochio, who published his own *De republica Hebraeorum* in 1648. Menochio, however, criticized the Protestant (or "heterodox") authors in this tradition for making use of what he regarded as corrupt, degenerate rabbinic materials. See Menochio, *De republica Hebraeorum libri octo* (Paris, 1648), Preface to the Reader.

71. See McCuaig, *Sigonio,* p. 91.

72. The consequence is that Sigonio replicates the errors of these earlier texts. See Ziskind, "Cornelius Bertram and Carlo Sigonio."

73. Joachim Stephani, *De iurisdictione Judaeorum, Graecorum, Romanorum et Ecclesiasticorum libri IV* (Frankfurt, 1604). I am grateful to Alexander Schmidt for calling this text to my attention.

74. Hugo Grotius, "De republica emendanda," ed. Arthur Eyffinger et al., *Grotiana* n.s. 5 (1984). This treatise was not printed in Grotius's lifetime.

75. Cunaeus, *De republica Hebraeorum libri III* (Amsterdam, 1617).

76. On this, see Arthur Eyffinger's Introduction to Cunaeus, *The Hebrew Republic,* ed. Arthur Eyffinger, trans. Peter Wyetzner (Jerusalem, 2006), p. xix.

77. See Boralevi, "Classical Foundational Myths of European Republicanism," p. 258; and Katchen, *Christian Hebraists and Dutch Rabbis,* pp. 38–39.

78. Schickard created a mechanical calculating device, which he described in detail to his friend Johannes Kepler. Neither of the two prototypes survived his death in 1635; it was not until 1955 that scholars reconstructed a working version of his machine. On Schickard, see Friedrich Seck, ed., *Wissenschaftsgeschichte um Wilhelm Schickard: Vorträge bei dem Symposion der Universität Tübingen im 500. Jahr ihres Bestehens* (Tübingen, 1981); Seck, ed., *Zum 400. Geburtstag von Wilhelm Schickard: Zweites Tübinger Schickard-Symposion* (Sigmaringen, 1995). Seck has also edited Schickard's correspondence. See Seck, ed., *Wilhelm Schickard: Briefwechsel,* 2 vols. (Stuttgart–Bad Cannstatt, 2002).

79. Wilhelm Schickard, *Mishpat ha-melekh, Jus regium Hebraeorum e tenebris rabbinicis* (Strasbourg, 1625).

80. The first important English text in this idiom was Edmund Bunny, *The scepter of Judah: or, what manner of government it was, that unto the common-wealth or Church of Israel was by the law of God appointed* (London, 1584). It should also be stressed that further publications continued to pour out of European presses, including the German Aristotelian Herman Conring's *De politia sive republica Hebraeorum exercitation* (Helmstadt, Germany, 1648) and Joachim Ludwig Reimer's *Respublica Ebraeorum, ex Sigonio, Bertramo, Cunaeo aliisque concinnata* (Leipzig, 1657).

81. For Selden's political use of his Hebraic scholarship, see G. J. Toomer, *John Selden: A Life in Scholarship,* 2 vols. (Oxford, 2009), esp. vol. 2, pp. 441–562 and pp. 692–788. See also Reid Barbour, *John Selden: Measures of the Holy Commonwealth in Seventeenth-Century England* (Toronto, 2003); Jason Rosenblatt, *John Selden: Renaissance England's Chief Rabbi* (Oxford, 2006); Rosenblatt, "John Selden's *De*

Jure Naturali . . . Juxta Disciplinam Ebraeorum and Religious Toleration," in *Hebraica Veritas? Christian Hebraists and the Study of Judaism in Early Modern Europe,* ed. Allison Coudert and Jeffrey Shoulson (Philadelphia, 2004), pp. 102–124; Sommerville, "Hobbes, Selden, Erastianism, and the History of the Jews"; and Richard Tuck, *Natural Rights Theories* (Cambridge, 1979), pp. 82–100, and Tuck, *Philosophy and Government,* pp. 205–221.

82. Anon., *Articles of High Treason . . . Likewise, The manner of administering Justice; and in case any Lawyer shall take either Money, or Bribes, to dye as a Traytor to the Commonwealth; and the Government to be established, as the Commonwealth of Israel was, in Mose's time* (London, 1652). For an introductory account of Hebraism during the Interregnum, see Nigel Smith, "The Uses of Hebrew in the English Revolution," in *Language, Self, and Society,* ed. Peter Burke and Roy Porter (Cambridge, 1991), pp. 51–71.

83. "The truth is," Harrington admitted, that "in all that is talmudical I am assisted by Selden, Grotius, and their quotations out of the rabbys, having in this learning so little skill, that if I miscall'd none of them, I shew'd a good part of my acquaintance with them." See Harrington, *Political Works,* p. 520.

84. Spinoza certainly read Hobbes's *De cive* (1642) long before composing the *Tractatus Theologico-Politicus* (1670); moreover, although he did not read English—and therefore could not have read *Leviathan* in the original—he was close friends with the man who translated it into Dutch (1665–1667), and probably read the Latin version (1668) in time to incorporate its arguments into the TTP. See Noel Malcolm, *Aspects of Hobbes* (Oxford, 2002), pp. 47, 390–392.

1. "TALMUDICAL COMMONWEALTHSMEN" AND THE RISE OF REPUBLICAN EXCLUSIVISM

1. *Leonardo Brunis Rede auf Nanni Strozzi: Einleitung, Edition, und Kommentar,* ed. Susanne Daub (Stuttgart, 1996), pp. 285–286. See the analysis of this speech in James Hankins, "Rhetoric, History, and Ideology: The Civic Panegyrics of Leonardo Bruni," in *Renaissance Civic Humanism,* ed. James Hankins (Cambridge, 2000), pp. 151–178. Hankins is also to be credited with having first noticed the turn toward *exclusivism* in seventeenth-century republican thought. I am greatly indebted to his essay "Exclusivist Republicanism and the Non-Monarchical Republic," forthcoming in *Political Theory* 38 (2010).

2. David Wootton has suggested that the Venetian Traiano Boccalini (1556–1613) should be regarded as an exclusivist in my sense—that is, one who did not merely prefer republican government, but instead insisted on "the destruction of monarchy" (Wootton, *Paolo Sarpi: Between Renaissance and Enlightenment* (Cambridge, 1983), p. 74). His evidence comes from Boccalini's posthumously published *Osservazioni politiche sopra i sei libri degli Annali de Cornelio Tacito* (1669), in which Boccalini writes that "Good kings, who deserve the name of God's lieutenants on Earth, who are images of the gods, who are sought after, and are depicted with the

pen, are in fact like the Sirens, the Hippogriffs, the Tritons, and unicorns who are likewise depicted. They are the stuff of fables, and cannot be found" (*I Principi buoni che meritano nome di Luogotenenti di Dio in Terra, che* sint instar Deorum, *si desiderano, si dipingono, con la penna, sono à guisa delle Sirene, de gli Hippogriffi, delli Tritoni, delli Alicorni che si dipingono, sono favolosi, e non si trovano*) (Traiano Boccalini, *La bilancia politica di tutte le opere di Traiano Boccalini*, 3 vols., ed. Ludovico Du May (Castellana, 1678), vol. 1, p. 344). This is indeed a strong statement—Boccalini's seventeenth-century editor apologetically characterizes it in a footnote as "troppo ardito"—but Boccalini makes clear that he is talking only about absolute monarchs. He immediately distinguishes the government he has in mind from "un Principato misto," which he regards as perfectly acceptable. Indeed, he begins the text by noting that the title of king has been distorted in the modern world, so that it refers only to the rank of an absolute monarch *(un assoluto Monarca)*— and not, as it did in ancient times, to a "king with greatly limited authority" *(Rè con autorità molto limitata)* (*La bilancia politica*, sig. A1ᵛ). Boccalini was not alone, of course, in regarding *absolute* monarchy as an illicit constitutional form, indistinguishable in practice from tyranny. But this is very far from the view that monarchy per se is illegitimate.

3. The classical text that most closely approximates such a position is Cicero's *De officiis*, but even here the theoretical possibility of an acceptable monarchy is retained (see, e.g., *De officiis*, ed. and trans. Walter Miller [Cambridge, MA, 1913], I.64–65; III.84–86). Moreover, Cicero offers an unreserved endorsement of Aristotelian constitutional analysis in *De republica* I.25. (Although most of this text was lost until the nineteenth century, this passage was well known to early-modern readers because it is quoted in Augustine, *City of God* II.21.) For a recent discussion of Cicero's antimonarchism, see Peter Stacey, *Roman Monarchy and the Renaissance Prince* (Cambridge, 2007), pp. 23–30. In the *Prince* (1513), Machiavelli famously dissolves the distinction between prince and tyrant, but he certainly has no interest in arguing that one-man rule is illegitimate.

4. Hobbes, *Leviathan*, ed. Richard Tuck, rev. ed. (Cambridge, 1996), pp. 227–228.

5. Ibid., p. 282.

6. Ibid., pp. 282–283.

7. Robert Filmer, "Observations Concerning the Originall of Government," in *Patriarcha and Other Writings*, ed. Johann Sommerville (Cambridge, 1991), p. 196.

8. Edward Hyde, Earl of Clarendon, *A brief view and survey of the dangerous and pernicious errors to church and state, in Mr. Hobbes's book, entitled Leviathan* (Oxford, 1676), p. 74.

9. Hobbes, *Opera omnia philosophica quae latine scripsit omnia*, 3 vols., ed. William Molesworth (London, 1841), vol. 3, pp. 294–298. Hobbes cuts similar material from chap. 38, where the English version records that God was king in Israel "till in the days of Samuel they rebelled, and would have a mortall man for their King, after the manner of other Nations" (Cf. Hobbes, *Leviathan*, p. 309; *Opera omnia*, vol. 3, p. 329), and where it has "in the time before the Jews had deposed God" (Cf. Hobbes, *Leviathan*, p. 314; *Opera omnia*, vol. 3, p. 324). He also tellingly alters a

passage in chap. 36: where the English version has "after the people of the Jews, had rejected God, that he should not reign over them," the Latin substitutes the vague phrase "after the Israelites had relieved themselves of the divine yoke" *(postquam autem jugum Dei excusserant Israelitae)* (cf. Hobbes, *Leviathan,* p. 294; *Opera omnia,* vol. 3, p. 306). Hobbes did not, however, remove all traces of this earlier reading. See, for example, *Opera omnia,* vol. 3, p. 95. My argument assumes (as I think we must) that Tricaud is mistaken in his view that the Latin *Leviathan* was written before the English. See Hobbes, *Léviathan,* ed. and trans. François Tricaud (Paris, 1971). It is also worth noting that Hobbes's discussion in chap. 35 of the English *Leviathan* is itself milder than the analogous discussion in *De cive* (1642). There, Hobbes had defended his gloss on I Sam. 8 by citing an inflammatory passage from Josephus: "It is also the teaching of *Judas of Galilee,* mentioned at Josephus, Jewish Antiquities 18.2, in these words: *Judas of Galilee was the founder of the fourth sect of seekers of wisdom. They agree with the Pharisees in everything except that they burn with a constant passion for liberty, believing that God alone is to be regarded as Lord and Prince*" (Hobbes, *De cive,* ed. Richard Tuck, trans. Michael Silverthorne [Cambridge, 1998], p. 192). Even here, however, Hobbes makes clear that he understands Judas's position to refer only to Israelite governance.

10. Hobbes, *Leviathan,* pp. 280–282. Hobbes's position is that, while God is lord of the universe in general by virtue of his power, he was only the civil sovereign over his "peculiar" people, Israel, by virtue of covenant. This is also Spinoza's view. See Spinoza, *A theologico-political treatise and A political treatise,* ed. and trans. R. H. M. Elwes (New York, 1951), pp. 219–226, 237–238.

11. Hobbes would certainly not have been pleased to find himself cited as a defender of the republican reading in James Harrington's *Prerogative of Popular Government* (1658). See Harrington, *The Political Works of James Harrington,* ed. J. G. A. Pocock (Cambridge, 1978), p. 423.

12. See the rich analysis of Christian exegesis on these verses in Annette Weber-Möckl, *"Das Recht des Königs, der über euch herrschen soll": Studien zu I Sam 8, 11ff. in der Literatur der frühen Neuzeit* (Berlin, 1986). I reach different conclusions from Dr. Weber-Möckl in several important respects, but I am greatly indebted to her scholarship. See also the able summary in Diego Quaglioni, "L'iniquo diritto: 'Regimen regis' e 'ius regis' nell'esegesi di I *Sam.* 8, 11–17 e negli 'specula principum' del tardo Medioevo," in *Specula principum,* ed. Angela De Benedictis, Studien zur europäischen Rechtsgeschichte 117 (Frankfurt, 1999), pp. 209–242.

13. I have a welcome opportunity here to correct an error in the first published version of this argument. There, I had attributed the *glossa ordinaria* to the ninth-century exegete Walafrid Strabo (Eric Nelson, "'Talmudical Commonwealthsmen' and the Rise of Republican Exclusivism," *The Historical Journal* 50 (2007): 809–835; see esp. p. 814). In fact, this attribution (originating in the sixteenth century) has recently been discredited. On this, see Karlfried Froehlich, "Walafrid Strabo and the Glossa Ordinaria: The Making of a Myth," *Studia Patristica* 28 (1993): 192–196. Frans van Liere points out, however, that this Renaissance error contained within it a kernel of truth: the gloss was deeply influenced by Carolingian materials, including most

especially the works of Walafrid's teacher, Hrabanus Maurus (787–856). See Frans van Liere, "The Literal Sense of the Books of Samuel and Kings: From Andrew of St. Victor to Nicholas of Lyra," in *Nicholas of Lyra: The Senses of Scripture*, ed. Philip D. W. Krey and Lesley Smith (Leiden, 2000), pp. 59–81 (esp. pp. 63–64).

14. "Quaeri potest cur displicuit populus Deo, cum regem desideravit, cum hic inveniatur esse permissus? Sed intelligendum est merito non fuisse secundum voluntatem Dei, quia hoc fieri non praecepit, sed desiderantibus permisit." See J.-P. Migne, *Patrologia Latina,* 221 vols. (Paris, 1844–1855), vol. 113. Cf. Augustine, *Quaestiones in Heptateuchum* V.26. All translations are my own, unless otherwise noted.

15. "Habitatores terrae constituunt sibi regem contra Dei sententiam."

16. John of Salisbury, *Policraticus,* VIII.18. See John of Salisbury, *Policraticus,* ed. and trans. Cary Nederman (Cambridge, 1990), pp. 201–202.

17. Aquinas, *De reg.* 1.5–6. See *On the Government of Rulers: De Regimine Principum,* ed. and trans. James M. Blythe (Philadelphia, 1997). Aquinas's authorship of the first part of this important treatise continues to be disputed, but no consensus has emerged. Cf. Aquinas, *Summa theologiae,* Ia IIae q. CV a.1.

18. Erasmus, *Collected Works of Erasmus,* 86 vols., ed. A. H. T. Levi (Toronto, 1986), vol. 27, pp. 226–227. Another version of this position is found in Henry Ainsworth, *Annotations upon the five bookes of Moses, the booke of Psalmes, and the Song of Songs, Or Canticles* (London, 1627). He writes in his gloss on Deut. 17:14: "Thus God, who had set Judges over his people, permitteth them also to have a king, if they saw it so meet, and would; and should doe this thing after an holy and orderly manner. But when they sought it amisse, it displeaseth the Lord, I *Sam.* 8.5, 6, 7. and 12.12, 17, 19. Then God gave them a king in his anger, and took him away in his wrath, *Hos.* 13.11." As we will see, Ainsworth's account is influenced in part by Maimonides.

19. I use the term *Pauline* here to denote the view that all magistrates rule by divine providence, and that there is accordingly a generalized Christian duty of obedience.

20. Warren Chernaik is correct to stress that these Protestants tended to read I Sam. 8 through the lens of Romans 13:1–2: "Let every soul be subject unto the higher powers. For there is no power but of God: the powers that be are ordained of God. Whosoever therefore resisteth the power, resisteth the ordinance of God: and they that resist shall receive to themselves damnation." See Chernaik, "Biblical republicanism," *Prose Studies* 23 (2000): 147–160.

21. Jean Calvin, *Institutes of the Christian religion,* 2 vols., trans. John Allen (Philadelphia, 1955), vol. 2, IV.7.

22. Bodin, *Les six livres de la république,* ed. Christiane Frémont, Marie-Dominique Couzinet, and Henri Rochais, 6 vols. (Paris, 1986), I.10. English translation is taken from Jean Bodin, *On Sovereignty,* trans. Julian Franklin (Cambridge, 1992), p. 46). A related view is that the Israelites sinned in asking that their king be chosen by Samuel instead of God. See, for example, Balthasar Hubmaier, "On the Sword" [1527], in *The Radical Reformation,* ed. Michael Baylor (Cambridge, 1991), p. 192.

23. Aquinas, *De reg.* 2.15.2. See *On the government of rulers,* pp. 139–140.

24. For a recent discussion of Ptolemy's republicanism, see James Blythe, "'Civic Humanism' and Medieval Political Thought," in *Renaissance Civic Humanism,* ed. James Hankins (Cambridge, 2000), pp. 30–74.

25. Josephus, *Contra Apionem* 2:163–168. See Josephus, *The Life. Against Apion,* ed. and trans. H. St. J. Thackeray (Cambridge, MA, 1926).

26. τὸν μὲν θεὸν ἀποχειροτονοῦσι τῆς βασιλείας. Josephus, *De ant. iud.* 6:60. See Josephus, *Jewish Antiquities,* 8 vols., ed. and trans. H. St. J. Thackeray and Louis H. Feldman (Cambridge, MA, 1930–1965). Josephus was, in effect, reading I Sam. 8:7 in light of I Sam. 12:12.

27. It would be more precise to say that Christian exegetes understood Josephus's position in this manner; Josephus himself may well have regarded Israel as a model for other nations to emulate (although he does not seem to have regarded monarchy as illicit). See, for example, *De. ant. iud.* 14:38; 18:6; *De bello iud.* 2:2.

28. See Julian Franklin, ed., *Constitutionalism and Resistance in the Sixteenth Century: Three Treatises by Hotman, Beza, & Mornay* (New York, 1969), p. 116.

29. See ibid., pp. 158–159.

30. It is worth noting that certain sixteenth-century Protestant radicals read I Sam. 8 (in conjunction with Hosea 13) to suggest that earthly, secular rule itself was the object of God's displeasure. See, for example, Thomas Müntzer, "Testimony of the first chapter of the gospel of Luke" [c. 1524], in *The Collected Works of Thomas Müntzer,* ed. and trans. Peter Matheson (Edinburgh, 1988), p. 283. This theme was later emphasized by English Fifth Monarchists. John Eliot, for example, exhorts his readers to "throw down that great Idol of Humane Wisdom in Governments" and to govern themselves by Scripture alone (see John Eliot, *The Christian Commonwealth: or, The civil polity of the rising kingdom of Jesus* [London, 1659], sig. D2ʳ.

31. Here it is important to note the central rabbinic distinction between *pshat* (the literal meaning of the Biblical text) and *drash* (interpretive exegesis). This gloss is clearly an instance of the latter. My thanks to Shulamite Valler for prompting me to focus on this issue.

32. This is, importantly, how the Vulgate renders the line: "cum ingressus fueris terram quam Dominus Deus tuus dabit tibi et possederis eam habitaverisque in illa et dixeris constituam super me regem sicut habent omnes per circuitum nationes."

33. There are, however, exceptions to this rule. One is Salmasius, to whom I will turn below.

34. Rav and Rav Yehudah are "Amoraim," writing two centuries later.

35. Not to be confused with Rav Yehudah, who lived over a century later.

36. I have drawn from two English translations of this discussion. The first is that of Jacob Shachter in the *Soncino Hebrew-English Edition of The Babylonian Talmud* (London, 1994); the second is that provided in volume 1 of *The Jewish Political Tradition,* ed. Michael Walzer and Menachem Lorberbaum (New Haven, CT, 2000), pp. 141–142. For the rabbinic debate over monarchy see Gerald Blidstein, "The Monarchic Imperative In Rabbinic Perspective," *Association for Jewish Studies Review* 7–8 (1982–1983): 15–39.

37. "Observarunt Hebraei tria praecepta fuisse Isrealitis cum ingressuri essent Terram promissionis, nempe ut super se constituerent Regem, exterminarent semen Amalec, & exstruerent Domino Templum. Quaestionem quoque hic movent Hebraei, Cur Dominus aegre tulerit quod tempore Samuelis Regem postularint, cum tamen hoc loco aut praecipiat, aut ius faciat eius constituendi? Ad hoc quidam respondent, Seniores quidem qui eo tempore erant, non male & impie Regem postulasse, cum dicerent ad Samuelem, *Da nobis Regem, qui iudicet nos,* &c. sed vulgus peccavisse, quod nollet audire vocem Samuelis, sed dicebat, *Nequaquam: sed Rex erit super nos, ut & nos simus sicut caetera gentes . . ."* See John Pearson, ed., *Critici sacri, sive, Doctissimorum virorum in ss. Biblia annotationes* (London, 1660), vol. 1, p. 1247. This nine-volume work is a compendium of famous Biblical commentaries.

38. "Tradunt Iudaeorum magistri, tria injuncta fuisse Israelitis quae facere eos oporteret postquam introducti essent in terram sactam, *regem sibi constituere, exscindere Amalechitas, templum exstruere."* See Claude de Saumaise (Salmasius), *C. L. Salmasii Defensio pro Carolo I* (Cambridge, 1684), p. 63. This work was originally published in November 1649. Maimonides also repeats this dictum in his *Mishneh Torah;* as a result, various Christian authors atttributed it to him. For example, Peter van der Cun (Cunaeus) writes in his *De republica Hebraeorum libri III* (Amsterdam, 1617): "Ait Rabbi Maimonides in parte postrema Misnae, Israelitas tria mandata accepisse a numine, quae exequerentur cum Palaestinam tenerent. e quibus primum erat, uti regem sibi constituerent; alterum, uti memoriam obliterarent Amalekitarum; tertium de templi aedificatione fuit." See *Petrus Cunaeus of the commonwealth of the Hebrews,* trans. Clement Barksdale (London, 1653), p. 124.

39. "Plurimi eorum scribunt recte & ordine Seniores illius temporis regem postulasse, sed in eo peccasse vulgus hominum quod ad instar regum quos haberent caeterae nationes, sibi dari eum petierint" (Salmasius, *Defensio,* p. 63). See also Filmer's remarks in the *Observations:* "The sin of the Children of Israel did lye, not in Desiring a King, but in desiring such a King like as the Nations round about had." Filmer, *Observations concerning the original and various forms of government* (London, 1696), p. 191 (cf. Filmer, *Patriarcha* [London, 1680], pp. 51–52). This view was endorsed earlier by the Scottish Hebraist John Weemes, who tried to harmonize it with the Pauline position: "They [the rabbis] say, that he [God] gave them three things in commandement when they entered into *Canaan;* first, to choose a King; secondly, to roote out the *Canaanites* [sic] and thirdly, to build a Temple for his worship: God was angry with them that they sought a King so long as good *Samuel* ruled over them; he was angry with them because they would have a King to reigne over them after the manner of the Nations" (Weemes, *An explication of the iudiciall lavves of Moses* [London, 1636], p. 12).

40. "In hanc sententiam recte omnino de R. Iose in Gemara Sanhedrin scriptum est, ita illum senisse. Quidquid dicitur in capite de rege, eum regum ius habere" (Salmasius, *Defensio,* pp. 48–49). By the time Salmasius was writing, the Talmudic tractate *Sanhedrin* had been completely translated into Latin. See Johannes Coccejus, *Duo tituli thalmudici: Sanhedrin et Maccoth* (Amsterdam, 1629).

41. Cunaeus, *De republica Hebraeorum libri III* (1617), p. 273. The English translation is from the edition of 1653. "Sed illis erudite respondit Maimonides, atque indignationem numinis ex eo esse ortam ait [Hebrew text follows], *quia regem concupivissent per ambiguas querelas, seditiosasque voces, non uti legis praeceptum peragerent, sed quod displicebat illis sanctissimus vates Samuel, ad quem vox illa numinis extat, Non te illi, sed me fastidiverunt.*" The quotation is from Maimonides, MT, *Melakhim* 1:1–2.

42. "Cur igitur haec petitio displicuit Domino? Quia malo animo eum petierunt, non propter praeceptum . . . per murmurationem, non tam ut iudicaret eos quam ut bella eorum bellaret" (*Critici sacri,* vol. 2, p. 2257). Drusius's commentary was written about 1600.

43. Edmund Bunny, *The scepter of Judah: or, what manner of government it was, that unto the common-wealth or Church of Israel was by the law of God appointed* (London, 1584), p. 130.

44. "Leges autem de Rege, de Templo, & excidio Amalecitarum pertinent ad tempora possessae Terrae" (*Critici sacri,* vol. 1, p. 1253). For a general account of Grotius's use of rabbinica in his *Annotationes,* see Peter T. van Rooden, *Theology, Biblical Scholarship and Rabbinical Studies in the Seventeenth Century: Constantijn L'Empereur (1591–1648), Professor of Hebrew and Theology at Leiden* (Leiden, 1989), pp. 142–148.

45. "Alio tempore Regem sibi facere sine culpa potuissent" (*Critici sacri,* vol. 2, p. 2260).

46. "Licebat ergo ipsis Regem expetere, sed non quo tempore Interregem habebant a Deo constitutum" (*Critici sacri,* vol. 1, p. 1253). Grotius's view seems to follow an argument of Nahmanides's, which appears in the latter's gloss on Genesis 49:10.

47. See John Locke, *Two Treatises of Government and A Letter Concerning Toleration,* ed. Ian Shapiro (New Haven, CT, 2003), p. 150.

48. פרוסטיה, prob. from the Greek προστασία.

49. Once again, I have drawn together elements from two different translations of this text. The first is that of Rabbi J. Rabbinowitz in *Midrash rabbah,* 10 vols., ed. Rabbi H. Freedman and Maurice Simon (London, 1939), vol. 7, pp. 109–113. The second is the excerpted version found in *The Jewish Political Tradition,* pp. 148–149. The Hebrew text is taken from *Midrash debarim rabbah,* ed. S. Lieberman (Jerusalem, 1940); however, it is important to note that the Lieberman version reproduces a different recension of the text (although with no significant differences for our purposes). There are also other Midrashic passages that suggest the same orientation: *Bereshith Rabbah,* for example, has R. Samuel b. Nahman claim that Abraham declined the title of king, declaring "Let the world not be without its [true] king." See *Genesis Rabbah,* 2nd ed., 3 vols., ed. Julius Theodor and Chanoch Albeck (Jerusalem, 1965), 1:419, 2:624. I should also note that, in the penultimate paragraph, the phrase translated as "idolatry" is *'avodat kokhavim,* which literally means "worship of the stars." It is a later formulation that often stands in for the more conventional term for idolatry: *'avodah zarah* (literally, strange worship). Early-modern readers were well aware of this fact. John Selden, for example, makes the point as follows: "Pro עבודה זרה *culto extraneo* in Maimonidis editis aliquot libris aliorumque

saepius occurrit . . . עֲבוֹדַת כּוֹכָבִים וּמַזָּלוֹת *Cultus astrorum & Planetarum."*
Selden, *De synedriis & praefecturis iuridicis veterum Ebraeorum,* 3 vols. (London, 1650–1955), vol. 1, p. 9. For Selden's Hebrew scholarship, see Jason Rosenblatt, *John Selden: Renaissance England's Chief Rabbi* (Oxford, 2006).

50. It is important to note that the rabbis of the Midrash never explicitly state that, as a juridical matter, monarchy is equivalent to idolatry; that would have committed them to the view that defenders of monarchy had to be put to death.

51. See, for example, Blair Worden, "Milton's Republicanism and the Tyranny of Heaven," in *Machiavelli and Republicanism,* ed. Gisela Bock, Quentin Skinner, and Maurizio Viroli (Cambridge, 1990), pp. 225–245; Martin Dzelzainis, "Milton's Classical Republicanism," in *Milton and Republicanism,* ed. David Armitage, Armand Himy, and Quentin Skinner (Cambridge, 1995), pp. 3–24; Thomas N. Corns, "Milton and the Characteristics of a Free Commonwealth," in *Milton and Republicanism,* pp. 25–42; and Quentin Skinner, "John Milton and the Politics of Slavery," in *Visions of Politics,* 3 vols. (Cambridge, 2002), vol. 2, *Renaissance Virtues,* pp. 286–307.

52. It is indeed very striking that, even in the heated environment of 1649, radical republican pamphleteers continued to defend the basic legitimacy of monarchy. Consider, for example, Eleutherius Philodemius, who states in *The armies vindication . . . in Reply to Mr. William Sedgwick* (London, 1649) that "it is an unquestionable truth, that Monarchy, Democratie, and Aristocratie, are the powers of God, each in it self a lawfull form of Government," arguing only that "it is as unquestionable, that so the case may be, as the use of one may be laid aside, and another set up, and God much seen and honoured in the change" (p. 5). Even at his most incendiary, when he claims that "we know, and experience shews it, that there is no kind of civil government more averse and opposite to the Kingdom of Christ and lesse helpful to it than Monarchie," he nonetheless immediately adds that "we grant that true religion is not inconsistent with monarchie" (p. 15). Marchamont Nedham likewise aims only to vindicate "the Excellency of a Free State above a Kingly Government," by arguing that "it is the most commodious and profitable way of government, conducing to the enlargement of a nation every way in wealth and dominion" (*The Case of the Commonwealth of England, Stated,* ed. Philip Knachel [Charlottesville, VA, 1969], p. 117). Although his antimonarchical rhetoric is often quite strident, he never actually claims that monarchy per se is illegitimate— indeed, his strongly de facto theory of political obligation rules out this argument (see esp. pp. 28–29, 32–33). Nedham's pamphlet was published in 1650. Consider also John Hall (*The grounds and reasons of monarchy considered* [London, 1651]), who inveighs quite boldly against the "slavish" condition of subjects (and even once refers parenthetically to monarchy as "a disease of Government" (p. 54), but nonetheless argues only that "republicks may be as Just and Authoritative, as Kingships" (pp. 12–13). He also distinguishes sharply between "absolute" monarchy, in which "my very naturall liberty is taken away from me," and "mixt and limited" monarchy. In the case of the second sort of monarch, Hall exclaims "Ile be the first man shall sweare him Allegiance" (p. 17).

53. Milton, *Complete Prose Works of John Milton,* vol. 3, ed. Merritt Hughes (New Haven, CT, 1962), p. 207. This had become a standard monarchomach reading of the verses. See Quentin Skinner, *Foundations of Modern Political Thought,* 2 vols. (Cambridge, 1978), vol. 2, pp. 206-238. For Milton's use of this topos, see Walter S. H. Lim, *John Milton, Radical Politics, and Biblical Republicanism* (Newark, NJ, 2006), pp. 41-68.

54. *Complete Prose,* vol. 5, p. 208.

55. Ibid., p. 236.

56. Ibid., p. 256.

57. See, for example, ibid., pp. 343-344. There are also several instances in Milton's later writings in which he entertains the possibility of an acceptable monarchy (see, e.g., *Complete Prose,* vol. 7, ed. Robert Ayers [New Haven, CT, 1980], pp. 377-378). My argument is simply that Milton was the first to make the exclusivist argument, and that it remained a dominant feature of his political theory after 1650. For Milton's vacillation on the subject, see Blair Worden, *Literature and Politics in Cromwellian England: John Milton, Andrew Marvell, Marchamont Nedham* (Oxford, 2007), esp. pp. 227-239.

58. For a similarly emphatic presentation of this view, see Filmer, *Patriarcha,* pp. 80-81.

59. "Deo irato, non solum quod regem vellent ad exemplum gentium, et non suae legis, sed plane quod vellent regem." Milton, *Pro populo anglicano defensio* (London, 1651), p. 19. Most English translations from Milton's *Defensio* are taken from *Complete Prose,* vol. 4:1, ed. Don Wolfe, trans. Donald Mackenzie (New Haven, CT, 1966). In this instance, however, I have had to replace Mackenzie's with my own. His version is found on p. 347.

60. "Idem Theologi omnes Orthodoxi, idem Iurisconsulti, idem Rabbini plerique, ut ex Sichardo didicisse potuisti, de explicatione huius loci sentiunt; ne Rabbinorum enim quisquam ius regis absolutum isto loco tractari dixit" (Milton, *Defensio,* p. 21). *Complete Prose,* vol. 4:1, pp. 349-350.

61. "Nam caput illud de rege in quo R. Ioses ius regium aiebat contineri, Deuteronomii esse, non Samuelis, manifestum est. Samuelis enim ad terrorem duntaxat populo iniiciendum pertinere rectissime quidem & contra te dixit R. Iudas" (Milton, *Defensio,* p. 25). *Complete Prose,* vol. 4:1, p. 353.

62. Leonard R. Mendelsohn takes this as evidence that Milton did not have direct access to the Talmud or failed to understand it. I see it, rather, as an intrepid forensic move. See Mendelsohn, "Milton and the Rabbis: A Later Inquiry," *Studies in English Literature* 18 (1978):125-135 (esp. p. 130).

63. *Complete Prose,* vol. 1, ed. Don M. Wolfe (New Haven, CT, 1953), p. 460.

64. "Reges autem Hebraeorum iudicari posse, atque etiam ad verbera damnari fuse docet Sichardus ex libris Rabbinicis, cui tu haec omnia debes, & tamen obstrepere non erubescis" (Milton, *Defensio,* p. 27). *Complete Prose,* vol. 4:1, p. 355.

65. "Ut omnes autem videant te nullo modo ex Hebraeourm scriptis id probare, quod probandum hoc capite susceperas, esse ex magistris tua sponte confiteris, qui negant alium suis majoribus regem agnoscendum fuisse praeter Deum, datum autem in poenam fuisse. Quorum ego in sententiam pedibus eo" (Milton, *Defensio,*

p. 35). *Complete Prose,* vol. 4:1, p. 366. The third and fourth lines reproduce Salmasius's words almost verbatim.

66. The literature on this question is quite large and is motivated by the desire to explain Milton's frequent use of Midrashic material in *Paradise Lost.* Important contributions include Harris Fletcher, *Milton's Rabbinical Readings* (Urbana, IL, 1930); Kitty Cohen, *The Throne and the Chariot: Studies in Milton's Hebraism* (The Hague, 1975); Jason Rosenblatt, *Torah and Law in Paradise Lost* (Princeton, NJ, 1994); Golda Werman, *Milton and Midrash* (Washington, DC, 1995); and Jeffrey S. Shoulson, *Milton and the Rabbis: Hebraism, Hellensim, & Christianity* (New York, 2001). That Milton knew Biblical Hebrew and the Aramaic targums is certain; the question is whether his command of the language was sufficient to enable him to consult rabbinic commentaries in the original, and in conventional italic script (as they appear, for instance, in Johannes Buxtorf's 1618 Rabbinical Bible).

67. "Non is populum increpabat, quia Regem peterent sed quia non legitime peterent." See Wilhelm Schickard, *Mishpat ha-melekh, Jus regium hebraeorum e tenebris rabbinicis* (Strasbourg, 1625), p. 6.

68. "Tamen non desunt inter Judaeos qui contradicunt & putant, Regibus majores suos minime indiguisse. Rationes illorum diversae sunt, quas distincte videbimus" (Schickard, *Mishpat ha-melekh,* p. 4).

69. "R. Bechai existimat, DEUM Opt. Max. sufficere ipsis; nec nisi poenam Reges indulsisse. forte ut ranis Jupiter Ciconiam apud Aesopum. sic autem ille ad Parsch. Schoph. col. 6 [Hebrew text follows] *Non erat voluntas Dei O. M. ut esset Rex in Israel aliusque ipsemet. Ipse enim Altissimus est Rex ille, qui ambulat in medio castrorum & provide attendit ad particularissima quaeque. Nec opus erat illis Rege alio. Nam populus electus, cuius Rex est Dominus universi, quid faceret cum Rege qui caro tantum est & sanguis? . . . Scriptum est* (Hos. 13.11) *do tibi Regem in ira mea . . .*" (Schickard, *Mishpat ha-melekh,* p. 4). For the way in which the fable Schickard mentions made its way into seventeenth-century politics, see Mark Kishlansky, "Turning Frogs into Princes: Aesop's Fables and the Political Culture of Early-Modern England," in *Political Culture and Cultural Politics in Early Modern England,* ed. Susan Amussen and Mark Kishlansky (Manchester, U.K., 1995), pp. 338–360. Bahya's commentary on Deut. 17:14 can be found in *Midrash Rabeinu Bahya 'al Hamishah Humshei Torah,* 2 vols. (Jerusalem, 1988), vol. 2.

70. This is an erroneous attribution. The figure Shickard has in mind is certainly not the great thirteenth-century scholar Rabbi Moshe ben Nahman (Nahmanides), since the latter endorses the majority view in the Talmud (and Schickard, a good Hebraist, would have known this). The most likely explanation for the mistake is that Schickard is referencing a tradition, exemplified by a gloss to the *Sefer ha-Kabbalah* of the twelfth-century scholar Abraham Ibn Daud (translated into Latin in 1527), which incorrectly attributed primary authorship of *Bereshit Rabbah* and the other *Rabbot* to Rabba bar Nahmani, a Babylonian rabbi of the Talmud (who, in fact, had no connection to these texts). That is, this tradition took the title *Bereshit Rabbah* to mean "Rabba's commentary on Genesis," rather than what it actually means: "The great commentary on Genesis" (see Abraham Ibn Daud, *Sefer*

ha-Qabbalah, ed. and trans. Gerson Cohen [Oxford, 2005], p. 123). This explanation seems particularly plausible because Grotius likewise attributes authorship of *Devarim Rabbah* as a whole to "Barnachmon" in the *De iure belli ac pacis* (for Grotius's attribution, see Phyllis Lachs, "Hugo Grotius's Use of Jewish Sources in *On the Law of War and Peace,*" *Renaissance Quarterly* 30 [1977]: 181–200 [esp. pp. 196–197]). If this is correct, then Schickard here is likely quoting directly from the Midrash, and not from an excerpted version in another commentary.

71. "Rabba B. Nachmoni arbitratur hoc pugnare cum libertate populi Judaeici, quorum conditio non sit regi ab alio, ut a pastore pecora. Sed instar ferarum liberrime circum vagari. paulo ante loc. supra citat. [Hebrew text follows] *ait DEUS O. M. Israeli, mi fili! Sic cogitavi, ut essetis liberi ab imperiis. unde hoc? quia dicitur* (Jerem. 2.v.24) *Onager asssuetus deserto. Sicut ergo asinus sylvestris adolescit in deserto, nec timet ullum hominem super se: sic reputavi, ne esset metus regni super vos. At vos non hoc quaesivistis. Sed (ut in textu sequitur) in desiderio animae suae sorbuit ventum. non est his ventus aliud quam Regnum. unde hoc? quia dicitur* (Dan. 7.2) *ecce quatuor venti coeli pugnabant ad mare magnum*" (Schickard, *Mishpat ha-melekh,* p. 5).

72. "*Abi & disce quid contigerit nobis sub manu regum. sic enim concionantur Doctores nostri p.m. Saul cecidit in monte Gilboah, David causatus est plagam, sicut dicitur* (2 Sam 24.15) *deditque Dominus pestem in Israel. Achab cohibuit pluvies ab eis, ut scribitur* (I. Reg. 17.1 *vivit Dominus) si erit hisce annis ros aut pluvia &c. Zidkiah desolari fecit sanctuarium*" (Schickard, *Mishpat ha-melekh,* p. 5).

73. "Tandem fuerunt Reges illi causa deceptionis Israeli, ut alienarentur a Domine Deo, usque dum abducerentur in exilium a terra sua" (Schickard, *Mishpat ha-melekh,* p. 5). Another author who clearly uses Schickard to cite this Midrash is John Weemes. Weemes, like Schickard, defends monarchy, but he also feels compelled to note (confusing rabbinic authorities) that "*Levi ben Gerson* upon the I *Sam.* 8. holdeth that Aristocraticall Government is best, and to be preferred to Kingly Government; learne saith hee what hath befallen us under the hand of Kings; *David* caused the plague to come upon the people, 2 *Sam.* 24.15. *Ahab* restrained the raine for three yeares, I *King.* 17. and *Zedekiah* caused the Sanctuary to be burnt, 2 *Chro.* 36.14. and the *Iewes* apply the saying of *Hosea, I gave them a King in mine anger,* and tooke him away in my wrath, *Hos.* 13 11. That is, I gave them their first King *Saul* in mine anger, and I tooke away their last King *Zedekiah* in my indignation" (Weemes, *Explication,* p. 5). As we have seen, Weemes is actually quoting Bahya; the confusion derives from the fact that Schickard quotes Levi ben Gershom in the adjacent sentence.

74. The *editio princeps* of *Devarim Rabbah* dates to 1512 (Constantinople), and it was frequently reprinted thereafter. An important edition for our purposes is that printed in Amsterdam in 1640 (*Sefer Rabot: . . . midrashot 'al Hamishah Humshe Torah,* 2 vols. [Amsterdam, 1640]), which employed standard Hebrew lettering, rather than italic script. There is also uniform agreement that Milton knew the Midrash to Genesis (*Bereshit Rabbah*), which echoes the relevant paragraph in the Midrash to Deut. 17:14 quite clearly in places. He also probably knew the midrashic *Pirkei de Rabbi Eliezer,* which had been translated into Latin by G. H. Vorstius in

1644 (*Chronologia sacra-profana . . . Cui addita sunt Pirke vel Capitula R. Elieser* [Leiden, 1644]). A description of the Messianic age in chap. 11 of that work explains that it "will restore the sovereignty to its owner. He who was the first king will be the last king, as it is said, 'Thus saith the Lord, the King . . . I am the first, and I am the last; and beside me there is no God' (Isa. 44:6); and it is written, 'And the Lord shall be king over all the earth' (Zech. 14:9) and the sovereignty shall return to its (right-ful) heir and then, 'The idols shall utterly pass away. And the Lord alone shall be exalted in that day' (Isa. 2:18–19)." See *Pirke de Rabbi Eliezer*, 4th ed., ed. and trans. George Friedlander (New York, 1981), p. 83. On Milton's Midrashic materials, see Werman, *Milton and Midrash,* pp. 27–41, 42–92. It is interesting to note that the Midrashic view is not canvassed in Menasseh ben Israel's extensive gloss on Deut. 17:14 in the *Conciliator;* Menasseh does, however, include copious quotations from the Biblical commentary of the fifteenth-century scholar Isaac Abravanel—an anti-monarchical exegete whom Schickard neglected. See Menasseh ben Israel, *Menasseh Ben Israel conciliator: Sive, de convenientia locorum S. Scripturae, quae pugnare inter se videntur* (Amsterdam, 1633).

75. The closest thing to a precedent I have been able to find is John Lilburne's *Regall tyrannie discovered* (London, 1647). Lilburne writes that "*Monarks* assume unto themselves, the very *Soveraignty, Stile, Office,* and name of GOD himself, whose *Soveraign Prerogative* it is, only, and alone, *to rule and govern by his Will*" (p. 11), and then he offers the following piece of evidence: the Israelites, not content with God's bounty and protection, "*Would have a King to reigne over them, when* (saith Samuel) *the Lord your God was your King:* therefore [I Sam.] chap. 10.19 saith *Samuel, ye have this day rejected your God, who himself saved you out of all your adversities,* &c. yea, and (in the 19. verse of the 12. chap.) the People acknowledged that they had added unto all their sins, this evill, *even to ask a King;* Whereby we may evidently perceive, that this office of a King, is not in the least of Gods institution; neither is it to be given to any man upon earth: Because none must rule by his will but God alone; And there-fore the Scripture saith, He gave them a King in his anger, and took him away in his wrath, *Hosa* 13.11" (pp. 13–14). Lilburne's analysis certainly resembles Bahya as quoted by Schickard (note the identical use of Hosea 13.11); nonetheless he does not actually refer to monarchy as a form of "idolatry." See also John Goodwin, *Anti-cavalierisme or, Truth Pleading As well the Necessity, as the Lawfulness of this present War* (London, 1642), esp. pp. 4–5; and (after the release of Milton's *Defensio*) John Cook, *Monarchy, No creature of Gods making* (Waterford, Ireland, 1651), esp. pp. 29–35, 50, 53, and 93. All of these texts (including Lilburne's) distinguish sharply be-tween absolute monarchs who rule according to their will and legitimate monarchs who rule by law. As we shall see, Milton's eventual view is more radical than this.

76. "Passim enim testatur Deus valde sibi displicuisse quod regem petissent. ver. 7. *Non te sed me spreverunt ne regnem super ipsos, secundum illa facta quibus dereliquerunt me & coluerunt Deos alienos:* ac si species quaedam idololatriae videretur regem petere, qui adorari se, & honores prope divinos tribui sibi postulat. Sane qui supra omnes leges terrenum sibi dominum imponit, prope est ut sibi Deum statuat alie-num; Deum utique haud saepe rationabilem, sed profligata saepius ratione brutum

& belluinum. Sic I Sam. 10.19. *Vos sprevistis Deum vestrum qui ipse servat vos ab omnibus malis, & angustiis vestris, cum dixistis ei, regem praeponens nobis . . .* plane ac si simul docuisset, non hominis esse dominari in homines, sed solius Dei" (Milton, *Defensio,* pp. 38–39).

77. "Populus denique resipiscens apud Isaiam 26.13. calamitosum hoc sibi fuisse queritur, quod alios praeter Deum dominos habuerat. Indicio sunt haec omnia regem irato Deo Israelitis fuisse datum" (Milton, *Defensio,* p. 39). I have altered the translation here.

78. I owe this point to Bernard Septimus.

79. *Complete Prose,* vol. 1, p. 432.

80. *Complete Prose,* vol. 3, p. 343.

81. On this, see Barbara Lewalski, "Milton and Idolatry," Studies in *English Literature* 43 (2003): 213–232 (esp. pp. 220–222). See also Richard F. Hardin, *Civil Idolatry: Desacralizing and Monarchy in Spenser, Shakespeare, and Milton* (London, 1992), esp. pp. 164–201.

82. Milton had likewise related these verses in the first Defense (*Complete Prose,* vol. 4:1, pp. 377–378), but here his reading of Luke 22:25 becomes more radical.

83. *Complete Prose,* vol. 7, pp. 360–361. Calvin directly attacks this reading of Luke 22:25 in Institutes IV.7.

84. Ibid., p. 374.

85. Ibid., p. 387.

86. Quotations from *Paradise Lost* are taken from *John Milton: A Critical Edition of the Major Works,* ed. Stephen Orgel and Jonathan Goldberg (Oxford, 1991).

87. Compare *Samson Agonistes* 268–271: "But what more oft in nations grown corrupt,/ And by their vices brought to servitude,/ Than to love bondage more than liberty;/ Bondage with ease than strenuous liberty."

88. See Milton, *Complete Prose,* vol. 7, p. 363.

89. On this, see Roger Lejosne, "Milton, Satan, Salmasius and Abdiel," in *Milton and Republicanism,* ed. David Armitage, Armand Himy, and Quentin Skinner (Cambridge, 1995), pp. 106–117.

90. God's kingship is, for Milton, utterly unlike human kingship, but it is not allegorical. God actually rules us as a sovereign, and we should be governed by his will, rather than our own. It is Satan who, in *Paradise Regain'd,* tempts the Son to embrace human kingship by wondering aloud whether the kingdom of God is merely "allegoric" (PR IV.389–390).

91. Cf. PR IV.163–194.

92. Here he is invoking an ancient tradition, common both to Christian and Jewish exegetes. See, for example, Jean Bodin, *Les six livres de la république,* 6 vols., ed. Christiane Frémont, Marie-Dominique Couzinet, and Henri Rochais, vol. 2 (Paris, 1986), p. 35.

93. *Complete Prose,* vol. 4:1, pp. 366–367. "Non decet enim, neque dignum est regem esse, nisi qui caeteris omnibus longe antecellit; ubi multi sunt aequales, ut sunt in omni civitate plurimi, imperium ex aequo atque per vices dandum esse arbitror: aequali, aut plerumque deteriori, ac saepissime stulto servire omnes, quis non indignissimum putet . . . Rex est Messias: agnoscimus, gaudemus, & quam citissime

veniat oramus; dignus enim est, nec ei quisquam similis aut secundus" (Milton, *Defensio,* pp. 35–36). Note that, according to Milton, men are equal in every state *(in omni civitate),* not, as the Yale edition has it, "in most states." Early readers of the poem were quick to notice that these verses recalled arguments from Milton's revolutionary prose. For the important example of John Beale, see Nicholas von Maltzahn, "Laureate, Republican, Calvinist: An Early Response to Milton and *Paradise Lost* (1667)," *Milton Studies* 29 (1993): 181–198 (see esp. pp. 189–190).

94. See, for example, *Bereshit Rabba* XXIII.7 (p. 197); XXVI.4 (pp. 211–212); XLII.4 (p. 346); *Pirkei de Rabbi Eliezer* 34 (pp. 174–178); Josephus, *Jewish Antiquities* I.113–119. See also Werman, *Milton and Midrash,* pp. 69–71. This view also appears in Augustine (*City of God* XVI.4).

95. See, for example, *Bereshit Rabba* XXXVIII.13 (pp. 310–311); XLIV.2 (p. 361); XLIV.7 (p. 365); and *Zohar Bereshit* 74a. The first two texts, as we have seen, were certainly known to Milton. For the European reception of this tradition, see Hardin, *Civil Idolatry,* pp. 48–49.

96. Cf. Nedham, *The Case of the Commonwealth of England, Stated,* pp. 15–16.

97. Diodati renders the verse as follows: "Quando tu sarai entrato nel paese che'l Signore Iddio tuo ti dà, e lo possederai, e v'habiterai dentro: se tu vieni a dire, Io voglio constituire un rè sopra me, come hanno tutte le genti che son d'intorno a me . . ." See Giovanni Diodati, trans., *La sacra Bibbia tradotta in lingua italiana e commentata da Giovanni Diodati,* 3 vols., ed. Michele Ranchetti (Milan, 1999), vol. 1, p. 577. It is important to note, however, that Diodati himself did not adopt the Midrashic reading of Deut. 17 and I Sam. 8. See, for example, Diodati, *Pious and learned annotations upon the Holy Bible,* trans. R. G. (London, 1648), p. 168. Diodati's Hebrew scholarship is discussed in Milka Ventura Avanzinelli, "Giovanni Diodati, traduttore della Bibbia," in Diodati, *La sacra Bibbia,* vol. 1, esp. pp. lxxx–xc.

98. J. G. A. Pocock, ed., *The Political Works of James Harrington* (Cambridge, 1978), p. 575. See also ibid., p. 581.

99. See also John Cook's observation that Royalists "read those words, I will set a King over me, which is spoken by the people, Thou shalt set a King over thee, as if God had commanded a kingly Government in *Canaan* which was only permissive as the sin of *Adam*" (Cook, *Monarchy, No creature of Gods making,* p. 34).

100. Ibid., p. 574. Harrington here seems to be paraphrasing Carlo Sigonio's analysis from the *De republica Hebraeorum* (1582), itself shaped by rabbinic materials. He glosses Deut. 17:14 as follows: "Significavit enim aperte, Iudicibus rerum summam ex lege habentibus regnasse Deum super Hebraeos, quia lex dominata esset; imperio vero ad regem gentium more translato, Deum non regnaturum, cum non penes legem, sed penes voluntatem unius hominis summa rerum esset futura. probe. etenim, ut optime dixit Aristoteles in Politicis, *Qui legem vult imperare, Deum vult imperare, qui regem, id est hominem, belluam: quod non semper ratione, sed plerunque cupiditate ducatur."* *Caroli Sigonii de republica Hebraeorum libri VII, ad Gregorium XIII pontificem maximum* (Frankfurt, 1585, pp. 40–41. The quotation at the end is from Aristotle, *Pol.* III (1287a). Aristotle here is discussing tyranny, which he sharply distinguishes from monarchy—as Harrington well knew.

101. Algernon Sidney, *Court Maxims*, ed. Hans Blom, Eco Haitsma Mulier, and Ronald Janse (Cambridge, 1996), p. 65. Even Sidney, however, was not always consistent. Earlier in the same treatise he writes: "Let us have such kings [as described in Deut. 17:14] and we will not complain; and that we may have none but such, let us have means of punishing them if they be not so and I am content with that government" (p. 49). An earlier endorsement of the Miltonic reading, this time by a Digger, can be found in Gerrard Winstanley, *The Law of Freedom in a Platform, or, True Magistracy Restored* (London, 1652), pp. 28–29. See also Marchamont Nedham, *Mercurius Politicus* 56 (26 June–3 July 1651), pp. 885–887.

102. Ibid., p. 48.

103. Algernon Sidney, *Discourses Concerning Government,* ed. Thomas G. West (Indianapolis, 1996), p. 338. Interestingly, Sidney cites Abravanel to defend this view (*Discourses*, p. 124); as we have seen, Abravanel tended not to be invoked in this context, simply because Schickard had not excerpted him.

104. Thomas Paine, *The Essential Thomas Paine,* ed. Sidney Hook (Harmondsworth, U.K., 1984), pp. 29–30. Paine himself acknowledged that he owed this argument to Milton. John Adams reports the following conversation with Paine: "I told him further that his Reasoning from the Old Testament [in *Common Sense*] was ridiculous, and I could hardly think him sincere. At this he laughed, and said he had taken his ideas in part from Milton: and then expressed a Contempt for the Old Testament and indeed of the Bible at large, which surprized me." See John Adams, *Diary and Autobiography of John Adams,* 3 vols., ed. L. H. Butterfield (Cambridge, MA, 1961), vol. 3, p. 333. For Paine's use of the Israelite example in his polemical writings, see Maria Teresa Pichetto, "La 'respublica Hebraeorum' nella rivoluzione americana," *Il pensiero politico* 35 (2002): 481–500 (esp. pp. 497–500). See also David Wootton, "Introduction," in *Republicanism, Liberty, and Commercial Society, 1649–1776,* ed. David Wootton (Stanford, 1994), esp. pp. 26–41.

105. Rousseau insisted strongly on the distinction between "sovereignty" (which must always reside in the "general will") and "government" (which may be entrusted to one man, a few, or many). Speaking of forms of government, he argued that "each of the possible forms is the best in some cases and the worst in others." See Rousseau, *The Social Contract,* trans. Maurice Cranston (Harmondsworth, U.K., 1968), p. 111 (III.3). Kant's notoriously opaque version of this argument appears in *Toward Perpetual Peace* (1795). See Kant, *Practical Philosophy,* ed. and trans. Mary J. Gregor (Cambridge, 1996), pp. 322–323.

106. For the role played by the Hebraic exclusivist argument I have sketched out in the wholesale delegitimization of monarchy during the American Revolution, see Nathan Perl-Rosenthal, "'The Divine Right of Republics': Hebraic Republicanism and the Legitimization of Kingless Government in America," *William and Mary Quarterly* 66 (2009): 535–564. For the Hebrew republic as a constitutional model in Revolutionary America, see Eran Shalev, "'A Perfect Republic': The Mosaic Constitution in Revolutionary New England, 1775-1788," *The New England Quarterly* 82 (2009): 235–263.

107. See, for example, Paul Rahe, "The Classical Republicanism of John Milton," *History of Political Thought* 25 (2004): 243–275, reprinted in Rahe, *Against Throne and*

Altar: Machiavelli and Political Theory under the English Republic (Cambridge, 2008), pp. 104–138.

108. Thomas Hobbes, *De Cive: The English Version,* ed. Howard Warrender (Oxford, 1983), p. 37. This is Charles Cotton's translation. The Latin text reads: "ne civitati Aristocraticae, vel Democraticae, minorem a civibus obedientiam deberi quam Monarchicae existimare viderer." See Hobbes, *De Cive: The Latin Version,* ed. Howard Warrender (Oxford, 1983), p. 83.

109. Ibid. The Latin text reads: "Licet enim Monarchiam caeteris civitatis speciebus capite decimo commodiorem esse argumentis aliquot suadere conatus sim (quam rem unam in hoc libro non demonstratam sed probabiliter positam esse confiteor) . . ."

110. Hobbes, *Leviathan,* pp. 114–115, 120, and 129–138.

111. Ibid., p. 108.

112. Ibid., p. 173.

113. Ibid., p. 131.

114. Ibid., p. 132. Hobbes also gives several other arguments concerning the stability of monarchies.

115. See Noel Malcolm, *Aspects of Hobbes* (Oxford, 2002), pp. 16–21.

116. *Eight bookes of the Peloponnesian warre written by Thucydides. . . . Interpreted with faith and diligence immediately out of the Greeke by Thomas Hobbes secretary to ye late earle of Devonshire* (London, 1629). For Hobbes's humanist education, see Quentin Skinner, *Reason and Rhetoric in the Philosophy of Hobbes* (Cambridge, 1996), pp. 215–249.

117. See *Thomas Hobbes: Translations of Homer,* ed. Eric Nelson, 2 vols. (Oxford, 2008). Hobbes published his translation of books 9–12 of the *Odysses* first in 1673; he then released the full *Odysses* in 1675 (with a learned explanatory essay and with a number of alterations to the 1673 text), the full *Iliads* in 1676, and a joint edition in 1677.

118. John Aubrey, *Brief Lives,* ed. Oliver Lawson Dick (London, 1949), p. 158. Although he added that Aristotle's *Rhetoric* was "rare."

119. It should go without saying that this is simply one relevant perspective. One might well conclude, for example, that Hobbes's metaphysics were a good deal more "modern" than Milton's. One could also focus instead on the novelty of Hobbes's conception of the state. See, for example, Quentin Skinner, "Hobbes and the Purely Artificial Person of the State," in *Visions of Politics,* 3 vols. (Cambridge, 2002), vol. 3, pp. 177–208.

2. "FOR THE LAND IS MINE"

1. Philip Pettit, *Republicanism: A Theory of Freedom and Government* (Oxford, 1997), esp. pp. 140–146. See also Cass Sunstein, *Free Markets and Social Justice* (Oxford, 1997), esp. pp. 13–31, 61–62, and 207–211.

2. Gerald F. Gaus, "Backwards into the Future: Neorepublicanism as a Postsocialist Critique of Market Society," *Social Philosophy & Policy* 20 (2003): 59–92 (esp. pp. 64–65).

3. Thomas A. Spragens Jr., "The Limits of Libertarianism," in *The Essential Communitarian Reader,* ed. Amitai Etzioni (Lanham, MD, 1998), p. 33.

4. John Rawls, *A Theory of Justice* (Oxford, 1972), pp. 75–80, 100–108. Rawls does say that the "distribution branch" should use the tools of taxation to "prevent concentrations of power detrimental to the fair value of political liberty and fair equality of opportunity" (p. 277), but it appears that such concentrations would have to be very great indeed in order for Rawls to reject an economic arrangement that would make the least well-off maximally better off. "The essential thing," as he puts it, "is that as far as possible inequalities . . . should satisfy the difference principle" (p. 278).

5. This section relies on material found in Eric Nelson, *The Greek Tradition in Republican Thought* (Cambridge, 2004), pp. 52–73, 89–93. See also Nelson, "Republican Visions," in *The Oxford Handbook of Political Theory,* ed. John Dryzek, Bonnie Honig, and Anne Phillips (Oxford, 2006), pp. 191–210.

6. For the agrarian laws, see Ernst Badian, *Foreign Clientelae* (Oxford, 1958), esp. pp. 168–191; Badian, "From the Gracchi to Sulla: 1940–59," *Historia* 11 (1962): 197–245; Badian, "Tiberius Gracchus and the Beginning of the Roman Revolution," in *Aufstieg und Niedergang der römische Welt,* 37 vols., ed. Hildegard Temporini (Berlin, 1972), vol. 1:1, pp. 668–731; A. H. Bernstein, *Tiberius Gracchus: Tradition and Apostasy* (Ithaca, NY, 1978); Jérome Carcopino, *Autour des Gracques: Études critiques* (Paris, 1967); Giuseppe Cardinali, *Studi Graccani* (Rome, 1912); D. Kontchalkovsy, "Recherches sur l'histoire du mouvement agraire des Gracques," *Revue Historique* 153 (1926): 161–186; Ronald T. Ridley, *"Leges Agrariae:* Myths Ancient and Modern," *Classical Philology* 95 (2000): 459–467; David Stockton, *The Gracchi* (Oxford, 1979), esp. chaps. 1–4; and Gianfranco Tibiletti, "Il possesso dell'*ager publicus* e le norme *de modo agrorum* sino ai Gracchi," *Athenaeum* 26 (1948): 173–236; 27 (1949): 3–42.

7. All quotations from Livy are taken from Livy, *History of Rome,* 14 vols., ed. and trans. B. O. Foster et al. (London, 1919–1959). "Tum primum lex agraria promulgata est, numquam deinde usque ad hanc memoriam sine maximis motibus rerum agitata."

8. Lucan, *The Civil War,* ed. and trans. J. D. Duff (London, 1924), p. 383.

9. Quotations from Velleius are taken from Velleius Paterculus, *Res gestae divi Augusti,* ed. and trans. Frederick W. Shipley (New York, 1924). "Simul etiam promulgatis agrariis legibus, omnibus statim concupiscentibus, summa imis miscuit et in praeruptum atque anceps periculum adduxit rem publicam."

10. II.i.13. See L. Annaeus Florus, *Epitome,* ed. and trans. Edward Seymour Forster (Cambridge, MA, 1929). "Et reduci plebs in agros unde poterat sine possidentium eversione, qui ipsi pars populi erant, et iam relictas sibi a maioribus sedes aetate quasi iure possidebant?"

11. For Cicero's views on property, see Julia Annas, "Cicero on Stoic Moral Philosophy and Private Property," in *Philosophia Togata,* vol. 1: *Essays on Philosophy and Roman Society,* ed. Miriam Griffin and Jonathan Barnes (Oxford, 1989), pp. 151–173; Neal Wood, "The Economic Dimension of Cicero's Political Thought: Property and State," *Canadian Journal of Political Science* 16 (1983): 739–756; and N. Wood,

Cicero's Social and Political Thought (Berkeley, 1988). Cicero notoriously softened his view when addressing a plebeian audience in 64 BCE (*De lege agraria* II.10), but, when unconstrained by tactical considerations, his anti-Gracchan position was both consistent and strident. On this aberrant speech, see Robert Morstein-Marx, *Mass Oratory and Political Power in the Late Roman Republic* (New York, 2004), p. 200.

12. Quotations from Cicero are taken from Cicero, *De officiis*, ed. and trans. Walter Miller (Cambridge, MA, 1939). "Quod cuique obtigit, id quisque teneat; e quo si quis sibi appetet, violabit ius humanae societatis."

13. "In primis autem videndum erit ei, qui rem publicam administrabit, ut suum quisque teneat neque de bonis privatorum publice deminutio fiat."

14. Cicero, *De re publica, De legibus,* ed. and trans. C. W. Keyes, Loeb Classical Library (Cambridge, MA, 1928). "Nonne omnem rei publicae statum permutavit."

15. "Quid est aliud aliis sua eripere, aliis dare aliena?"

16. Giovanni Boccaccio, *De mulieribus claris,* ed. and trans. Virginia Brown, I Tatti Renaissance Library (Cambridge, MA, 2001), p. 10.

17. Leonardo Bruni, *Opere letterarie e politiche di Leonardo Bruni,* ed. Paulo Viti (Torino, 1996), p. 432. "Per hunc modum lex agraria, que primum a T. Graccho introducta, et per singulos fere annos tribunitiis furoribus et summis contentionibus agitata, patres et plebem assidue collidebat, per Ciceronis prudentiam et eloquentiam facile sopita." The English translation is taken from *The Humanism of Leonardo Bruni: Selected Texts,* ed. and trans. Gordon Griffiths, James Hankins, and David Thompson, Medieval and Renaissance Texts and Studies (Binghamton, NY, 1987), p. 186. Revealingly, this is one of the passages in which Bruni completely departs from his classical source: Plutarch's *Life of Cicero.* Plutarch, as we shall see, had a very different attitude toward the agrarian laws.

18. Platina, *De optimo cive,* Book 1, in *Platinae cremonensis de vita & moribus summarum pontificum historia . . . eiusdem de optimo cive* (Cologne, 1529). "Testes sunt autem Saturninus tribunus plebis, Sp. Melius, Gracchi duo, M. Drusus, quorum vita tota in ostentatione fundata erat."

19. Ibid. *De falso et vero bono,* Book II. "Nam ut malo contagione quadam malos fieri dicimus, sic bono meliores effici necesse est. Verum tantum abest ut bonos magistratus faciant, ut etiam plerosque ad supremam saevitiam, libidinem & avaritiam perduxerint, ut de Appio illo decemviro, qui Virginiam Virginii filiam ob magistratum & potentiam stuprare est ausus. Quid vero egerint duo Gracchi, quid Saturninus, quid Spurius Melius, quid Clodius, quid plerique alii apud Romanos in magistratibus constituti, ex rebus eorum gestis facillime deprehendimus."

20. Francesco Patrizi [of Siena], *Francisci Patricii Senensis, pontificis Caietani, de institutione reipublicae libri IX. Ad senatum populumque Senesem scripti* (Strasbourg, 1594), p. 36. "Titus Grachus pater, summae probitatis vir extitit . . . hic tamen filios habuit Tiberium & Caium Grachos, qui turbulentissimi, & seditiosissimi extiterunt."

21. Ibid. "Et alter in Capitolio ob Reip. salutem a Scipione Nasica oppressus est, alter ad voluntariam mortem compulsus."

22. One striking possible exception is the Italian humanist Aurelio Lippo Brandolini, who authored a manuscript dialogue entitled *De comparatione regni et rei publicae* in 1489 while living in Budapest under the patronage of Matthias Corvinus (Corvinus died later that year, and Brandolini returned to Florence, ultimately dedicating his manuscript to Lorenzo de'Medici). Brandolini is a defender of monarchy, so he stands outside of the tradition with which we are concerned. Nonetheless, he bases his theory of good government on Plato's *Laws* (becoming perhaps the first European to do so—the text had only become widely available in 1484)—and endorses a system of laws requiring equality of holdings. However, this treatise was never printed and survives in only two manuscripts. See Brandolini, *Republics and Kingdoms Compared,* ed. James Hankins (Cambridge, MA, 2009).

23. Thomas More, *Utopia,* ed. and trans. George M. Logan, Robert M. Adams, and Clarence H. Miller (Cambridge, 1995), p. 102. "Nempe si statuatur ne quis supra certum agri modum possideat et uti sit legitimus cuique census pecuniae."

24. Ibid. "Talibus, inquam, legibus, quemadmodum aegra assiduis solent fomentis fulciri corpora deploratae valetudinis." More's scorn for this sort of remedy may perhaps complicate the view that he intentionally dated the Utopian founding to 244 BCE in order to honor the land reforms of Agis IV of Sparta. Agis is precisely the sort of figure Hythloday means to criticize here. See R. J. Schoek, "More, Plutarch, and King Agis: Spartan History and the Meaning of *Utopia,*" *Philological Quarterly* 35 (1956): 366–375.

25. Machiavelli, *Discorsi sopra la prima deca di Tito Livio,* ed. Giogio Inglese (Milan, 1984), p. 140. "Le republiche bene ordinate hanno a tenere ricco il publico e gli loro cittadini poveri."

26. Ibid. "Da questo nacque il morbo che partorì la contenzione della legge agraria, che infine fu causa della distruzione della Republica."

27. James Harrington, *The Political Works of James Harrington,* ed. J. G. A. Pocock (Cambridge, 1978), p. 231.

28. William Fulbecke, *An Historicall Collection of the Continuall Factions, Tumults, and Massacres of the Romans and Italians during the space of one hundred and twentie yeares next before the peaceable Empire of Augustus Caesar* (London, 1601), pp. 21, 27.

29. Sir Walter Raleigh, "A Discourse of the Original and Fundamental Causes of Natural, Arbitrary, Necessary, and Unnatural War," in *The Works of Sir Walter Raleigh, Kt.,* ed. T. Birch and W. Oldys, 8 vols. (Oxford, 1829), vol. 8, p. 292.

30. Raleigh's discussion here follows Machiavelli, *Discorsi* I.37.3.

31. Thomas May, *The Reigne of King Henry the Second Written in Seauen Bookes,* ed. Götz Schmitz (Tempe, AZ, 1999), p. 17.

32. Edmund Waller, *A Speech Made by Master Waller Esquire . . . Concerning Episcopacie* (London, 1641), p. 5.

33. Marchamont Nedham, *The Case of the Commonwealth of England, Stated,* ed. Philip A. Knachel (Charlottesville, VA, 1969), p. 109. Actually, the agrarian law proposed by C. Licinius Stolo limited parcels of *ager publicus* to 500 *iugera.*

34. Nelson, *The Greek Tradition.*

35. For the sixteenth-century publication history of these authors, see Peter Burke, "A Survey of the Popularity of Ancient Historians, 1450–1700," *History and Theory* 5 (1966): 135–152. Twenty-seven editions of Plutarch were published between 1550 and 1599, the most influential of them being Thomas North's English translation of 1579. As is well known, North's edition became an extremely important source for Shakespeare's plays. The *editio princeps* of Appian's history was published in 1551, and he was widely read thereafter.

36. This is, to a great extent, an elaboration of a point I initially made in *The Greek Tradition,* p. 94n29.

37. Rashi, *Hamishah humshe Torah ʿim kol ha-haftarot: The Rashi Chumash,* ed. and trans. Shraga Silverstein (Jerusalem, 1997). Cf. *Bereshith Rabba* I.2–3. See *Midrash Rabba,* ed. Rabbi H. Freeman and Maurice Simon, 10 vols. (London, 1939), vol. 1, pp. 4–5.

38. This is Rashi's gloss on what causes God to "will" the transfer of land from one people to another.

39. There is some debate among Biblical scholars as to when exactly the word *tzedakah* came to refer specifically to almsgiving. It seems that it had already acquired this connotation in the later Biblical books (particularly Psalms, Proverbs, and Daniel). See, for example, Gary A. Anderson, "Redeem Your Sins by the Giving of Alms: Sin, Debt, and the 'Treasury of Merit' in Early Jewish and Christian Tradition," *Letter & Spirit* 3 (2007): 39–69 (esp. pp. 45–51). The classic discussion of the semantics of this term remains Franz Rosenthal, "*Sedaqah,* Charity," *Hebrew Union College Annual* 23 (1950/1951): 411–430. Maimonides notes that one who refuses to give alms may be compelled to do so by a court. The court is even allowed to seize the offender's property. See Maimonides, MT, *Hilkhot Matanot ʿAniyim* 7.10.

40. This is not, of course, to say that all rabbinic commentators took this precise view of the relationship between justice and charity. Maimonides, for example, makes the Platonist case that *tzedakah* refers to almsgiving because "when we walk in the way of virtue we act justly toward our intellectual faculty, and pay what is due unto it . . . every virtue is thus *tzedakah*" (Maimonides, *Guide* III.53). See Moses Maimonides, *Guide for the Perplexed,* ed. and trans. M. Friedländer, 2nd ed. (New York, 1956), p. 393. I have altered the translation somewhat for the sake of clarity.

41. English translations of Biblical passages are taken from the King James Version, unless otherwise indicated. See also Philo, *Special Laws* XXII.

42. See, for example, Asher Gulak, *Prolegomena to the Study of the History of Jewish Law in the Talmudic Age. Part I: The Law of Immoveable Property* (Jerusalem, 1929); and Martin John Lauré, *The Property Concepts of the Early Hebrews* (Iowa City, IA, 1915).

43. Interestingly, a tradition of rabbinic commentary understood this law to apply only to the generation of Zelophehad's daughters (whose complaint in Num. 27 prompts God to formulate the law allowing women to inherit property in the absence of a male heir). See BT Taʿanit 30b.

44. I have altered the translation here for the sake of clarity. The Talmud notes that there are, in fact, two different sabbatical years. The first, involving the remission of

debts, is referred to as *shemittah* (release) or, more precisely, *shemittat kesafim* (release of money); the second, in which the land is left uncultivated, is referred to as *shemittat karka'ot* (release of land). The remission of debts occurs at the end of every seven-year period, while the *shemittat karka'ot* occurs at the start of every seventh year. The rabbis ruled that land release applies only to the land of Israel, while debt release applies to the diaspora as well.

45. BT Gittin 36a. Talmudic references are taken from the *Soncino Hebrew-English Edition of the Babylonian Talmud* (London, 1994). Maimonides endorses this view in *Mishneh Torah, Hilkhot shemittah ve-yovel* VII.9. See Maimonides, *The Code of Maimonides,* 32 vols., ed. and trans. Rabbi Isaac Klein (New Haven, CT, 1979), vol. 21, p. 282. As Maimonides points out, however, it is likewise a rabbinic ruling (a *mitzvah d'rabbanan*) that in the diaspora the remission of debts should be observed, even though the jubilee cannot be, so that the ancient land laws are not forgotten by the Jewish people. On this, see below.

46. See also Josephus, *Antiquities.* 8 vols., ed. and trans. H. St. J. Thackeray and Louis H. Feldman (Cambridge, MA, 1930–1965), III.280–286.

47. I have altered the translation here for the sake of clarity.

48. See Bergsma, *The Jubilee,* pp. 152–153. Cf. Ezekiel 46:16–18.

49. Perhaps from the Greek πρὸς βουλήν, "by decree of the council." The Talmud records a number of fanciful etymologies.

50. On this development, see Michael Walzer and Menachem Lorberbaum, eds., *The Jewish Political Tradition,* 2 vols. (New Haven, CT, 2000), vol. 1, pp. 275–281. The Talmud records a further series of exceptions to the *shemittah* requirement (see, e.g., Gittin 36a–37a).

51. For the *fortuna* of Maimonides's *Mishneh Torah* in early-modern Europe, see Aaron Katchen, *Christian Hebraists and Dutch Rabbis: Seventeenth Century Apologetics and the Study of Maimonides' Mishneh Torah* (Cambridge, MA, 1984). Interestingly, early-modern Hebraists seem to have paid virtually no attention to Maimonides's rather different characterization of the land laws in Maimonides, *Guide for the Perplexed,* III.39, esp. p. 340.

52. Sigonio is, however, the exception in the late sixteenth century. To take another example, the land laws are not mentioned at all in William Wellwood's *Juris divini Judaeorum ac juris civilis Romanorum parallela* (Leiden, 1594).

53. On this, see Anthony Grafton, *Joseph Scaliger: A Study in the History of Classical Scholarship,* 2 vols. (Oxford, 1983), vol. 2: *Historical Chronology,* pp. 355–356. Biblical dating was a major preoccupation of Scaliger's *De emendatione temporum* (1583), and, in the later *Thesaurus temporum* (1606), he attempted to draw up a complete table of jubilee and sabbatical years, ending in 68 CE. As Grafton points out, Scaliger used Talmudic sources to argue that the Jubilee was observed during the Second Temple period (p. 670).

54. The imperative to establish a correct chronology of Roman history animated Sigonio's early commentary on the *Fasti,* and meticulous chronological reconstruction was likewise a central feature of his work on ancient Greece (e.g., the *De Atheniensium Lacedaemoniorumque temporibus liber* of 1564). See William McCuaig, *Carlo*

Sigonio: The Changing World of the Late Renaissance (Princeton, NJ, 1989), pp. 24–30.

55. Carlo Sigonio, *De republica Hebraeorum libri VII: Ad Gregorium XIII pontificem maximum* (Bologna, 1582), p. 88. The most recent study of this text is Guido Barto-lucci, *La repubblica ebraica di Carlo Sigonio: Modelli politici dell'età moderna* (Florence, 2007). Sigonio, unlike Bertram and Junius, knew no Hebrew.

56. Ibid. "Pertinuit ad hanc etiam observationem Annus septimus, qui Sabbatarius dictus est, quia eo remissio terrae a cultura concedebatur. De eo vero sic praeceptum est [Ex. 23; Lev. 35] . . . Quomodo vero remissio septimo quoque anno esset facienda, deinceps docetur XV Deuteronomii his verbis: *Septimo anno facies remissionem . . .*"

57. Ibid. "Quinquagesimus item annus Sabbatarius fuit, quia remissio dabatur servis a ministerio servili. atque ager alienatus redibat ad veterem possessorem: De eo vero sic scriptum est Levitici XXV: *Numerabis quoque tibi septem hebdomades annorum . . .*"

58. Ibid., p. 90. "Quinquagesimus autem annus dictus est Iobeleus, quod eum Levitae per tubas arietinas, quae dicuntur Hebraeis Iobelim, convocato populo, ut super scriptum est, indicerent. unde illud est VI Iosue: *Septimo die sacerdotes tollent septem buccinas, quarum usus est in iubileo.* Atque hae quidem celebritates a Deo institutae sunt."

59. On this, see, for example, Frank Manuel, *The Broken Staff: Judaism through Christian Eyes* (Cambridge, MA, 1992), pp. 92–98; and Kalman Neuman, "Political Hebraism and the Early Modern 'Respublica Hebraeorum': On Defining the Field," *Hebraic Political Studies* 1 (2005): 57–70.

60. Franciscus Junius, *De politiae Mosis observatione* (Leiden, 1593), p. 105. "Quia Deus se mancipem illius terrae, & terram vel regionem illam optima lege mancipii ad se pertinere, nec ad alium quenquam, ceremoniali observatione voluit ostendere."

61. Ibid. "& Israelitas hoc pacto iussit constantissime profiteri beneficium Dei: quemadmodum Domini vassalis suis quos vocant Feudatarios, aut etiam Emphyteutis solent imponere legem aliquam fiduciariam, aut aliam quamvis, & sibi dominium merum semper vindicare." This claim is very reminiscent of a reading found in the *Sefer ha-Hinuch,* a 13th-century commentary on the 613 Biblical commandments (quite popular among early-modern Hebraists): "This matter of the jubilee is somewhat similar to a custom practiced in the earthly kingdom [*b'malkhuta d'ara*]: from time to time, the rule over fortified cities belonging to their [the kings'] noblemen is taken away, to remind them of the reverence due to the ruler [*yirat ha-adon*]. So in this matter: for the Lord wished that every landed property should return to the one who had original possession of the land from Him (blessed be He)." See the rubric *Mitzvah sephirat sheva' shabbatot shanim (shin-lamed; §330). Sefer haHinnuch,* ed. and trans. Charles Wengrov (Jerusalem, 1984), pp. 370–371. I have altered the translation for the sake of clarity.

62. On this practice, see William R. Johnston, "Emphyteusis: A Roman 'Perpetual' Tenure," *University of Toronto Law Journal* 3 (1940): 323–347. As Johnston makes clear, both the practice itself and the word designating it are Greek imports.

63. Ibid., p. 106. "Ut se regionis Dominum, illos Emphyteutas, sive colonos perpetuarios (ut Iurisconsulti vocant) ex beneficio Dei & Domini ipsorum sese ostenderet."

64. Sigonio, *De republica Hebraeorum*, p. 2. "Est enim mihi, ut dixi, consilium, his libris Hebraicorum sacrorum, sacerdotumque descriptionem, consiliorum, Iudiciorum, & Magistratuum rationem, totamque pacis, bellique disciplinam ex sacris litterarum monumentis erutam aperire. Feci hoc idem olim iuvenis in Atheniensibus, & Romanis, ut eorum leges, instituta, civitatem, & remp. variis eorum voluminibus abdita palam facerem." The two works in question are the *De antiquo iure civium Romanorum, Italiae, provinciarum* (1560) and the *De republica Atheniensium libri IV* (1564).

65. Johannes Althusius, *Politica methodice digesta,* ed. Carl Joachim Friedrich (Cambridge, MA, 1932), p. 198. "Similiter lex de anno jubilaeo lata: *Lev.c.25. Deut.c.15.* Haec enim moralis erat, quatenus continebat & praestabat σεισάχθειαν καὶ ἄφεσιν debitorum & onerum excussionem, qua pauperes juvabantur."

66. John Pearson, ed., *Critici sacri, sive, Doctissimorum virorum in ss. Biblia annotations,* 9 vols. (London, 1660), vol. 1, p. 891. "*Remissionem cunctis habitatoribus terrae tuae Σεισάχθειαν,* medicam inaequalitatis quam mala fortuna induxerat. *Revertetur homo ad possessionem suam.* Erant enim Israelitiae usufructuarii sive feudatarii; Deus, sive Lex eius, Dominus."

67. Ainsworth published his annotations on each Biblical book separately. The edition of Leviticus was published in 1618, but it would certainly have been written before Ainsworth could have read Cunaeus's *De republica Hebraeorum.*

68. Henry Ainsworth, *Annotations upon the five bookes of Moses, the booke of Psalmes, and the Song of Songs, or Canticles* (London, 1627), Preface.

69. For Ainsworth's pioneering use of the Code, see Katchen, *Christian Hebraists and Dutch Rabbis,* pp. 35–37. For another contemporary English discussion of the jubilee (which remains uninflected by Cunaeus), see Thomas Godwyn, *Moses and Aaron: Civil and ecclesiastical rites Used by the Ancient Hebrews* (London, 1685 [orig. 1625]), pp. 135–136.

70. The fact that Cunaeus was the first to describe the jubilee as an agrarian law has not, I think, been noticed before. His views on the land laws are, however, nicely summarized in Jonathan Ziskind, "Petrus Cunaeus on Theocracy, Jubilee and Latifundia," *Jewish Quarterly Review* 48 (1978): 235–254. See also Lea Campos Boralevi's introduction to Petrus Cunaeus, *De Republica Hebraeorum,* ed. Lea Campos Boralevi (Florence, 1996), pp. vii–lxvii; Vittorio Conti, *Consociatio civitatum: Le repubbliche nei testi elzeviriani (1625–1649)* (Florence, 1997), pp. 105–117; François Laplanche, "L'érudition Chrétienne aux XVIe et XVIIe siècles et l'état des Hebreux," in *L'écriture sainte au temps de Spinoza et dans le système Spinoziste* (Paris, 1992), pp. 133–147; Fania Oz-Salzberger, "The Jewish Roots of Western Freedom," *Azure* 13 (2002): 88–132, esp. pp. 100–103; Anna Strumia, *L'immaginazione repubblicana: Sparta e Israele nel dibattito filosofico-politico dell'età di Cromwell* (Turin, 1991), esp. pp. 31–35; and the important discussion in Richard Tuck, *Philosophy and Government: 1572–1651* (Cambridge, 1993), pp. 167–169.

71. Cunaeus, *De republica Hebraeorum*, p. 5. "Offero rempublicam, qua nulla unquam in terris sanctior, nec bonis exemplis ditior fuit. Hujus initia, & incrementa

perdidicisse, omnino vestrum est, quoniam illa hercle non hominem quenquam mortali concretione satum, sed ipsum deum immortalem, autorem fundatoremque habet, cujus vos venerationem, atque intemeratum cultum suscepistis ac tuemini."

72. Ibid., pp. 5–7. "Profecto habuit is populus regundae reipublicae instituta quaedam ejusmodi, quae omnium essent prudentum praeceptis potiora. Eorum nos magnam partem posse ex sacris voluminibus erui ostendimus."

73. Ibid., p. 46. "De lege agraria, deque eius inaestimabili utilitate. Redemptio agro- rum. Beneficium Iubilaei. Restitutio gratuita agrorum. Iuris Talmudici quaedam sanctiones super ea re. De Maimonide, eiusque luculentissimis commentionibus."

74. Cunaeus acquired the 1574 Venice edition of the *Mishneh Torah* from his friend Jo- hannes Boreel (Borelius) in (or shortly before) 1615. On this, see Lea Campos Bora- levi, "Classical Foundational Myths of European Republicanism: The Jewish Com- monwealth," in *Republicanism: A Shared European Heritage,* 2 vols., ed. Martin van Gelderen and Quentin Skinner (Cambridge, 2002), vol. 1, p. 258; Katchen, *Christian Hebraists and Dutch Rabbis,* pp. 38–39.

75. It is, indeed, highly revealing that Cunaeus returned to the subject of the Jubilee over twenty years later in his final lecture as university rector in Leiden (1638). See Cunaeus, "De annis climacteribus et eorum vi in rerumpublicarum et civitatum conversione," in *Orationes, argumenti varii* (Wittenberg, 1643), pp. 60–81. I am grateful to Arthur Eyffinger for calling this speech to my attention.

76. Ibid., pp. 47–49. Barksdale incorrectly translates this figure as "three hundred thou- sand Acres." Josephus, whose Greek Cunaeus simply reprints here, has $\tau \rho \iota \alpha \kappa o \sigma \iota \alpha \varsigma$ $\mu \upsilon \rho \iota \dot{\alpha} \delta \alpha \varsigma$, which literally means "three-hundred ten-thousands," or three million. "Saepe Flavius Josephus Hecataeum Abderiten laudat . . . illud ad rem, de qua dic- turi sumus, pertinet, quod regionem optimam, frugumque feracissimam habitari a Iudaeis ait, cujus amplitudo continet $\tau \rho \iota \alpha \kappa o \sigma \iota \alpha \varsigma$ $\mu \upsilon \rho \iota \dot{\alpha} \delta \alpha \varsigma$ $\dot{\alpha} \rho \gamma \rho \tilde{\omega} \nu$ [*sic*]." Cf. Josephus, *Contra Ap.* I.195.

77. "Inter initia, cum promissam pridem Palaestinam occupasset armis sacer populus, illico Mosis iussa secutus summus dux Iosua est. Universam enim regionem in duo- decim partes divisit, atque habitandam totidem tribuus dedit. Mox singularum tribuum familias numeravit, & pro capitum multitudine certum cuique modum agri, atque proprios fines dedit."

78. Ibid., p. 51. "Ita provisum est, uti eadem aequalitate omnes continerentur. quae esse prima cura omnis reipublicae moderatoribus solet."

79. "Quod si occupatione suum quidque fecissent ii, qui primi in vacua venissent, iam necesse fuisset pugnas motusque civium ingentes existere. Quicquid enim eius- modi est, quod ex communi facere proprium possis, in eo fit plerumque tanta con- tentio, ut difficillimum sit servare sanctam societatem."

80. Ibid., pp. 51–53. "Porro, quoniam sapientis est non praesentia modo ordinare, sed ea statuere etiam, quae profutura alteri seculo sunt, praeclaram legem quandam Moses tulit, qua effectum est ne paucorum opulentia quandoque caeteros opprim- eret, neu mutatis studiis cives ad novas artes peregrinasque ab innoxio labore se converterent. Ea fuit lex agraria, quae vetuit ne quis venditione aut ullo contractu plenum dominum fundi sui transferret in alium. Nam & iis, qui egestate compulsi

agrum vendidissent, redimendi jus quovis tempore concessit. & ni redemtus esset, restitui eum gratis in Iubilaei celebritate jussit."

81. Ibid., p. 53. "Scriptor maximus, Rabbi Moses Ben Maimon, is qui Talmudicam doctrinam sepositis nugamentis feliciter complexus est divino illo opere, quod ipse *Mishneh Torah* appellat. Nunquam ita magnifice quidquam de illo autore dicemus, quin id virtus superet ejus." Cunaeus gives the title of Maimonides's code in Hebrew characters: משנה תורה.

82. Ibid., p. 55. "Multa ille de Iubilaei beneficio tradidit, aitque id positum in eo fuisse, quod omnes agri ad veteres dominos redibant, etiam si centies emptorem mutaverant. Nec eos excipit eruditissimus scriptor, quos ex donatione acceperit aliquis."

83. Ibid., p. 61. "Sane . . . interfuit reipublicae, ne in possessiones optime positas divisasque paucorum avaritia irrumperet. Ferme enim egentiorem quemque ditior aliquis pretio expellit. atque is, dum rura in immensum spatiis supervacuis extendit, alios necessariis excludit."

84. Ibid., pp. 61–63. "Ex qua causa incessere interdum rerum conversio solet. Ita enim est profecto. plena hostibus ea respublica est, in qua cives plurimi, possessionibus avitis nudati, priscas fortunas votis expetunt. Hi odio rerum suarum mutari omnia student, neque in ea conditione, cuius eos poenitet, diutius, quam necesse sit, manent."

85. Ibid., p. 63. "Ac Romae quidem, cum primores patrum omnia ad se trahebant, prope ut singuli possiderent trecentorum civium agros, lege Stolonis cautum fuit, ne quis plus quingenta iugera haberet. Sed statim evagata rectum ordinem fraus est. Primum enim ipse Stolo sanctiones suas violavit, damnatusque est quod mille jugerum cum filio tenebat, quem ob hoc emancipaverat. Et postea quam plurimi cives diversa arte callidi sententiam legis circumvenerunt. Aliis enim ad emendum agrum submissis, ipsi possederunt. Vidit istaec, & stabilire legem conatus est C. Laelius, insigni sapientia vir, & Africani Scipionis maximus amicus. sed impar adversantium factioni, cum in contentiones discordiasque iretur, ab incepto destitit. Ita in aevum erupit licentia, neque occupandi agros modus fuit. Ac tandem sane eo deventum est, ut pauci quidam totam Italiam vicinasque provincias velut proprium patrimonium tenerent."

86. "Huius rei testimonia recitare, quae plurima ubique extant, nihil nunc necesse est."

87. Plutarch, *Ti. Gracc.* 8:1–4. See Plutarch, *Lives,* 11 vols., ed. and trans. B. Perrin (Cambridge, MA, 1914), vol. 10, pp. 158–161. It is true that, in the *Praecepta gerendae reipublicae* (818c), Plutarch argues that statesmen should allow "no confiscation of others' property" (οὐδὲ δήμευσιν ἀλλοτρίων), but this isolated comment does not seem to refer to the issue of agrarian laws. Plutarch's praise for these measures, and for the Gracchi in particular, is a consistent theme in his writings. See Plutarch, *Moralia,* 17 vols., ed. and trans. Harold North Fowler (Cambridge, MA, 1936), vol. 10, p. 260.

88. The only text published before Harrington's *Oceana* that offers a similar reassessment is *A copy of a letter from an officer of the Army in Ireland, to his Highness the Lord Protector, concerning his changing of the government* (1656), attributed to the enigmatic "R. G." (most often thought to be the Digger Richard Goodgroom). This pamphlet reasons as follows: "our unhappiness is that great alterations seldom

come without intestine wars, it being hard (especially in populous and flourishing Cities, to bring the multitude to give so great a power to one man as is necessary to redress a disordered State, and for that men are generally short sighted, and cannot foresee great inconveniences till they are too late to remedy, but by force, this makes the cure oftentimes miscarry, as in the case of the *Gracchi* at *Rome,* and of *Agis* and *Cleomenes* at *Sparta,* in both which examples, there was an endeavour to reduce those two excellent States, to their first principles, but it was too late attempted, when the corruption was growne to too great a height, which if they had found, and would have been contented to erect a new form more suitable to the inequalitie of mens estates at that time, they might possiblie have succeeded, if not to have introduced so good and excellent a model as they fell from, yet one able to have prevented the ruine and slaverie which soon after befell both these people" (p. 7). This discussion is so overtly Harringtonian (it was published only months before *Oceana* and also contains Harrington's analysis of the process by which Henry VII altered the English balance) that accusations of plagiarism were raised even in the late 1650s. Pocock offers much the most reasonable conjecture, viz. that this pamphlet was influenced by the as yet unpublished *Oceana.* On this, see Harrington, *Political Works,* pp. 10–13. The reassessment is perhaps already underway in John Lilburne's *The upright mans vindication: or, An epistle writ by John Lilburn Gent. prisoner in Newgate* (London, 1653), which likens one of its proposals to "the Law *Agraria* amongst the Romans" (p. 21), but Lilburne does not develop the thought. Consider also the case of the Digger Gerrard Winstanley, who endorsed the Israelite land laws, but did not refer to them as agrarian laws (see Gerrard Winstanley, *The Law of Freedom in a Platform, or, True Magistracy Restored* [London, 1652], pp. 18–23).

89. Harrington, *Political Works,* p. 276.
90. Ibid., p. 231.
91. Ibid., p. 174. The classic discussion of Harrington's use of the Israelite example remains S. B. Liljegren, "Harrington and the Jews," *Bulletin de la societé royale des lettres de Lund* 4 (1931–1932): 656–692. See also Gary Remer, "Machiavelli and Hobbes: James Harrington's Commonwealth of Israel," *Hebraic Political Studies* 4 (2006): 440–461; and Adam Sutcliffe, *Judaism and Enlightenment* (New York, 2003), pp. 51–57.
92. Harrington, *Political Works,* p. 373.
93. Ibid., p. 464.
94. Ibid., p. 164.
95. Ibid., pp. 462–463. Writing a decade later, Spinoza likewise emphasized this aspect of the Hebrew republic: "there was one feature peculiar to this state and of great importance in retaining the affections of the citizens, and checking all thoughts of desertion, or abandonment of the country: namely self-interest, the strength and life of all human action. This was particularly engaged in the Hebrew state, for nowhere else did citizens possess their goods so securely as did the subjects of this community, for the latter possessed as large a share in the land and the fields as did their chiefs, and were owners of their plots of ground in perpetuity; for if any man was

compelled by poverty to sell his farm or his pasture, he received it back again intact as the year of jubilee: there were other similar enactments against the possibility of alienating real property. Again, poverty was nowhere more endurable than in a country where duty towards one's neighbour, that is, one's fellow citizen, was practised with the utmost piety, as a means of gaining the favour of God the King." See Baruch Spinoza, *A theologico-political treatise and A political treatise,* ed. and trans. R. H. M. Elwes (New York, 1951), p. 230.

96. Harrington, *Political Works,* p. 573.

97. Ibid., p. 373.

98. Ibid., p. 379.

99. Cunaeus, *De Republica Hebraeorum,* pp. 46–51.

100. Harrington, *Political Works,* p. 379.

101. Ibid., p. 201.

102. Ibid., pp. 604–605.

103. Ibid., p. 634.

104. On this, see Nelson, *The Greek Tradition,* pp. 87–126.

105. Harrington, *Political Works,* p. 188.

106. Ibid.

107. Ibid., p. 235.

108. Sigonio, *De antiquo iure civium Romanorum* (Paris, 1576), esp. pp. 61–75. For Sigonio's use of Appian and his broader pro-Gracchan sympathies, see McCuaig, *Carlo Sigonio,* pp. 153–173.

109. Harrington, *Political Works,* p. 689.

110. Ibid., p. 607.

111. Ibid., p. 276.

112. Ibid., p. 202.

113. Ibid., p. 182.

114. Ibid., p. 178.

115. Henry Neville, *Plato Redivivus,* in *Two English Republican Tracts,* ed. Caroline Robbins (Cambridge, 1969), p. 94.

116. Thomas Allen, *A proposal for a free and unexpensive election of Parliament men* (London, 1753), pp. 29, 39. Allen reproduces a lengthy block quotation from Barksdale's translation of Cunaeus's text. Also noteworthy is Allen's use of the following argument: "And whereas it is commonly objected by the great ones, *That they may do what they will with their own*; we grant this to be true in other things, but not in lands, unless they will aver, *That the earth is not the Lord's, nor the fulness thereof,* and that he has not made a reservation to himself of any part thereof, or of the produce of it" (p. 29). For an illuminating discussion of this text, and the role of agrarian laws in the eighteenth-century enclosure debate more broadly, see S. J. Thompson, "Parliamentary Enclosure, Property, Population, and the Decline of Classical Republicanism in Eighteenth-Century Britain," *The Historical Journal* 51 (2008): 621–642.

117. Charles S. Hyneman and Donald S. Lutz, eds., *American Political Writing during the Founding Era: 1760–1805,* 2 vols. (Indianapolis, 1983), vol. 2, p. 1002.

3. HEBREW THEOCRACY AND THE RISE OF TOLERATION

1. Mark Lilla, *The Stillborn God: Religion, Politics, and the Modern West* (New York, 2007), p. 8.
2. Ibid., p. 103. For another prominent endorsement of this position see Jonathan Israel, *Enlightenment Contested: Philosophy, Modernity, and the Emancipation of Man, 1670–1752* (Oxford, 2006), esp. pp. 11, 51–60, and 138–163. See also Israel, *Radical Enlightenment: Philosophy and the Making of Modernity, 1650–1750* (Oxford, 2001); and Israel, "Religious Toleration and Radical Philosophy in the Later Dutch Golden Age (1668–1710)," in *Calvinism and Religious Toleration in the Dutch Golden Age.* ed. R. Po-Chia Hsia and H. F. K. Van Nierop (Cambridge, 2002), pp. 148–158. For the contrary view, see, for example, Blair Worden's observation that "the development of religious toleration looks to be not evidence of a decline of religious conviction, but rather a part of the process by which the Protestant God changes his character" (Blair Worden, "Toleration and the Cromwellian Protectorate," in *Persecution and Toleration,* ed. W. J. Sheils, Studies in Church History 21 (Oxford, 1984), pp. 199–233; see esp. p. 233). See also Mark Goldie, "Civil Religion and the English Enlightenment," in *Politics, Politeness, and Patriotism,* ed. Gordon Schochet (Washington, DC, 1993), pp. 31–46; and Hugh Trevor-Roper, "The Religious Origins of the Enlightenment," in *The Crisis of the Seventeenth Century: Religion, the Reformation, and Social Change* (New York, 1967), pp. 193–236.
3. Peréz Zagorin, *How the Idea of Religious Toleration Came to the West* (Princeton, NJ, 2003), pp. 171, 175. Cary Nederman likewise considers "establishmentarianism" to be "a doctrine generally inimical to religious toleration" (Nederman, *Worlds of Difference: European Discourses of Toleration, c. 1100–c.1550* [University Park, PA, 2000], p. 76). For an eloquent statement of the view that toleration and "civil religion" did in fact go hand-in-hand in Whig political thought, see Simone Zurbuchen, "Republicanism and Toleration," in *Republicanism: A Shared European Heritage,* 2 vols., ed. Martin Van Gelderen and Quentin Skinner (Cambridge, 2002), vol. 2, pp. 47–71.
4. Examples include Lipsius, l'Hôpital, and Bodin. Their position was that the sovereign should establish as much uniformity as was consistent with civil peace—not because this was precisely the amount God wanted, but because God's wishes had to be balanced against the imperative to avoid dissension. On the *politique* position, see John Marshall, *John Locke, Toleration, and Enlightenment Culture* (Cambridge, 2006), pp. 275–280; see also G. Güldner, *Das Toleranz-Problem in den Niederlanden im Ausgang des 16. Jahrhunderts* (Lübeck, Germany, 1968), esp. pp. 13–30; and Richard Tuck, "Scepticism and Toleration in the Seventeenth Century," in *Justifying Toleration: Conceptual and Historical Perspectives,* ed. Susan Mendus (Cambridge, 1988), pp. 21–35.
5. It is also worth pointing out that the degree of toleration endorsed by such radical sects was often greater than that defended by Erastians.
6. For Josephus's biography, see, for example, Shaye J. D. Cohen, *Josephus in Galilee and Rome: His Vita and Development as a Historian* (Leiden, 1979); R. Laqueur,

Der Jüdische Historiker Flavius Josephus (Darmstadt, Germany, 1970; orig. Gissen, Germany, 1920); and Seth Schwartz, *Josephus and Judaean Politics* (Leiden, 1990).

7. On Josephus's account, when Moses descended from Mount Sinai, he brought with him God's "rules for a happy life and an ordered *politeia*" (βίον τε ὑμῖν εὐδαίμονα καί πολιτείας κόσμον ὑπαγορεύσας πάρεστι). Josephus, *Jewish Ant.* III.84. See Josephus, *Jewish Antiquities*, 8 vols., ed. and trans. H. St. J. Thackeray and Ralph Marcus (Cambridge, MA, 1934), vol. 5, p. 356. Moses is described as a *nomothetes* at *Jewish. Ant.* III.180, and at III.213 Josephus tells us that "he [Moses] wrote down their politeia and laws" (ἔτι δέ τὴν πολιτείαν καί νόμους ἔγραφε).

8. Josephus, *Contra Ap.* II.164–166. "οὐκοῦν ἄπειροι μέν αἱ κατά μέρος τῶν ἐθῶν καί τῶν νόμων παρά τοῖς ἅπασιν ἀνθρώποις διαφοραί. κεφαλαιωδῶς δ' ἄν ἐπίοι τις. οἱ μέν γάρ μοναρχίαις, οἱ δέ ταῖς ὀλίγων δυναστείαις, ἄλλοι δέ τοῖς πλήθεσιν ἐπέτρεψαν τήν ἐξουσίαν τῶν πολιτευμάτων. ὁ δ' ἡμέτερος νομοθέτης εἰς μέν τούτων οὐδοτιοῦν ἀπεῖδεν, ὡς δ' ἄν τις εἴποι βιασάμενος τόν λόγον, θεοκρατίαν ἀπέδειξε τό πολίτευμα, θεῷ τήν ἀρχήν καί τό κράτος ἀναθείς. καί πείσας εἰς ἐκεῖνον ἅπαντας ἀφορᾶν ὡς αἴτιον μέν ἀπάντων ὄντα τῶν ἀγαθῶν, ἃ κοινῇ τε πᾶσιν ἀνθρώποις ὑπάρχει καί ὅσων ἔτυχον αὐτοί δεηθέντες ἐν ἀμηχάνοις." See Josephus, *The Life. Against Apion*, ed. and trans. H. St. J. Thackeray (Cambridge, MA, 1926), p. 359.

9. "τόν μέν θεόν ἀποχειροτονοῦσι τῆς βασιλείας." Josephus, *Jewish Ant.* VI.60–61. See Josephus, *Jewish Antiquities*, vol. 6, p. 357. Cf. *Jewish Ant.* XIV.40–42.

10. Ibid., p. 357. "οὐκ εἰδότες ὡς συμφορώτατον ὑπό τοῦ πάντων ἀρίστου προστατεῖσθαι, θεός δέ πάντων ἄριστος, αἱροῦνται δ' ἔχειν ἄνθρωπον βασιλέα, ὅς ὡς κτήματι τοῖς ὑποτεταγμένοις κατά βούλησιν . . . ἀλλ' οὐχ ὡς ἴδιον ἔργον καί κατασκεύασμα τό τῶν ἀνθρώπων γένος οὕτως διατηρῆσαι σπουδάσει."

11. This is not to say that Josephus was always consistent on this point. Elsewhere, he describes the initial Hebrew polity as an aristocracy—a view which would also find early-modern adherents. See, for example, Thomas Godwyn, *Moses and Aaron: Civil and ecclesiastical rites Used by the Ancient Hebrews* (London, 1685; orig. 1625), p. 2. The relevant passages are *Jewish Ant.* IV.223–224 and VI.36.

12. Josephus, *Contra Ap.* II.179. "τό γάρ μίαν μέν ἔχειν καί τήν αὐτήν δόξαν περί θεοῦ." See Josephus, *The Life. Against Apion*, p. 365.

13. Josephus's precise level of agreement with this last claim (viz. that God gave supreme jurisdiction to the civil magistrate) is difficult to establish. In the *Jewish Antiquities*, he seems to take something like this position: no political or juridical function is listed among the duties of priests (III.190–192); Moses is said to have deputized a class of "chiefs" (ἄρχοντες), not priests, to act as judges in mundane matters, reserving jurisdiction to himself in more serious cases (following Jethro's advice) (III.70–71). He emphasizes that Moses bestowed the guardianship of both the "laws" (νόμοι) and "divine matters" (τό θεῖον) on his own successor, Joshua, not on the high priest Eleazar (IV.165). He makes clear that, after entry into the land

of Israel, the priests were to have no legislative or judicial role, apart from a responsibility to hear the most difficult cases in collaboration with the prophet and the
"senate of elders" (γερουσία) (IV.214–218). Finally, he describes God as the sovereign of Israel (ἡγεμών) and the post-Mosaic/pre-monarchic constitution of the Israelites as an "aristocracy" (IV.223–224). On the other hand, even in the *Jewish Antiquities*, Josephus strikingly assigns the high priest the responsibility of reading the
Law at Israelite convocations (a detail not found in the Bible itself; see Deut.
XXXI.11), and he certainly assigns the priests a much more prominent political role
in *Against Apion* (see, e.g., *Contra Ap.* II.185). Suffice it to say that a great many
early-modern authors attributed an Erastian commitment of this sort to Josephus,
whether or not he himself in fact held it. For the contentious early-modern reception
of Josephus's notion of theocracy (and a welcome recognition of the fact that the
term "theocracy" was sharply distinguished from "priestcraft" during the period),
see Wolfgang Hübener, "Die verlorene Unschuld der Theokratie," in *Religionstheorie und politische Theologie*, 3 vols., ed. Jacob Taubes (Munich, 1987), vol. 3,
Theokratie, pp. 29–64.

14. Ibid., p. 367. "ἐξ ἀρχῆς τεθῆναι τὸν νόμον κατὰ θεοῦ βούλησιν."
15. Ibid. "τί γὰρ αὐτοῦ τις ἂν μετακινήσειεν, ἢ τί κάλλιον ἐξεῦρεν, ἢ τί παρ᾽
    ἑτέρων ὡς ἄμεινον μετήνεγκεν; ἀρά γε τὴν ὅλην κατάστασιν τοῦ πο-
    λιτεύματος; καὶ τίς ἂν καλλίων ἢ δικαιοτέρα γένοιτο . . ."
16. See Josephus, *Jewish Ant.* 3.214–224.
17. It should go without saying that not all early-modern Hebraists shared this view. To
    take just one example, Cornelius Bertram (the very first author to write a treatise on
    the Hebrew republic) was an orthodox Calvinist and friend of Beza's, who used He-
    brew sources to argue in favor of an independent ecclesiastical jurisdiction. See Ber-
    tram, *De politia iudaica tam civili quam ecclesiastica* (Geneva, 1574). It is well known
    that Hebrew theocracy was often interpreted as a model of intolerance; I want to
    show that there was another, equally important understanding of religious life in the
    Hebrew republic that led early-modern readers in a very different direction.
18. It is important to note that it does not *follow* from the view that the civil sovereign is
    uniquely authorized to make religious law that the number of such laws must be
    small—or that the laws themselves should aim only at the preservation of peace. It
    would be perfectly possible to imagine a deeply intolerant Erastianism: one in which
    the care of souls was regarded as a civic purpose, and in which that objective was
    thought to require the use of coercive law by the civil magistrate. That the authors
    we will be considering did *not* take this view is a result, rather, of their meditation on
    the Erastian model of the Hebrew republic. After all, if God desires us to make reli-
    gious law for civic purposes alone, and if the laws that he himself gave to Israel as
    civil sovereign reveal that he construed these purposes quite narrowly, then we have
    a *religious* reason to privilege the demands of peace over those of doctrinal unifor-
    mity. I am grateful to Allen Patten for prompting me to focus on this point.
19. Another way of putting this thought is that the traditional opposition between *theoc-
    racy* and *toleration* (as in the title of Douglas Nobbs's classic account of the Dutch
    Remonstrant debates) is misguided. It was, rather, a particular understanding of

Israelite theocracy that served to justify toleration for a broad range of Erastian authors. This is my suggestion for how we ought to understand what Mark Goldie has called "a paradoxical fusion of the belief in an erastian national church and a tolerant indifferentism, a union which persists through the eighteenth century" (Goldie, "Civil Religion and the English Enlightenment," p. 37).

20. See, for example, Jeffrey Collins, *The Allegiance of Thomas Hobbes* (Oxford, 2005), p. 171.

21. This text brought together Erastus's initial seventy-five *Theses* and his reply to Theodore Beza, the *Confirmatio thesium*. To say that Erastianism properly begins with Erastus is not, of course, to deny that he had important antecedents. Without question, the most important of these was the fourteenth-century conciliarist Marsilius of Padua. For Marsilius's argument that the "human legislator" must possess a monopoly on coercive power, see Marsilius, *Defensor pacis* II.21 (*The Defender of the Peace*, ed. and trans. Annabel Brett [Cambridge, 2005]). See also Quentin Skinner, *Foundations of Modern Political Thought*, 2 vols. (Cambridge, 1978), vol. 1, pp. 21–22; and Nederman, *Worlds of Difference*, pp. 69–84.

22. The classic account remains John Neville Figgis, "Erastus and Erastianism," *Journal of Theological Studies* 2 (1900): 66–101. That said, I believe that Figgis considerably overstates the distance between Erastus's own views and those of later Erastians. See esp. p. 81 and the caricature of Selden's position on p. 82. Selden certainly is not one who "utterly denies any rights of conscience to either individual or church."

23. Thomas Erastus, *The Nullity of Church-Censures: or A Dispute Writtem by that Illustrious Philosopher, Expert Physician, and Pious Divine, Dr Thomas Erastus* (London, 1659), B2^r. The Latin text is taken from Erastus, *Explicatio gravissimae quaestionis utrum excommunicatio, quatenus religionem intelligentes et amplexantes, a sacramentorum usu, propter admissum facinus arcet, mandato nitatur divino, an excogitata sit ab hominibus* (London, 1589). "Ergo relictis interpretibus ad sacra literas redii: atque inter legendum pro captu meo diligenter notavi, quid dissentaneum vel consentaneum receptae opinioni esset" (A4^v).

24. Ibid. "In qua re non vulgariter me adiuvit contemplatio status Reipublicae & Ecclesiae Iudaicae. Sic enim apud me cogitabam: Deus ipse testatur Deut. 4. populum suum statuta, & leges habere tam iustas & sapientes, ut cum illis nullarum gentium instituta, nullius Reipublicae sanctiones, nullae ordinationes, quantumvis sapienter excogitatae, contendere possint" (Erastus, *Explicatio*, A4^v).

25. Ibid. "praeclarissime, sapientissimeque disposita sit Ecclesia, quae ad Iudaicae formam proxime accedit" (Erastus, *Explicatio,* B2^v).

26. Ibid. "At in hac ita fuerunt constitutae res a Deo, ut duo diversa de moribus iudicia, Politicum, & Ecclesiasticum, nusquam reperiantur. . . . Neque sub hoc, neque sub Mose, vel Iudicibus, vel aliis Regibus, vel optimatum vocata procuratione duo nos ita discrepantia iudicia invenire" (Erastus, *Explicatio*, B2^v–B3^r).

27. Ibid., p. 55. "Permiserunt Romani omnibus populis, nominatim autem Iudaeis, intra & extra Iudaeam habitantibus, in rebus ad religionem pertinentibus, suis uti legibus, suisque ritibus & moribus libere vivere, teste Ioseph. lib. Antiq. 14. cap. 12.16 & 17" (Erastus, *Explicatio*, p. 38).

28. Ibid., p. 56. "Nam in politicis rebus & causis iniuriarum, ubi lex nihil certi statuisset, non ambigo, quin ad se Romani vel omnia vel certe pleraque rapuerint sibique usurparint" (Erastus, *Explicatio,* p. 39).

29. Ibid., p. 49. ". . . quoad constat Christum formam iudiciorum & gubernationis, quae secundum leges administrabatur, non novasse" (Erastus, *Explicatio,* p. 34).

30. Ibid., p. 52. "Emittit armatos ad comprehendendum Iesum: Testes contra eum examinat secundum praeceptum legis: ut videri volebat: Iubet Christum coram se iudicio sisti" (Erastus, *Explicatio,* p. 36).

31. Ibid., p. 87. "Non video cur hodie non debeat Magistratus Christianus, quod in Rep. Iudaeorum facere a Deo iussus est. An putamus nos Reipub. & Ecclesiae formam meliorem constituere posse?" (Erastus, *Explicatio,* p. 60).

32. Ibid. "In 4 cap. Deut. legimus propter iudicia & statuta, quae populo Israelitico Deus dederit, omnes gentes admiraturas & praedicaturas sapientiam & intelligentiam eorum."

33. Ibid. ". . . ac potestas coercendi spurcos & facinorosos penes Magistratum fuit: cuius erat non modo hos ex praescripto legis Dei punire, verumetiam religionem omne externam constituere."

34. Ibid., p. 6. "Equidem nullum unquam propter dictam causam legimus apud Iudaeos a Sacerdotibus, Levitis, Prophetis, Scribis, Pharisaeis, prohibitum venire ad sacrificia, ceremonias, & Sacramenta" (Erastus, *Explicatio,* pp. 4–5).

35. Ibid., p. 90. "Quis enim corda iudicat praeter Deus?" (Erastus, *Explicatio,* p. 62). This would seem to answer Figgis's claim that "there is no hint of toleration in his [Erastus's] writings" (Figgis, "Erastus and Erastianism," p. 91).

36. Richard Hooker, *Of the Laws of Ecclesiastical Polity,* ed. Arthur Stephen McGrade (Cambridge, 1989) p. 128.

37. Ibid.

38. Ibid.

39. Ibid., pp. 128–129.

40. Ibid., p. 129.

41. Ibid., p. 153.

42. Ibid., p. 138.

43. Ibid., pp. 182–183.

44. Ibid., p. 183.

45. Ibid.

46. The classic account remains Douglas Nobbs, *Theocracy and Toleration: A Study of the Disputes in Dutch Calvinism from 1600–1650* (Cambridge, 1938), esp. pp. 1–49. See also Zagorin, *How the Idea of Religious Toleration Came to the West,* pp. 165–169; and Richard Tuck, *Philosophy and Government: 1572–1651* (Cambridge, 1993), pp. 179–190. An important new study of the controversy and its effects is Mark Somos, "The History and Implications of Secularisation: The Leiden Circle, 1575–1618," unpublished PhD dissertation, Harvard University, 2007. Jonathan Israel is, however, right to point out that, when the Remonstrants were themselves in power under Oldenbarnevelt, they were not energetically tolerant in practice (although certainly more tolerant than the Counter-Remonstrants after 1618). See Israel, "The

Intellectual Debate about Toleration in the Dutch Republic," in *The Emergence of Tolerance in the Dutch Republic,* ed. C. Berkvens-Stevelinck, J. Israel, and G. H. M. Posthumus Meyjes (Leiden, 1997), pp. 3–36 (see esp. pp. 10–11).

47. Uytenbogaert also composed his own important defense of Erastianism and toleration, the *Tractaet van't Ampt ende Authoriteyt eener hooger Christelijcker Overheydt in Kercklycke Saeken* (s'Graven-Haghe, 1610). This text also made extensive use of the model of Hebrew theocracy.

48. Hugo Grotius, "De republica emendanda," ed. Arthur Eyffinger, et al., *Grotiana* n.s. 5 (1984): 67. "Quod si qua inveniri possit respublica quae verum Deum vere auctorem praeferret, dubium non est quin eam omnes sibi imitandam et quam proxime exprimendam debeant proponere."

49. Ibid., p. 69. "Hebraicum igitur imperium cuius fuisse generis dicemus? Nam quot sint apud philosophos regendi differentiae et quae illis imposita nomina minime ignoratur."

50. Ibid. "An forte istis parum credemus, ut qui in omni civili doctrina nec verum principium nec finem attigerint, quasi quispiam ubi carcer, ubi meta sit ignarus in stadio velit decurrere? Quid enim faciunt aliud, qui loco divinae providentiae humanam statuunt prudentiam et ad usum referunt operis, quod ad gloriam debuissent auctoris?"

51. Ibid. "Puto igitur in re veteribus istis incognita voce utendum nova, quam commodissimam invenit Iosephus, vir et patriae antiquitatis scientissimus et externae elegantiae non rudis, qui illam reipublicae formam theocratiam ausus est dicere, significans nimirum summum solumque in ea imperium Dei fuisse, cuius cultui omnia famularentur."

52. Ibid., p. 71. "Populus Hebraeus a Deo leges habuit tum ad cultum suum, tum ad vitam civilem pertinentes."

53. Ibid., p. 101. "Ius autem huius senatus magistri Thalmudici ita explicant, leges divinas interpretandi, condendi novas potestatem penes eum fuisse regimenque publicum, non tantum sub regibus et principibus sed etiam si rex aut princeps esset nullus . . ." Grotius is referring to the summary of the Sanhedrin's jurisdiction found in the opening of the tractate. The Talmud includes within it such religious matters as ordination (BT Sanhedrin 13b–14a), the trial of false prophets and high priests (16a), construction on or alteration of the Temple complex, sanctification of the new month and the jubilee, and intercalation.

54. Grotius, *De republica emendanda.* "Ius etiam dandae veniae et administrandae aequitatis contra summi iuris rigorem penes senatum fuisse inde colligo, quod iuramentorum gratiam fecerint et votorum. Quin diserte in explicatione praeceptorum iubentium legis tradunt Iudaei posse synedrion rei prohibitae temporariam licentiam ex causa permittere."

55. Grotius, *De imperio summarum potestatum circa sacra,* 2 vols., ed. and trans. Harm-Jan van Dam (Leiden, 2001), vol. 1, p. 391. "Reges Hebraeos facta quaedam ab ipsa divina lege quasi excepisse: nam cum lex esset ne *quis impuratus pascha mandicaret* [Levit. VII.10 et XXII], Ezechias tamen fusis ad Deum precibus concessit adhuc immundis de sacro vesci [II Chron. XXX.18]. Item lex erat ut iugularentur pecudes per

sacerdotes [Levit. I.5]; attamen bis sub Ezechia Levitae ob penuriam sacerdotum huic sacerdotali officio admoti reperiuntur [II. Chron. XXIX.34 et XXX.17]. Non quod reges quemquem divinae legis vinculo solverint (id enim homini nefas), sed quod κατ' ἐπιεικείαν, optimam divini humanique iuris interpretem, declaraverint legem divinam tali rerum constitutione ex Dei ipsius mente non obligare." Another version of this argument can be found in Lancelot Andrewes, *Tortura Torti sive ad Matthaei Torti librum responsio* (1609). See *The Works of Lancelot Andrewes*, 11 vols., ed. J. P. Wilson and J. Bliss (Oxford, 1841–1854), vol. 7, pp. 445ff.

56. Grotius, *De imperio*, vol. 1, p. 395. ". . . ergo etiam in eos qui circa sacra delinquunt."

57. Ibid. "Ut enim Esdras Persae regis concessu omnimodam iurisdictionem ita populi Romani posteaque imperatorum permissu hanc iurisdictionis partem retinuit Iudaeorum synedrium cum vinciendi flagellandique iure."

58. Ibid. "Docent nos Hebraeorum magistri tres fuisse gradus ἀποσυναγωγίας, quorum primus dicitur גּוּדִי; ea poena affectum seorsim in synagoga stare iussum loco ignobiliore; alter חֵרֶם; cui id esset irrogatum, eum nefas fuisse in synagoga conspici neque opera eius ad ullam rem usos ceteros neque datum ei quicquam nisi quo tenuissime vitam sustentaret. Tertius gradus Chaldaico vocabulo שַׁמָּתָא; appellatur: ei proprius qui ex lege Mosis mortem meruisset, sed sublata capitalium iudiciorum potestate nequiret interfici; huius contactum atque commercium defugisse omnes."

59. The richest Talmudic discussion of *shammata* is found in BT Mo'ed Katan 17a. The rabbis offered several possible etymologies for the term, including *sham-mita* (death is there) and *shemamah yihye* (he shall be a desolation). See BT Berakhot 19a for the canonical list of offenses which could incur this penalty. A third type of ban that Grotius does not mention is the milder *nezifah*, which did not require physical separation from the community. An important summary of rabbinic law on the topic is found in *Shulkhan 'Arukh Yoreh De'ah*, Nidduy ve-Herem, §334, 43.

60. Grotius, *De imperio*, vol. 1, p. 577. "Ad magnum synedrium veniamus, quod quidam duplex constituunt: alterum civile, alterum ecclesiasticum. Et habent auctores sententiae suae magnos, sed recentes."

61. Ibid. "Primum omnium, quibus magis par est credi in re historica ad Iudaicam rempublicam pertinente quam Iudaeis ipsis."

62. Ibid., vol. 1, p. 579. "Hebraei magistri, non spernendi in his talibus auctores, aiunt synedrium hoc magnum de omnibus quidem causis ad se relatis respondisse."

63. Ibid., vol. 1, p. 587. "Tamen Scripturis congruentius arbitror per 'Dei res' intellegere ea omnia quae lege Dei definita sunt et de quibus ex lege iudicandum est."

64. Ibid., vol. 1, p. 397. "Ostensum ergo est iurisdictionem de sacris competere summis potestatibus utpote imperii late sumpti partem . . . naturaliter sacerdotibus nulla iurisdictio, hoc est iudicium coactivum sive imperativum competit, quia tota illa functio nihil tale suapte natura includit."

65. Ibid., vol. 1, p. 481. "Quin et pontificem maximum non successionis iure id muneris adeptum sed electione magni synedrii certis tamen familiis astricta doctissimus Hebraeorum Maimonides observat, ut et vicarium summi pontificis simili ratione constitutum." Cf. BT Middot 37b.

66. Ibid. "Hoc ipsum synedrii ius regni tempore videtur fuisse penes reges. Alioqui vix est ut recte interpretemur quod dicit Scriptura *Sadocum a rege constitutum qui Abiatharo succederet,* eodem plane loquendi genere quo Benaia *constitutus* dicitur, *qui in belli ducatum succederet Ioabo.*"

67. Ibid. "Et qui postea adepti sunt ius regium Syro-Macedones, Romani posterique Herodis pontificum maximorum creationem eiusdem iuris obtentu sibi vindicavere, cum ceteris in rebus Iudaeis αὐτονομίαν relinquerent." I have altered the translation here.

68. Ibid., vol. 1, pp. 481–483. "Neque illud est indignum memoratu: sicut olim in captivitate Babylonica Iudaei ducem habuerunt qui 'Ras Galiuth' vocabatur, ita post destructa Hierosolyma Iudaeis praefuisse patriarchas diversos in diversis mundi partibus, quos ipsi ex Davidis stirpe ortos crederent et quibus proinde quasi legitimis principibus parerent. . . . Hi ergo patriarchae ut cetera fecerunt quasi regio iure, ita archisynagogos quoque et presbyteros . . . synagogis praeposuerunt."

69. For the office of *resh galuta* (i.e., Babylonian exilarch), and the rabbinic argument that these rulers should be regarded as successors of David (fulfillments of the prophecy that "the scepter shall not depart from Judah" [Gen. 49:10]) see BT Sanhedrin 5a.

70. See, for example, Grotius, *De imperio*, vol. 1, pp. 313, 317, 321.

71. Grotius, *The Rights of War and Peace,* 3 vols., ed. Richard Tuck, trans. Jean Barbeyrac (Indianapolis, IN, 2005), vol. 2, p. 1028. "Religio autem quanquam per se ad conciliandam Dei gratiam valet, habet tamen et suos in societate humana effectus maximos" (Grotius, *De iure belli ac pacis libri tres* [Amsterdam, 1626], p. 340).

72. Ibid., vol. 2, p. 1031. "Iam vero maiorem etiam usum habet religio in maiori illa quam in civili societate" (Grotius, *De iure,* p. 341).

73. The text was discovered by G. H. M. Posthumus Meyjes in 1984, and then published in 1988. See Grotius, *Meletius, De iis quae inter Christianos conveniunt Epistola,* ed. and trans. G. H. M. Posthumus Meyjes (Leiden, 1988).

74. Grotius, *The Rights of War and Peace,* vol. 2, p. 1032. "Notandum est religionem veram, quae omnium aetatum communis est, quatuor praecipue pronuntiatis niti, quorum primum est Deum esse et esse unum. Secundum Deum nihil esse eorum quae videntur, sed his aliquid sublimius; tertium a Deo curari res humanas, et aequissimis arbitriis diiudicari; quartum eundem Deum opificem esse rerum omnium extra se" (Grotius, *De iure,* p. 341).

75. "Nam id iurisiurandi fundamentum est. Deus enim testis, etiam cordis, et si quis fallat vindex invocatur, quo ipso simul et justitia Dei significatur et potentia" (Grotius, *De iure,* p. 342).

76. Grotius, *The Rights of War and Peace,* vol. 2, p. 1033. ". . . bonitatem eius et sapientiam et aeternitatem et potentiam tacite indicat" (Grotius, *De iure,* p. 342).

77. Ibid., vol. 2, p. 1035. ". . . ad honestum sint duces" (Grotius, *De iure,* p. 342).

78. Ibid., vol. 2, p. 1037. "Has igitur notitias qui primi incipiunt tollere, sicut in bene constitutis civitatibus coerceri solent . . . ita et coerceri posse arbitror nomine humanae societatis quam sine ratione probabili violant" (Grotius, *De iure,* p. 343).

79. There were, however, limits to Grotius's embrace of toleration in practice. His 1613 *Remonstrantie,* recommending the admission of the Jews to Holland and advocating freedom of worship for them, came with no fewer than forty-nine caveats (including, for example, a requirement that Christian preachers be allowed to give sermons in synagogues—sermons that the Jews would be obliged to attend). See J. Meijer, "Hugo Grotius' Remonstrantie," *Jewish Social Studies* 17 (1955): 91–104.

80. Grotius, *The Rights of War and Peace,* vol. 2, p. 1038. ". . . ut sine qua aliqua saltem consistere religio posset" (Grotius, *De iure,* p. 344).

81. Ibid., vol. 2, pp. 1038–1039. "Ipsa lex Dei illi populo data quem Prophetae et prodigia partim conspecta, partim non dubitandae auctoritatis fama ad ipsos perlata, cognitione harum rerum nec obscura, nec incerta imbuerant, quanquam falsorum deorum cultus maxime detestatur, non tamen omnes eius culpae convictos morte punit, sed eos demum quorum facta circumstantiam habent singularem, ut eum qui princeps alios seduxerit. Deut. XIII,16. civitatem quae incepit colere deos ante ignotos. Deut. XII,23. eum qui astra colit ut legem totam ac proinde Dei veri cultum deserat. Deut. XVII,2. . . . Cananaeos vero et vicinos illis populos pridem delapsos ad pravas superstitiones non statim Deus puniendos iudicavit, sed tum demum cum hanc culpam magnis sceleribus cumulassent, Gen. XV, 16" (Grotius, *De iure,* p. 344).

82. Ibid., vol. 1, p. 169. "Quia inter ipsos Hebraeos vixerunt semper aliqui exteri homines. . . . Hebraice חסידי אומות, pii ex gentibus, ut legitur titulo Thalmudico de Rege . . . Hi, ut narrant ipsi Hebraeorum magistri, leges ad Adamo et Noae datas servare tenebantur, abstinere ab idolis et sanguine, et aliis quae infra suo loco memorabuntur, ut non item leges proprias Israelitorum" (Grotius, *De iure,* p. 7). Grotius makes an error here: the "Title of the King" to which he refers is the section *Melakhim* in Maimonides's *Mishneh Torah*—not part of the Talmud. Barbeyrac corrects Grotius on this point (see Jason Rosenblatt, *John Selden: Renaissance England's Chief Rabbi* (Oxford, 2006), pp. 147–149). Note also that the Hebrew phrase to which Grotius refers is incompletely reproduced here. It should read: *hasidei 'ummot ha-'olam.*

83. Cf. Josephus, *Contra Ap.* II.28.

84. Grotius, *The Rights of War and Peace,* vol. 2, p. 1045. ". . . sed de quibusdam quae aut extra legem sunt, aut in lege sensum videntur habere ambiguum, et ab antiquis Christianis non eundem in modum sunt exposita, dubitant aut errant" (Grotius, *De iure,* p. 346).

85. Ibid., vol. 2, p. 1046. "Iudaeorum exemplum vetus" (Grotius, *De iure,* p. 346). This is an argument that would be developed by the Arminian Simon Episcopius, who endorsed an even broader toleration than did Grotius. Episcopius likewise insisted that the toleration of numerous sects in the Hebrew republic should serve as a model for Christians: "Exemplo nobis est Ecclesia Judaica. Multae ibi Synagogae & diversae; multi cœtus & non levia inter eos dissidia: unum tamen templum, eadem sacrificia, iidem ritus, idem cultus. Quid impedit, quo minus Christiani hoc exemplum sequantur? Nullum maius periculum his est metuendum, quam istis." See Simon Episcopius, "Examen thesium theologicarum Jacobi Capelli," in *Opera theologica,* 2 vols. (London, 1678), vol. 2, p. 189.

86. Cunaeus would not have seen the *De republica emendanda,* and the *De imperio* was completed too late to influence his work—but Cunaeus certainly did read and comment on the *Meletius,* as well as on Grotius's *Ordinum pietas,* and we know that Grotius was actively involved in urging the completion and publication of the *De republica hebraeorum* (see Cunaeus, *The Hebrew Republic,* ed. Arthur Eyffinger, trans. Peter Wyetzner [Jerusalem, 2006], pp. xxx–xxxvii). It is important, however, to point out that not all Dutch Hebraists were Remonstrants and Erastians. Constantijn L'Empereur, for example, was an Orthodox Calvinist and an opponent of Arminius—at the same time, he was professor of Hebrew at Leiden from 1627 to 1646, and he published an annotated edition of Bertram's *De politia judaica* in 1644 (*not* of Cunaeus's *De republica Hebraeorum,* pace Frank Manuel [*The Broken Staff: Judaism through Christian Eyes* (Cambridge, MA, 1992), p. 120]). On L'Empereur, see Peter T. van Rooden, *Theology, Biblical Scholarship and Rabbinical Studies in the Seventeenth Century: Constantijn L'Empereur (1591–1648), Professor of Hebrew and Theology at Leiden* (Leiden, 1989), see esp. pp. 22–25. Gomarus himself taught L'Empereur his Hebrew (p. 42).

87. For an account of the importance of the "Zeeland connection," see Somos, "The History and Implications of Secularisation," pp. 209–218; see also Cunaeus, *The Hebrew Republic,* ed. Arthur Eyffinger, trans. Peter Wyetzner (Jerusalem, 2006), p. xxxi.

88. This was a commitment that came back to haunt Cunaeus in the wake of the book's publication. In 1632, the Dutch humanist Caspar Barlaeus wrote to him to inquire whether the frontispiece of that year's reissue of *De republica hebraeorum* (which portrayed Moses on the right and Aaron on the left) was meant to embody a particular ecclesiological position. Cunaeus wrote back on January 1, 1632, to deny having had any responsibility for its design. He then offered the following clarification: "my judgment on law and on the power of princes and kings in sacred matters appears readily, not from the frontispiece, but from the fourteenth chapter of Book I, with the result that this matter brought me great unpopularity and the indignation of some people" (*sententia mea super iure, ac super Principum & Regum potestate in rebus sacris, non ex picta editionis fronte, sed ex libris primi capite decimo quarto adeo manifeste appareat, ut haec res etiam invidiam mihi & quorundam indignationem pepererit*) (my translation). As we shall see, the discussion in that chapter is stridently Erastian. See *Praestantium ac Eruditorum virorum epistolae ecclesiasticae et theologicae* (Amsterdam, 1704), p. 765 [esp. p. 506].

89. It is worth recalling that Barksdale was also Grotius's great popularizer in England. He translated several of Grotius's works into English, including the *De iure belli ac pacis,* and also provided an English version of Grotius's biography. Barksdale himself defended an Arminian, latitudinarian Anglicanism.

90. Cunaeus, *Petrus Cunaeus of the commonwealth of the Hebrews,* trans. Clement Barksdale (London, 1653), A3ʳ. ". . . rempublicam, qua nulla unquam in terris sanctior, nec bonis exemplis ditior fuit. Huius initia, & incrementa perdidicisse, omnino vestrum est, quoniam illa hercle non hominem quenquam mortali concretione satum, sed ipsum deum immortalem, autorem fundatoremque habet, cuius vos venerationem,

atque intemeratum cultum suscepistis ac tuemini." For the view that, despite all of this, Cunaeus should in fact be regarded as a secularizer, see François Laplanche, "L'érudition Chrétienne aux XVIe et XVIIe siècles et l'état des Hebreux," in *L'écriture sainte au temps de Spinoza et dans le système Spinoziste* (Paris, 1992), pp. 133–147 (esp. pp. 143–146).

91. Cunaeus, *Petrus Cunaeus of the commonwealth of the Hebrews*, p. 6. "Ille rempublicam conditurus, quae in terris sanctissima foret, summam rerum potestatem numini detulit. &, cum alii nomina alia, ut res fert, reperiant, ac monarchiam modo oligarchiamque & interdum democratiam appellent, nihil ille horum fore pro natura atque indole intellexit tanti imperii. Igitur regiminis quendam modum constituit, quem persignificanter Flavius [Josephus] vocari posse θεοκρατίαν ait, quasi tu eiusmodi civitatem dixeris, cuius praeses rectorque solus Deus sit. Quae enim cunque gerebantur, huius geri iudicio ac numine professus est."

92. Ibid., p. 123. "Diximus antea, Iudaeos rempublicam eiusmodi habuisse, quae in Biblico codice regnum sacerdotale appellatur. Ex quo sit sane, ut reges eorum non res modo civicas domi militiaeque moderati sint, sed religionibus etiam, sacrisque, & ceremoniis praefuerint."

93. Ibid. "Erant enim personae ἱερομῆναι, quibus numinis iussus, & vatis vox, autoritatem, decus, atque imperium dabat."

94. Ibid. ". . . praefectura sacrorum, summaque potestas, & iudicium ad illos pertinuit."

95. Ibid., pp. 123–124. "Praeclare annotatum a Talmudicis est, quanto maior omnibus & prophetis & pontificibus rex fuerit. Nos id obiter ex Maimonide referemus, cuius haec verba sunt [Hebrew text follows: *mitzvah 'al ha-kohen gadol*]. Ea sententiam ferme habent eiusmodi: *sancitum fuit, uti pontifex maximus regem veneraretur, & locum illi suum ad sedendum cederet, atque ipse staret, si quando veniret ad eum rex. At e contra, rex non stat praesente pontifice.*"

96. Barksdale's translation included only Book I of the text; translations of all subsequent passages are taken from the Eyffinger/Wyetzner edition. This passage appears in *The Hebrew Republic,* p. 100. "In tractatu Talmudico, quem Massechta Middot appellant, traditum est, potestatem et iurisdictionem Senatorum, qui adscripti in magnum synedrium erant, sitam praecipue in hoc fuisse, quod in parte templi quae Gazith dicta est, iudices de sacerdotibus sedebant, quibus familiae et generis mota controversia est" (Cunaeus, *De republica Hebraeorum libri III* [Leiden, 1631], p. 176). Maimonides is referring to the final Mishnah in the tractate (BT Middot 37b), which outlines the role of the Sanhedrin in evaluating candidates for the priesthood.

97. Ibid. "In capite secundo eiusdem tractatus Talmudici scriptum est, cognovisse etiam eosdem Senatores de vitiis, morbisque, queis adfecti sacerdotes, tanquam mali ominis res, ex legis edicto reprobabantur" (Cunaeus, *De republica Hebraeorum libri III,* p. 177).

98. Cunaeus, *The Hebrew Republic,* p. 103. "Temporum iniquitas bellorumque aestus quadam fati lege causam deposuit ad aliud schema" (Cunaeus, *De republica Hebraeorum,* p. 182).

99. Cuneus, *Petrus Cunaeus of the commonwealth of the Hebrews,* p. 321. "Primum pontifices rebus gerundis prefuerunt, nullo principis aut regis nomine assumpto."

100. Ibid. "Apud hos omnis gratia, potentia, divitiae erant, aut ubi illi volebant. ceteri vulgus erant, sine honore, sine auctoritate."

101. Ibid., p. 327. "Et iam nihil prisci integrique moris supererat."

102. Cunaeus, *The Hebrew Republic,* p. 121. ". . . variis interpretationibus sacri codicis, dissensionibusque de religione, deque rebus divinis inter se pugnaverunt" (Cunaeus, *De republica Hebraeorum,* p. 214).

103. Ibid., pp. 121–122. "In partes enim se divisere varias homines male curiosi: atque uno ex errore infiniti, diversi omnes, et contrarii nati sunt. Iam primum Saducaeorum vesana opinio permultos tenuit, esse animas, ut corpora, mortales, neque post vitam praemia aut poenas bonos malosve sequi. Et rursus Pharisaei, homines supra modum factiosi, commentis suis legem divinam multo latius, quam summus Moses voluit, extenderunt. Ex quibus dehinc Essaei tertium genus orti, religionum sanctimoniam omnem paulo magis scrupulatim ad anxias quasdam superstitiones exegerunt" (Cunaeus, *De republica Hebraeorum libri III,* p. 214).

104. Ibid., p. 122. ". . . ardorem mentium ultra ad rimandum omnia tulere, et suis se tenebris involvit humana imbecilitas" (Cunaeus, *De republica Hebraeorum,* p. 216). This is very much in the same spirit as Cunaeus's earlier satirical attack on theological dogmatism, the *Sardi venales* (Leiden, 1612). This Menippean satire was inspired by the fierce controversy over the appointment of Conrad Vorstius to succeed Arminius after the latter's death in 1609. Partisans of Gomarus accused Vorstius of Socinianism and other heresies; in response, Cunaeus's text attacked the dogmatic assertion of abstruse theological positions on such issues as predestination and the nature of the Trinity, as did Grotius's own *Ordinum pietas* (1613). On this see Somos, "The History and Implications of Secularisation," pp. 219–238; and Cunaeus, *The Hebrew Republic,* pp. xx–xxi.

105. Cunaeus, *The Hebrew Republic,* p. 122. "Quare controversias et quaestiones ex sacris literis eruere, morbus esse coepit deterioris evi" (Cunaeus, *De republica Hebraeorum libri III,* p. 216).

106. Here we see an important point of contact between the Hebraic Erastian case and the *politique* defense of toleration. The key difference is that *politique* authors such as Lipsius, l'Hôpital, and Bodin endorsed intolerance in principle, only embracing toleration as a necessary concession to unfortunate practical realities. Their position was that the sovereign should establish as much uniformity as was consistent with civil peace—not because this was precisely the amount God wanted, but because God's wishes had to be balanced against the imperative to avoid dissension. Hebraic Erastian authors, in contrast, offered an affirmative, *religious* defense of toleration.

107. Cunaeus, *The Hebrew Republic,* p. 216. "Quae in universum vulgus Israëlitarum credere necesse habuit ea ferme istiusmodi sunt, Dei virtute res posse maximas et admirandas perfici: certa esse illius promissa: colendum illum non vultu et fronte, quibus simulatio facillime sustinetur, sed animi obsequio" (Cunaeus, *De republica Hebraeorum libri III,* p. 406).

108. Ibid.

109. Ibid. "Hinc discordia, iraeque, et nulla modestia contentionis" (Cunaeus, *De republica Hebraeorum libri III,* p. 407).

110. Ibid., pp. 216–217. "Apostoli et Evangeliorum scriptores, si brevi usura lucis ad mortalium coetus redirent, mirarentur ad libros suos interpretandos tot esse analyses methodosque, et ex sophistarum nugis tot insanas moles convectatas" (Cunaeus, *De republica Hebraeorum libri III,* p. 407).

111. ". . . in hoc mundi senio" (Cunaeus, *De republica Hebraeorum libri III,* p. 407).

112. For an important account of the Arminian influence in England during the Civil War, see Worden, "Toleration and the Cromwellian Protectorate," pp. 199–233.

113. See William Lamont, *Godly Rule: Politics and Religion, 1603–1660* (London, 1969), p. 115.

114. An important fourth was Bulstrode Whitelocke, also an accomplished Hebraist. As Gerald Toomer reminds us, Selden disliked the label "Erastian," on the grounds that he did not endorse all of Erastus's theses (although he did share Erastus's crucial commitments concerning the ecclesiastical authority of the civil magistrate and excommunication), and on the grounds that others had held some of these views before Erastus. See Toomer, *John Selden: A Life in Scholarship,* 2 vols. (Oxford, 2009), vol. 2, p. 569.

115. The most important exception (in this as in so many other respects) is John Milton. For the tellingly ambiguous case of Marchamont Nedham, see Blair Worden, *Literature and Politics in Cromwellian England: John Milton, Andrew Marvell, Marchamont Nedham* (Oxford, 2007), pp. 249–254.

116. John Lightfoot, *Some Genuine Remains of the Late Pious and Learned John Lightfoot, D.D.,* ed. John Strype (London, 1700), p. viii.

117. John Lightfoot, *Journal of the Proceedings of the Assembly of Divines,* in *The Whole Works of Rev John Lightfoot,* 13 vols., ed. John Rogers Pitman (London, 1824), vol. 13, p. 76. It is worth recalling that, by this time, the Talmudic tractate *Sanhedrin* had been completely translated into Latin. See Johannes Coccejus, *Duo tituli thalmudici: Sanhedrin et Maccoth* (Amsterdam, 1629).

118. Lightfoot, *The Whole Works,* vol. 13, p. 77.

119. Ibid., vol. 13, p. 78.

120. Ibid., p. 77.

121. William Lamont rightly emphasizes Coleman's central role in 1640s English Erastianism, and he is also quite right to stress that "the Erastian revival, far from being a reaction against the ideal of 'Godly Rule,' is a continuation of it in a different form" (Lamont, *Godly Rule,* p. 121). It seems to me, however, that his attempt to distinguish "true Erastians" (e.g., Coleman) from "cynics" masquerading as Erastians (e.g., Grotius, Selden, and Hobbes) obscures more than it illuminates. The rest of this chapter is, in effect, a defense of that proposition.

122. Lightfoot, *The Whole Works,* vol. 13, p. 78.

123. Ibid., vol. 13, pp. 106, 164–167. For the comparison of Erastus and Copernicus, see Selden, *Opera omnia,* 3 vols., ed. David Wilkins (London, 1726), vol. 1, col. 1076.

124. On this, see Tuck, *Philosophy and Government,* p. 210.

125. Selden, *The Historie of Tithes That is, The Practice of Payment of them, The Positiue Laws made for them, The Opinions touching the Right of them* (London, 1618), p. 18.

126. An important article on Selden's use of Jewish history, and his impact on other Erastian authors, is Johann Sommerville, "Hobbes, Selden, Erastianism, and the History of the Jews," in *Hobbes and History,* ed. G. A. J. Rogers and Tom Sorell (New York, 2000), pp. 160–188.

127. See Rosenblatt, *John Selden,* pp. 135–157, 161; Rosenblatt, "John Selden's *De Jure Naturali . . . Juxta Disciplinam Ebraeorum* and Religious Toleration," in *Hebraica Veritas? Christian Hebraists and the Study of Judaism in Early Modern Europe,* ed. Allison Coudert and Jeffrey Shoulson (Philadelphia, 2004), pp. 102–124; and Toomer, *John Selden,* vol. 2, pp. 490–562.

128. John Selden, *De jure naturali et gentium iuxta disciplinam Ebraeorum* (London, 1640), p. 141. "Bina fuere hominum ex Noachidis seu Gentibus genera, quibus sedes licitae in imperio Israelitico. Alterum eorum qui in ritus Ebraeorum prorsus transierant, seu iuris Mosaici corpori nomina palam, admissi iuxta modum statim indicatum, dederant. Alterum eorum, quibus sedes ibi citra aliquam Judaismi professionem permissae."

129. Also referred to as *gerei emet* (true proselytes) or *gerei ben br'it* (proselyte children of the covenant).

130. Also referred to as *gerei ha-sha'ar* (proselytes of the gate).

131. For an earlier discussion of this crucial distinction, see Godwyn, *Moses and Aaron,* pp. 9–10.

132. Selden, *De jure naturali,* p. 833. Selden once again quotes Maimonides, MT *Teshuvah* 3.5: "חסידי אומות העולם יש להן חלק לעולם הבא" *Piis ex Gentibus Mundi pars seu sors est in futuro seculo.* Quod in annotationibus adjectis de eis Praecepta Noachidarum observarint, explicatur. *Atque ipse alibi, Quicunque susceperit in se septem Praecepta, atque monitus ea cautius observaverit* (de Proselytis Domicilii recens factis loquitur) *ipse est ex eis qui vocantur Pii ex Gentibus Mundi, atque ei sors est in seculo futuro. Eum vero intelligimus qui ea observaverit ideo quod praeceperit Deus O.M. ut legislator. Nam & per Mosem Magistrum nostrum nobis notum fecit, imperatam fuisse antiquitus Noachidis eorum observationem. Ceterum si sponte solum, seu ex suo potius arbitratu* (non habita imperantis Numinis sanctissimi ratione) *ea observaverit, nec pro Proselyto Domicilii nec pro aliquo ex Piis ex Gentilibus Mundi habetur, neque in numero Sapientum eorum censendus est."* The second quotation is drawn from Maimonides, MT *Melakhim* 8:11.

133. Selden, *De jure naturali,* pp. 254, 262–263. "Scilicet, quando Sanctitas, Potestas, Veritas, Unitas Numinis aut convitio ultro ac diserte proscinditur, aut ex professione actuve aliquo palam ac procaciter negari consequenter deprehenditur" (p. 254). This was quite important, as it was commonplace for opponents of toleration to equate the "blasphemy" criminalized in the Mosaic law with heresy in general (and particularly with forms of anti-Trinitarianism). On this, see, for example, Marshall, *John Locke,* p. 211. Selden also discusses the crime of *hilul ha-Shem* (profaning God's name), which Jews commit when they publicly violate a provision of the Mosaic law in order to avoid martyrdom: "חלול את השם seu *profanare Nomen Divinum* dicebatur. Et ברבים seu *publice* atque בפרהסיה, quod ex Graeco desumtum *palam ac aperte* significat, id profanare dicebatur si in Ebraeorum decem praesentia commiserat . . ."

134. Selden, *De jure naturali,* p. 310. On this, see the able summary in Toomer, *John Selden,* vol. 2, p. 519.

135. Selden, *De jure naturali,* p. 139. Maimonides MT, *'Avodah Zarah* 7: "Imperatum est nobis ut persequamur Cultum extraneum usque dum eruatur e cuncta terra nostra. At vero extra terram nostram imperatum non est ut persequamur eum."

136. Henry Stubbe, *An Essay In Defence of the Good Old Cause, or A Discourse concerning the Rise and Extent of the power of the Civil Magistrate in reference to Spiritual Affairs* (London, 1659), p. 106. Stubbe makes clear that he is simply paraphrasing the relevant passages from Selden's *De iure.* On Stubbe as a reader of Selden, see Rosenblatt, *John Selden,* pp. 182–201.

137. Stubbe, *Essay in Defence of the Good Old Cause,* p. 115.

138. Selden, *De jure naturali,* p. 308.

139. James Harrington, *The Political Works of James Harrington,* ed. J. G. A. Pocock (Cambridge, 1978), p. 185.

140. Ibid., pp. 377–378. Harrington is once again relying on the rabbinic excerpts found in Wilhelm Schickard, *Mishpat ha-melekh, Jus regium Hebraeorum e tenebris rabbinicis* (Strasbourg, 1625).

141. Harrington, *The Political Works of James Harrington,* p. 633.

142. Ibid., p. 387.

143. Ibid., p. 384.

144. Ibid., p. 519.

145. Ibid., p. 520.

146. Ibid., p. 520n. See also S. B. Liljegren, "Harrington and the Jews," *Bulletin de la societé royale des lettres de Lund* 4 (1931–1932): 656–692.

147. On Harrington's fear of "priestcraft," see Mark Goldie, "The Civil Religion of James Harrington," in *The Languages of Political Theory in Early-Modern Europe,* ed. Anthony Pagden (Cambridge, 1987), pp. 197–222.

148. Harrington, *The Political Works of James Harrington,* p. 384.

149. Ibid.

150. Ibid., p. 713.

151. Ibid., p. 185.

152. Ibid., p. 681.

153. Ibid., p. 778. It is true that Harrington is only prepared to allow Jews "their own rites and laws" (p. 159) if they should settle in Ireland, not England; but his reason for this is *not* that Judaism is "contrary" to Christianity. He argues, rather, that the Jews "of all nations never incorporate but, taking up the room of a limb, are of no use or office unto the body, while they suck the nourishment which would sustain a natural and useful member" (ibid.). His objection, in short, is not doctrinal in character.

154. See, for example, the uses of this phrase in Henry Cary, ed., *Memorials of the Great Civil War in England,* 2 vols. (London, 1842), vol. 1, pp. 335–346. I am grateful to Anthony Milton for calling my attention to these texts.

155. This is how Bishop Warner glosses the term "destructive" in his reply to Charles I's query to the bishops concerning toleration in August, 1644. See Cary, *Memorials of the Great Civil War in England,* vol. 1, p. 346.

156. Harrington, *Political Works,* vol. 1, p. 681.

157. Ibid., vol. 1, p. 744.

158. Ibid., vol. 1, p. 844.

159. Ibid., vol. 1, p. 186.

160. Ibid., vol. 1, p. 370.

161. Ibid., vol. 1, p. 563. Harrington's understanding of ordination in ancient Israel as a form of election is clearly indebted to Hobbes's discussion in chapter 42 of *Leviathan.* On this, see Collins, *The Allegiance of Thomas Hobbes,* pp. 183–191. Several scholars have recently focused on Harrington's friendly remarks about Hobbes and have suggested deep (and, I think, implausible) levels of agreement between the two. See, for example, Paul Rahe, "Antiquity Surpassed: The Repudiation of Classical Republicanism," in *Republicanism, Liberty, and Commercial Society,* ed. David Wootton (Stanford, 1994), pp. 233–256; Gary Remer, "James Harrington's New Deliberative Rhetoric: Reflection of an Anti-Classical Republicanism," *History of Political Thought* 16 (1995): 532–557; Jonathan Scott, "The Rapture of Motion: James Harrington's Republicanism," in *Political Discourse in Early Modern Britain,* ed. Nicholas Phillipson and Quentin Skinner (Cambridge, 1993), pp. 139–163. For a contrasting account, see Nelson, *The Greek Tradition in Republican Thought* (Cambridge, 2004), pp. 87–126.

162. Indeed, Hobbes looked with some suspicion on the revival of Hebrew scholarship. In *Behemoth,* he worries that those who have studied Latin, Greek, and Hebrew will falsely be thought to have "a greater skill in the Scriptures than other men have" and will therefore threaten to constitute a rival authority in the commonwealth. He sums up his attitude as follows: "As for the Latin, Greek, and Hebrew languages, it was once (to the detection of Roman fraud, and to the ejection of the Romish power) very profitable, or rather necessary; but now that is done, and we have the Scripture in English and preaching in English, I see no great need of Greek, Latin, and Hebrew" (Hobbes, *Behemoth or the Long Parliament,* ed. Ferdinand Tönnies (Chicago, 1990 [orig. 1889]), p. 90.

163. For the view that Hobbes's ecclesiology was more or less consistent in the three major statements of his political theory, see Lodi Nauta, "Hobbes on Religion and the Church between *The Elements of Law* and *Leviathan:* A Dramatic Change of Direction?" *Journal of the History of Ideas* 63 (2002): 577–598 (see esp. pp. 586–592). For the opposing view, see, for example, Richard Tuck, "The Civil Religion of Thomas Hobbes," in *Political Discourse in Early Modern Britain,* ed. Nicholas Phillipson and Quentin Skinner (Cambridge, 1993), pp. 120–138; and Tuck, *Philosophy and Government,* pp. 319–335.

164. Thomas Hobbes, *De Cive: The English Version,* ed. Howard Warrender (Oxford, 1983), p. 171. "*Naturalis* ea est quam Deus omnibus hominibus patefecit, per *Verbum* suum *aeternum* ipsis innatum nimirum *Rationem naturalem.*" Latin text is taken from Hobbes, *De Cive: The Latin Version,* ed. Howard Warrender (Oxford, 1983). This passage is found on p. 207.

165. Ibid. ". . . leges quas tradidit *Iudaeis* circa politiam, & cultum divinum; possuntque appellari *leges divinae civiles,* quia civitati *Israelitarum* populi sui peculiaris, peculiares erant" (*De cive,* p. 207).

166. Ibid., p. 204 (*De cive*, p. 238).
167. Ibid., p. 205. "... atque etiam doctrina *Iudae Galilaei;* cuius mentio fit apud Ioseph. Ant. Iud. lib. 18. cap. 2. his verbis. *Quartae autem studium sapientiae sectantium viae primus author fuit Iudas Galilaeus. Hi caetera cum Pharisaeis consentiunt, nisi quod constantissimo libertatis amore flagrant, credentes solum Deum, Dominum habendum ac Principem, & facilius vel exquisitissima poenarum genera laturi, una cum cognatis suis ac charissimis, quam mortalem aliquem appellare Dominum*" (*De cive*, p. 239). For the view that Hobbes actually means to endorse Judas's position (a view I do not hold), see Warren Zev Harvey, "The Israelite Kingdom of God in Hobbes's Political Thought," *Hebraic Political Studies* 1 (2006): 310–327.
168. Hobbes, *De Cive*, p. 171. "*Humana lex* omnis *civilis* est ... *Civiles leges* possunt dividi pro diversitate subiectae materiae in *sacras* & *saeculares*" (*De cive*, p. 208).
169. Hobbes, *Leviathan*, rev. ed., ed. Richard Tuck (Cambridge, 1996), p. 233.
170. Ibid., p. 282.
171. Hobbes dissents from Grotius and Selden (and, later, Harrington) in arguing that God designated the high priest as his chief magistrate after the death of Moses (and before the period of the Judges). However, the central claim is that God retains complete jurisdiction over religious matters *as* civil sovereign.
172. Ibid., p. 326.
173. Ibid., p. 329.
174. Ibid., p. 326.
175. See Tuck, *Philosophy and Government,* p. 220.
176. Hobbes, *Leviathan*, p. 421.
177. Ibid., p. 353.
178. Ibid., pp. 321–322.
179. Ibid., p. 322.
180. Ibid., p. 252.
181. Ibid., p. 356.
182. Ibid., pp. 268, 325.
183. Ibid., pp. 349–355.
184. Ibid., p. 321.
185. Ibid., pp. 223, 343–344.
186. See, for example, Justin Champion, "'Le culte privé est libre quand il est rendu dans le secret': Hobbes, Locke at les limites de la tolérance, l'athéisme et l'hétérodoxie," in *Les fondements philosophiques de la tolérance en France et en Angleterre au xviie siècle,* ed. Yves Charles Zarka, Franck Lessay, and John Rogers (Paris, 2002), pp. 221–253; Edwin Curley, "Hobbes and the Cause of Religious Toleration," in *The Cambridge Companion to Hobbes's* Leviathan, ed. Patricia Springborg (Cambridge, 2007), pp. 309–334; Alan Ryan, "A More Tolerant Hobbes?" in *Justifying Toleration,* ed. Susan Mendus (Cambridge, 1988); and Richard Tuck, "Hobbes and Locke on Toleration," in *Thomas Hobbes and Political Theory,* ed. Mary Dietz (Lawrence, KS, 1990), pp. 153–170.
187. Hobbes, *Leviathan*, p. 239.

188. Ibid., p. 323.
189. Ibid., p. 446.
190. This was, in effect, to challenge the anti-tolerationist view that all heresy, idolatry, and blasphemy constituted *crimen laesae-majestatis divinae*. See Marshall, *John Locke,* p. 214.
191. Ibid., p. 356.
192. See also ibid., pp. 234–235.
193. Ibid., p. 360.
194. Ibid., pp. 479–480.
195. The literature on this question is quite large and is constantly growing. Important contributions include Collins, *The Allegiance of Thomas Hobbes;* Edwin Curley, "Calvin and Hobbes, or, Hobbes as an Orthodox Christian," *Journal of the History of Philosophy* 34 (1996): 257–283; Eldon Eisenach, "Hobbes on Church, State, and Religion," *History of Political Thought* 3 (1982): 215–243; James Farr, "Atomes of Scripture: Hobbes and the Politics of Biblical Interpretation," in *Thomas Hobbes and Political Theory,* ed. Mary Dietz (Lawrence, KS, 1990), pp. 172–196; Noel Malcolm, "Hobbes, Ezra, and the Bible: The History of a Subversive Idea," in *Aspects of Hobbes* (Oxford, 2002), pp. 383–431; A. P. Martinich, *The Two Gods of Leviathan: Thomas Hobbes on Religion and Politics* (Cambridge, 1992); Joshua Mitchell, "Luther and Hobbes on the Question: Who Was Moses, Who Was Christ?" *Journal of Politics* 53 (1991): 676–700; Mitchell, *Not by Reason Alone: Religion, History, and Identity in Early Modern Political Thought* (Chicago, 1993), esp. pp. 46–72; J. G. A. Pocock, "Time, History and Eschatology in the Thought of Thomas Hobbes," in *Politics, Language, and Time: Essays on Political Thought and History* [0](New York, 1973), pp. 148–201; Henning Graf Reventlow, *The Authority of the Bible and the Rise of the Modern World* (Philadelphia, 1985), pp. 194–222; Johann Sommerville, *Thomas Hobbes: Political Ideas in Historical Context* (London, 1992), esp. pp. 108–113 and 135–149; and Tuck, "The Civil Religion of Thomas Hobbes," pp. 120–138.
196. Hobbes, *Leviathan,* pp. 260–269.
197. Ibid., pp. 49, 256–257.
198. It does not, of course, follow from this that Hobbes was any kind of orthodox Christian, although this view of his thought has occasionally been defended (see, e.g., Martinich, *The Two Gods of Leviathan*). It is perfectly possible to argue that Hobbes was a deeply heterodox thinker who nonetheless retained some sort of belief in revealed religion. In this sense, my own position represents something of a midpoint between those of Martinich and Collins in their recent debate on Hobbes's religion (A. P. Martinich, "Interpreting the Religion of Thomas Hobbes: An Exchange. Hobbes's Erastianism and Interpretation," *Journal of the History of Ideas* 70 (2009): 143–164; and Jeffrey Collins, "Interpreting the Religion of Thomas Hobbes: An Exchange. Interpreting Hobbes in Competing Contexts," *Journal of the History of Ideas* 70 (2009): 165–188).
199. Hobbes, *Leviathan,* p. 262.
200. Ibid., p. 266.
201. Ibid., p. 280.

202. Ibid., p. 267.

203. Ibid., p. 259.

204. Ibid., p. 259.

205. See, for example, Machiavelli, *The Prince,* ed. Quentin Skinner, trans. Russell Price (Cambridge, 1988), pp. 20–21.

206. See Spinoza, *A theologico-political treatise and A political treatise,* ed. and trans. R. H. M. Elwes (New York, 1951), p. 212. "ius summum competere de religione statuendi, quicquid iudicat" (Spinoza, *Opera quae supersunt omnia,* ed. Carl Herman Bruder, 3 vols. [Leipzig, 1843–1846], vol. 3, p. 219).

207. Spinoza, *A theologico-political treatise,* p. 245. "Religionem vim iuris accipere ex solo eorum decreto, qui ius imperandi habent" (Spinoza, *Opera,* vol. 3, p. 251).

208. Spinoza, *A theologico-political treatise,* p. 251. "Ceterum adversariorum rationes, quibus ius sacrum a iure civili separare volunt, et hoc tantum penes summas potestas, illud autem penes universam ecclesiam esse contendunt, nihil moror; adeo namque frivolae sunt, ut nec refutari mereantur. Hoc unum silentio praeterire nequeo, quam misere ipsi decipiantur, quod ad hanc seditiosam opinionem (veniam verbo duriori precor) confirmandam exemplum sumant a summo Hebraeorum pontifice, penes quem olim ius sacra administrandi fuit; quasi pontifices illud ius a Mose non acceperint (qui, ut supra ostendimus, summum solus imperium retinuit), ex cuius etiam decreto eodem privari poterant . . . quam postea pontifices ita retinuerunt, ut nihilo minus Mosis, id est, summae potestatis substituti viderentur" (Spinoza, *Opera,* vol. 3, pp. 257–258).

209. Spinoza, *A theologico-political treatise,* p. 220. "Et de hac causa hoc imperium theocratia vocari potuit; quandoquidem eius cives nullo iure nisi a Deo revelato tenebantur" (Spinoza, *Opera,* vol. 3, pp. 225–226).

210. Although Jonathan Israel is right to stress the degree to which Spinoza transforms the demand for *religious* toleration into a more generalized demand for a *libertas philosophandi.* See Israel, "Religious Toleration and Radical Philosophy," pp. 150–151.

211. Spinoza, *A theologico-political treatise,* p. 245. ". . . et praeterea quod religionis cultus et pietatis exercitium reipublicae paci et utilitati accommodari, et consequenter a solis summis potestatibus determinari debet . . ." (Spinoza, *Opera,* vol. 3, pp. 251–252).

212. Spinoza, *A theologico-political treatise,* p. 118. "Nam quandoquidem ipsa non tam in actionibus externis, quam in animi simplicitate et veracitate consistit, nullius iuris neque auctoritatis publicae est" (Spinoza, *Opera,* vol. 3, p. 124).

213. Spinoza, *A theologico-political treatise,* p. 118. "Animi enim simplicitas et veracitas non imperio legum, neque auctoritate publica hominibus infunditur, et absolute nemo vi aut legibus potest cogi, ut fiat beatus . . ." (Spinoza, *Opera,* vol. 3, p. 124).

214. Spinoza, *A theologico-political treatise,* p. 119. "Nam nulla alia de causa summa auctoritas leges interpretandi et summum de rebus publicis iudicium penes magistratum est, quam quia publici iuris sunt" (Spinoza, *Opera,* vol. 3, p. 124).

215. Spinoza, *A theologico-political treatise,* p. 47. "Imo in lege pro obedientia nihil aliud promittitur, quam imperii continua felicitas et reliqua huius vitae commoda, et contra pro contumacia pactique ruptione imperii ruina maximaque incommoda" (Spinoza, *Opera,* vol. 3, p. 51).

216. Spinoza, *A theologico-political treatise,* p. 47. "Hebraeorum igitur societati nihil aliud pro constanti legum observatione promitti potuit, quam vitae securitas eiusque commoda, et contra pro contumacia nullum certius supplicium praedici, quam imperii ruina et mala, quae inde communiter sequuntur" (Spinoza, *Opera,* vol. 3, p. 52).

217. Spinoza certainly read Hobbes's *De cive* (1642) long before composing the *Tractatus Theologico-Politicus* (1670); moreover, although he did not read English—and therefore could not have read *Leviathan* in the original—he was close friends with the man who translated it into Dutch (1665–1667) and may have read the Latin version (1668) in time to incorporate its arguments into the TTP. See Malcolm, *Aspects of Hobbes,* pp. 47, 390–392.

218. Spinoza, *A theologico-political treatise,* pp. 219–220. "Imperium . . . Hebraeorum Deus solus tenuit, quodque adeo solum ex vi pacti regnum Dei iure vocabatur, et Deus iure etiam rex Hebraeorum; et consequenter huius imperii hostes hostes Dei, et cives, qui id usurpare vellent, rei laesae divinae maiestatis, et iura denique imperii iura et mandata Dei. Quare in hoc imperio ius civile et religio, quae, ut ostendimus, in sola obedientia erga Deum consistit, unum et idem erant. Videlicet religionis dogmata non documenta, sed iura et mandata erant, pietas iustitia, impietas crimen et iniustitia aestimabatur. Qui a religione deficiebat, civis esse desinebat, et eo solo hostis habebatur; et qui pro religione moriebatur, pro patria mori reputabatur, et absolute ius civile et religio nullo prorsus discrimine habebantur" (Spinoza, *Opera,* vol. 3, p. 225). I have altered the translation somewhat for the sake of clarity.

219. For an elegant summary of Spinoza's position, see Susan James, *Passion and Action: The Emotions in Seventeenth-Century Philosophy* (Oxford, 1997), pp. 136–145. See also Israel, *Radical Enlightenment,* pp. 159–174.

220. See, for example, J. Samuel Preus, *Spinoza and the Irrelevance of Biblical Authority* (Cambridge, 2001).

221. Spinoza, *A theologico-political treatise,* pp. 63–64. "De ipso Mose etiam dicendum est, eum ex revelatione vel ex fundamentis ei revelatis percepisse modum, quo populus Israëliticus in certa mundi plaga optime uniri posset, et integram societatem formare sive imperium erigere; deinde etiam modum, quo ille populus optime posset cogi ad obediendum, sed non percepisse, nec ipsi revelatum fuisse, modum illum optimum esse, neque etiam, quod ex populi communi obedientia in tali mundi plaga necesssario sequeretur scopus, ad quem collimabant. Quapropter haec omnia non ut aeternas veritates, sed ut praecepta et instituta percepit, et tanquam Dei leges praescripsit; et hinc factum est, ut Deum rectorem, legislatorem, regem, misericordem, iustum etc. imaginaretur, quum tamen haec omnia solius humanae naturae sint attributa et a natura divina prorsus removenda" (Spinoza, *Opera,* vol. 3, p. 68).

222. Spinoza, *A theologico-political treatise,* p. 69. ". . . stante eorum imperio" (Spinoza, *Opera,* vol. 3, p. 74).

223. Spinoza, *A theologico-political treatise,* p. 71.

224. For another prominent "deflator," John Toland, see Justin Champion, *Republican Learning: John Toland and the Crisis of Christian Culture, 1696–1722* (Manchester, U.K., 2003), esp. pp. 167–189.

225. On this point, see the wise remarks in C. R. Ligota, "Histoire à fondement théologique: La république des Hebreux," in *L'écriture sainte au temps de Spinoza et dans le système Spinoziste* (Paris, 1992), pp. 149–167.

226. Marshall, *John Locke*, p. 354.

227. John Locke, *Two Treatises of Government and A Letter Concerning Toleration*, ed. Ian Shapiro (New Haven, CT, 2003), p. 240. Locke developed these arguments in his contribution to the "Critical Notes on Stillingfleet," composed with John Tyrell and Sylvester Brounower. The manuscript is not dated, but since it comments both on Stillingfleet's *The mischief of separation* (1680) and *The unreasonableness of separation* (1681), it seems likely that it dates from 1681–1682 (during which time Locke was frequently at Oakley). See Locke MS c. 34 at the Bodleian Library, Oxford, fol. 79–84. I am grateful to Tim Stanton for calling this manuscript to my attention.

228. Locke, *Two Treatises . . . and A Letter*, p. 239. John Marshall points out that Pierre Bayle also took up this argument. See Marshall, *John Locke*, pp. 541–542. Marshall notes that Bayle likewise stressed the broad toleration practiced in the Hebrew commonwealth—a position Marshall traces back to Episcopius, whose works Locke read with care.

229. Locke, *Two Treatises . . . and A Letter*, p. 218.

230. Ibid., pp. 218, 233.

231. In a well-known letter dated December 11, 1660 (later incorporated into the *Two Tracts*), Locke insists that "the supreme magistrate of every nation what way soever created, must necessarily have an absolute and arbitrary power over all the indifferent actions of his people." See *John Locke: Selected Correspondence*, ed. Mark Goldie (Oxford, 2002), p. 23.

232. Locke, *Two Treatises . . . and A Letter*, p. 232. See also Locke's 1689 exchange with the Dutch Remonstrant Phillip van Limborch, in which he explicitly discusses the pursuit of toleration through the twin approaches of "Comprehension and Indulgence." "The former," Locke explains, "signifies extension of the boundaries of the [established] Church, with a view to including greater numbers by the removal of part of the ceremonies. The latter signifies toleration of those who are either unwilling or unable to unite themselves to the Church of England on the terms offered to them." See Locke, *Correspondence*, pp. 136–143. The passage quoted appears on p. 137. For Locke's defense of establishment as a means of guarding against faction and division, see, for example, David McCabe, "John Locke and the Argument against Strict Separation," *Review of Politics* 59 (1997): 233–258.

233. Figgis seems to have understood this (see Figgis, "Erastus and Erastianism," pp. 91–101).

234. Locke, *Two Treatises . . . and A Letter*, p. 245.

235. Ibid., p. 246.

236. Locke, *Two Treatises . . . and A Letter*, p. 102.

EPILOGUE

1. Examples include Melchior Leydekker, *De republica Hebraeorum libri XII* (Amsterdam, 1704); Olavus Celsius, *De statu Judaeorum recedente sceptro* (Uppsala, 1719); and Thomas Lewis, *Origines Hebraeae: The Antiquities of the Hebrew Republick in four books* (London, 1724).

2. On this, see Adam Sutcliffe, *Judaism and Enlightenment* (Cambridge, 2003), esp. pp. 223–278.

3. For the plurality of "Enlightenments," see J. G. A. Pocock's magisterial *Barbarism and Religion*, 4 vols. (Cambridge, 1999–2005). A fifth volume is forthcoming. For the role of revealed religion in Enlightened thought, see, for example, David Sorkin, *The Religious Enlightenment: Protestants, Jews, and Catholics from London to Vienna* (Princeton, NJ, 2008).

4. Voltaire, *Oeuvres complètes*, ed. Louis Moland, 52 vols. (Paris, 1877–1885), vol. 19, p. 242. "En quoi notre gouvernement, nos lois, nos fortunes, notre morale, notre bien-être, peuvent-ils être liés avec les chefs ignorés d'un malheureux pays barbare, appelé *Édom* ou *Idumée*, toujours habité par des voleurs!"

Acknowledgments

My first and chief thanks go to those scholars who read and commented on this book in manuscript: Bernard Bailyn, Jeffrey Collins, Anthony Grafton, James Hankins, Noel Malcolm, John McCormick, Bernard Septimus, Quentin Skinner, and Richard Tuck. I am indebted to each of them for many valuable suggestions and for offering much-needed encouragement along the way. To Bernard Septimus, however, my debt is greater still. It was while studying the Midrash to Deuteronomy with him in 2003 that the idea for Chapter 1 first occurred to me, and I have relied on him ever since for crucial guidance in all matters rabbinic.

During the course of my research, I received help and counsel from a remarkable number of colleagues. I cannot hope to list all of them here, but I do wish to single out David Armitage, Eric Beerbohm, Avner Ben-Zaken, Ann Blair, Annabel Brett, Shaye Cohen, Edwin Curley, Arthur Eyffinger, Noah Feldman, Michael Frazer, Benjamin Friedman, Bryan Garsten, Eric Gregory, Kinch Hoekstra, Istvan Hont, Jonathan Israel, Susan James, Mark Kishlansky, Charles Larmore, Jon Levenson, Harvey Mansfield, Leonidas Montes, Philip Pettit, J. G. A. Pocock, Efraim Podoksik, Alexander Rehding, Michael Rosen, Nancy Rosenblum, Emma Rothschild, Michael Sandel, Alexander Schmidt, Gordon Schochet, Jonathan Scott, Amartya Sen, Richard Serjeantson, Johann Sommerville,

Mark Somos, Michael Sonenscher, Daniel Stein Kokin, Tim Stanton, Dennis Thompson, Martin van Gelderen, Michael Walzer, Ruth Wisse, and Blair Worden. My sincere thanks go to each of them.

I also want to acknowledge my debt to the foundational work on early-modern political Hebraism that has been done by previous scholars. To Lea Campos Boralevi must go the credit for having revived scholarly interest in the model of the "Hebrew republic" after generations of neglect. I have learned a great deal from her work, and she has supported my own with exceptional generosity. In the same vein, I am delighted to thank Fania Oz-Salzberger, whose passion for the subject is infectious, and who has done so much to raise its profile in the academy. She too has read and commented on various parts of this study, and has been a valued interlocutor throughout.

An earlier and abridged version of Chapter 1 appeared as " 'Talmudical Commonwealthsmen' and the Rise of Republican Exclusivism" in *The Historical Journal* 50 (2007), pp. 809–835. I am grateful to the editors of the *Journal* for permission to reproduce part of that essay here. Material drawn from the book was presented at the following conferences: "Political Hebraism: Jewish Sources in the History of Political Thought," Princeton University (September 2008); The Annual Meeting of the American Political Science Association, Boston (September 2008); "Civil and Religious Liberty: Ideas of Rights and Tolerance in England c. 1640–1800," Yale University (July 2008); "Freedom and the Construction of Europe: New Perspectives on Philosophical, Religious, and Political Controversies," The European University Institute, Florence (July 2008); "Republicanism and Global Politics: Past, Present, Future," Cambridge, U.K. (May 2007); and the Conference on Renaissance Hellenism, Princeton University (April 2007). I also had the privilege of presenting material from this study to colloquia at Brown, Haifa, Harvard, and Princeton Universities, as well as at the University of Chicago, the Hebrew University of Jerusalem, and the Centro de Estudios Públicos in Santiago, Chile. My thanks go to all of these audiences for their warm encouragement and for many helpful comments.

I conducted most of the research for this book as a junior fellow in the Harvard Society of Fellows, and it is a pleasure to have the opportunity here to acknowledge my very great debt to that remarkable institution.

Much of the book itself was written during a full year of teaching leave in 2006–2007, made possible by the forbearance of my colleagues in the Harvard Government Department. And it simply would not have been possible to undertake this study without the help and solicitude of the staff at Harvard's Andover, Houghton, Langdell, and Widener libraries.

Last, I have been very well served indeed by Harvard University Press. My editor, Lindsay Waters, took an interest in this project at a very early stage and has championed it tirelessly ever since. I am deeply grateful to him and to Phoebe Kosman, his exceptionally diligent assistant, for making the publication process a genuine pleasure. I am also indebted to Duncan MacRae for expert assistance with the proofs.

This book is dedicated with love to my grandparents, who have enriched my life beyond measure.

Bibliography

Note: This bibliography lists only works that are directly cited in the text.

MANUSCRIPTS

Bodleian Library, Oxford
  Locke MS c. 34.

PRIMARY SOURCES

Adams, John. *Diary and Autobiography of John Adams.* 3 vols. Ed. L. H. Butterfield. Cambridge, MA, 1961.

Ainsworth, Henry. *Annotations upon the five bookes of Moses, the booke of Psalmes, and the Song of Songs, or Canticles.* London, 1627.

Allen, Thomas. *A proposal for a free and unexpensive election of Parliament men.* London, 1753.

Althusius, Johannes. *Politica methodice digesta.* Ed. Carl Joachim Friedrich. Cambridge, MA, 1932.

Amama, Sixtinus. *Anti-Barbarus Biblicus in vi libros distributos.* Amsterdam, 1628.

Andrewes, Lancelot. *The Works of Lancelot Andrewes.* 11 vols. Ed. J. P. Wilson and J. Bliss. Oxford, 1841–1854.

[Anon.]. *Articles of High Treason. . . . Likewise, The manner of administering Justice; and in case any Lawyer shall take either Money, or Bribes, to dye as a Traytor to the Commonwealth; and the Government to be established, as the Commonwealth of Israel was, in Mose's time.* London, 1652.

[Aquinas, Thomas]. *On the Government of Rulers: De Regimine Principum.* Ed. and trans. James M. Blythe. Philadelphia, 1997.

———. *Summa theologiae.* 5 vols. Ed. Institutum Studiorum Medievalium Ottaviensis. Ottawa, 1941–1945.

Aristotle. *Politics.* Rev. ed. Ed. and trans. H. Rackham. Cambridge, MA, 1932.

Aubrey, John. *Brief Lives.* Ed. Oliver Lawson Dick. London, 1949.

Augustine. *The City of God against the Pagans.* Ed. and trans. R. W. Dyson. Cambridge, 1998.

Bahya ben Asher. *Midrash Rabeinu Bahya 'al Hamishah Humshei Torah* [Hebrew]. 2 vols. Jerusalem, 1988.

Ben Israel, Menasseh. *Menasseh Ben Israel conciliator: Sive, de convenientia locorum S. Scripturae, quae pugnare inter se videntur.* Amsterdam, 1633.

Bertram, Cornelius Bonaventure. *La Bible: Qui est toute la saincte Escriture du Vieil & du Nouveau Testament, autrement L'Anciene & la Nouvelle Alliance. Le tout revueu & conferé sur les textes Hebrieux & Grecs par les pasteurs & Professeurs de l'Église de Geneve.* Geneva, 1588.

———. *Lucubrationes Frankentallenses, seu Specimen Expositionum in Difficiliora Utriusque Testamenti Loca.* Geneva, 1586.

———. *Comparatio grammaticae Hebraicae et Aramaicae.* Geneva, 1574.

———. *De politia judaica tam civili quam ecclesiastica.* Geneva, 1574.

Boccaccio, Giovanni. *De mulieribus claris.* Ed. and trans. Virginia Brown. I Tatti Renaissance Library. Cambridge, MA, 2001.

Boccalini, Traiano. *La bilancia politica di tutte le opere di Traiano Boccalini.* 3 vols. Ed. Ludovico Du May. Castellana, 1678.

Bodin, Jean. *On Sovereignty.* Ed. and trans. Julian Franklin. Cambridge, 1992.

———. *Les six livres de la république.* 6 vols. Ed. Christiane Frémont, Marie-Dominique Couzinet, and Henri Rochais. Paris, 1986.

———. *Methodus ad facilem historiarum cognitionem.* Amsterdam, 1967.

Brandolini, Aurelio Lippo. *Republics and Kingdoms Compared.* Ed. James Hankins. I Tatti Renaissance Library. Cambridge, MA, 2009.

Bruni, Leonardo. *Leonardo Brunis Rede auf Nanni Strozzi: Einleitung, Edition, und Kommentar.* Ed. Susanne Daub. Stuttgart, 1996.

———. *Opere letterarie e politiche di Leonardo Bruni.* Ed. Paolo Viti. Turin, 1996.

———. *The Humanism of Leonardo Bruni: Selected Texts.* Ed. and trans. Gordon Griffiths, James Hankins, and David Thompson. Medieval and Renaissance Texts and Studies. Binghamton, NY, 1987.

Bucer, Martin. *Regnum Christi: Libri duo.* Paris, 1550.

Bunny, Edmund. *The scepter of Judah: or, what manner of government it was, that unto the common-wealth or Church of Israel was by the law of God appointed.* London, 1584.

Calvin, Jean. *Institutes of the Christian Religion.* 2 vols. Trans. John Allen. Philadelphia, 1955.

Cary, Henry, ed. *Memorials of the Great Civil War in England.* 2 vols. London, 1842.

Celsius, Olavus. *De statu Judaeourm recedente sceptro.* Uppsala, 1719.

Cicero. *Pro Publio Quinctio, Pro Sexto Roscio Amerino, Pro Quinto Roscio Comoedo, De lege agraria.* Ed. and trans. J. H. Freese. London, 1930.

———. *De republica, De legibus.* Ed. and trans. C. W. Keyes. Cambridge, MA, 1928.

———. *De officiis.* Ed. and trans. Walter Miller. Cambridge, MA, 1913.

Coccejus, Johannes. *Duo tituli thalmudici: Sanhedrin et Maccoth.* Amsterdam, 1629.

Conring, Herman. *De politia sive republica Hebraeorum exercitation.* Helmstadt, Germany, 1648.

Cook, John. *Monarchy, No creature of Gods making.* Waterford, Ireland, 1651.

Cunaeus, Petrus. *The Hebrew Republic.* Ed. Arthur Eyffinger. Trans. Peter Wyetzner. Jerusalem, 2006.

———. *De Republica Hebraeorum.* Ed. Lea Campos Boralevi. Florence, 1996.

———. *Petrus Cunaeus of the commonwealth of the Hebrews.* Trans. Clement Barksdale. London, 1653.

———. *Orationes, argumenti varii.* Wittenberg, 1643.

———. *De republica Hebraeorum libri III.* Leiden, 1631.

———. *De republica Hebraeorum libri III.* Amsterdam, 1617.

———. *Sardi venales: Satyra menippea in huius seculi homines plerosque inepte eruditos.* Leiden, 1612.

Cunaeus, Petrus et al. *Praestantium ac Eruditorum virorum epistolae ecclesiasticae et theologicae.* Amsterdam, 1704.

D'Aquin, Phillipe, trans. *Sentenze: Parabole di Rabbini. Tradotti da Philippo Daquin.* Paris, 1620.

Diodati, Giovanni. *La sacra Bibbia tradotta in lingua italiana e commentata da Giovanni Diodati.* 3 vols. Ed. Michele Ranchetti. Milan, 1999.

———. *Pious and learned annotations upon the Holy Bible.* Trans. R. G. London, 1648.

Eliot, John. *The Christian Commonwealth: or, The civil polity of the rising kingdom of Jesus.* London, 1659.

Episcopius, Simon. *Opera theologica.* 2 vols. London, 1678.

Erasmus. *Collected Works of Erasmus.* 86 vols. Ed. A. H. T. Levi. Toronto, 1986.

Erastus, Thomas. *The Nullity of Church-Censures: or A Dispute Writtem by that Illustrious Philosopher, Expert Physician, and Pious Divine, Dr Thomas Erastus.* London, 1659.

———. *Explicatio gravissimae quaestionis utrum excommunicatio, quatenus religionem intelligentes et amplexantes, a sacramentorum usu, propter admissum facinus arcet, mandato nitatur divino, an excogitata sit ab hominibus.* London, 1589.

Fénelon, François de Salignac de la Mothe-. *Oeuvres.* 2 vols. Ed. Jacques Le Brun. Paris, 1983.

Ficino, Marsilio. *Platonic Theology.* 2 vols. Ed. James Hankins, trans. Michael J. B. Allen. Cambridge, MA, 2001.

Filmer, Robert. "Observations Concerning the Originall of Government." In *Patriarcha and Other Writings,* ed. Johann Sommerville. Cambridge, 1991.

———. *Observations concerning the original and various forms of government.* London, 1696.

———. *Patriarcha.* London, 1680.

Fleury, Claude. *The Manners of the Israelites in Three Parts.* London, 1683.

Florus, L. Annaeus. *Epitome.* Ed. and trans. Edward Seymour Forster. Cambridge, MA, 1929.

Franklin, Julian, ed. *Constitutionalism and Resistance in the Sixteenth Century: Three Treatises by Hotman, Beza, & Mornay.* New York, 1969.

Fulbecke, William. *An Historicall Collection of the Continuall Factions, Tumults, and Massacres of the Romans and Italians during the space of one hundred and twentie yeares next before the peaceable Empire of Augustus Caesar.* London, 1601.

Genesis Rabbah. 2nd ed. 3 vols. Ed. Julius Theodor and Chanoch Albeck. Jerusalem, 1965.

Godwyn, Thomas. *Moses and Aaron: Civil and ecclesiastical rites Used by the Ancient Hebrews.* London, 1685.

[Goodgroom, Richard]. *A copy of a letter from on officer of the Army in Ireland, to his Highness the Lord Protector, concerning his changing of the government.* London, 1656.

Goodwin, John. *Anti-cavalierisme, or, Truth Pleading As well the Necessity, as the Lawfulness of this present War.* London, 1642.

Grotius, Hugo. *The Rights of War and Peace.* 3 vols. Ed. Richard Tuck, trans. Jean Barbeyrac. Indianapolis, IN, 2005.

———. *De imperio summarum potestatum circa sacra.* 2 vols. Ed. and trans. Harm-Jan van Dam. Leiden, 2001.

———. *Meletius, De iis quae inter Christianos conveniunt Epistola.* Ed. and trans. G. H. M. Posthumus Meyjes. Leiden, 1988.

———. "De republica emendanda." Ed. Arthur Eyffinger et al. *Grotiana* n.s. 5 (1984).

———. *De iure belli ac pacis libri tres.* Amsterdam, 1626.

Hall, John. *The grounds and reasons of monarchy considered.* London, 1649.

Harrington, James. *The Political Works of James Harrington.* Ed. J. G. A. Pocock. Cambridge, 1978.

Hobbes, Thomas. *Thomas Hobbes: Translations of Homer.* 2 vols. Ed. Eric Nelson. The Clarendon Edition of the Works of Thomas Hobbes. Oxford, 2008.

———. *De cive.* Ed. Richard Tuck, trans. Michael Silverthorne. Cambridge, 1998.

———. *Leviathan.* Rev. ed. Ed. Richard Tuck. Cambridge, 1996.

———. *Behemoth or the Long Parliament.* Ed. Ferdinand Tönnies. Chicago, 1990 [orig. 1889].

———. *De Cive: The English Version.* Ed. Howard Warrender. The Clarendon Edition of the Works of Thomas Hobbes. Oxford, 1983.

———. *De Cive: The Latin Version.* Ed. Howard Warrender. The Clarendon Edition of the Works of Thomas Hobbes. Oxford, 1983.

———. *Léviathan.* Ed. and trans. François Tricaud. Paris, 1971.

———. *Opera omnia philosophica quae latine scripsit omnia.* 3 vols. Ed. William Molesworth. London, 1841.

———. *Eight bookes of the Peloponnesian warre written by Thucydides. . . . Interpreted with faith and diligence immediately out of the Greeke by Thomas Hobbes secretary to ye late earle of Devonshire.* London, 1629.

Hooker, Richard. *Of the Laws of Ecclesiastical Polity.* Ed. Arthur Stephen McGrade. Cambridge, 1989.

Hubmaier, Balthasar. "On the Sword" [1527]. In *The Radical Reformation,* ed. Michael Baylor. Cambridge, 1991, pp. 181–209.

Hyde, Edward, Earl of Clarendon. *A brief view and survey of the dangerous and pernicious errors to church and state, in Mr. Hobbes's book, entitled Leviathan.* Oxford, 1676.

Hyneman, Charles S., and Lutz, Donald S., eds. *American Political Writing during the Founding Era: 1760–1805.* 2 vols. Indianapolis, IN, 1983.

Ibn Daud, Abraham. *Sefer ha-Qabbalah.* Ed. and trans. Gerson Cohen. Oxford, 2005.

Imbonati, Carlo. *Bibliotheca latino-hebraica; Sive De scriptoribus latinis, qui ex diversis nationibus contra Iudaeos, vel de re hebraica utcumque scripsere.* Rome, 1694.

John of Salisbury. *Policraticus.* Ed. and trans. Cary Nederman. Cambridge, 1990.

Josephus. *Jewish Antiquities.* 8 vols. Ed. and trans. H. St. J. Thackeray and Louis H. Feldman. Cambridge, MA, 1930–1965.

———. *The Jewish War.* 3 vols. Ed. and trans. H. St. J. Thackeray. Cambridge, MA, 1927.

———. *The Life. Against Apion.* Ed. and trans. H. St. J. Thackeray. Cambridge, MA, 1926.

Junius, Franciscus. *De politiae Mosis observatione.* Leiden, 1593.

Kant, Immanuel. *Practical Philosophy.* Ed. and trans. Mary J. Gregor. The Cambridge Edition of the Works of Immanuel Kant. Cambridge, 1996.

Lewis, Thomas. *Origines Hebraeae: The Antiquities of the Hebrew Republic in four books.* London, 1724.

Lightfoot, John. *Journal of the Proceedings of the Assembly of Divines.* In *The Whole Works of Rev John Lightfoot.* 13 vols. Ed. John Rogers Pitman. London, 1824.

———. *Some Genuine Remains of the Late Pious and Learned John Lightfoot, D.D.* Ed. John Strype. London, 1700.

Lilburne, John. *The upright mans vindication: or, An epistle writ by John Lilburn Gent. prisoner in Newgate.* London, 1653.

———. *Regall tyrannie discovered.* London, 1647.

Livy. *History of Rome.* 14 vols. Ed. and trans. B. O. Foster et al. London, 1919–1959.

Locke, John. *Two Treatises of Government and A Letter Concerning Toleration.* Ed. Ian Shapiro. New Haven, CT, 2003.

———. *John Locke: Selected Correspondence.* Ed. Mark Goldie. Oxford, 2002.

Lucan. *The Civil War.* Ed. and trans. J. D. Duff. London, 1924.

Lydekker, Melchior. *De republica Hebraeorum libri XII.* Amsterdam, 1704.

Machiavelli, Niccolò. *The Prince.* Ed. Quentin Skinner, trans. Russell Price. Cambridge, 1988.

———. *Discorsi sopra la prima deca di Tito Livio.* Ed. Giogio Inglese. Milan, 1984.

Maimonides, Moses. *Guide for the Perplexed.* 2nd ed. Ed. and trans. M. Friedländer. New York, 1956.

———. *The Code of Maimonides.* 32 vols. Yale Judaica Series. New Haven, CT, 1949–.

Marsilius of Padua. *The Defender of the Peace.* Ed. and trans. Annabel Brett. Cambridge, 2005.

May, Thomas. *The Reigne of King Henry the Second Written in Seauen Bookes.* Ed. Götz Schmitz. Tempe, AZ, 1999.

Menochio, Giovanni Stefano. *De republica Hebraeorum libri octo.* Paris, 1648.

Midrash Debarim Rabbah [Hebrew]. Ed. S. Lieberman. Jerusalem, 1940.

Midrash Rabbah. 10 vols. Ed. Rabbi H. Freedman and Maurice Simon. Trans. Rabbi J. Rabbinowitz. London, 1939.

Migne, J.-P. *Patrologia Latina.* 221 vols. Paris, 1844–1855.

Milton, John. *John Milton: A Critical Edition of the Major Works.* Ed. Stephen Orgel and Jonathan Goldberg. Oxford, 1991.

———. *Complete Prose Works of John Milton.* 8 vols. Ed. Don M. Wolfe et al. New Haven, CT, 1953–1982.

———. *Pro populo Anglicano defensio*. London, 1651.

More, Thomas. *Life of John Picus*. In *The Complete Works of St. Thomas More*, vol. 2. Ed. Anthony S. G. Edwards, Katherine Gardiner Rodgers, and Clarence H. Miller. New Haven, CT, 1997.

———. *Utopia*. Ed. and trans. George M. Logan, Robert M. Adams, and Clarence H. Miller. Cambridge, 1995.

Müntzer, Thomas. *The Collected Works of Thomas Müntzer*. Ed. and trans. Peter Matheson. Edinburgh, 1988.

Nedham, Marchamont. *The Case of the Commonwealth of England, Stated*. Ed. Philip Knachel. Charlottesville, VA, 1969.

———. *Mercurius Politicus*. London, 1650–1660.

Neville, Henry. *Plato Redivivus* in *Two English Republican Tracts*. Ed. Caroline Robbins. Cambridge, 1969.

Paine, Thomas. *The Essential Thomas Paine*. Ed. Sidney Hook. Harmondsworth, U.K., 1984.

Patrizi, Francesco [of Siena]. *Francisci Patricii Senensis, pontificis Caietani, de institutione reipublicae libri IX. Ad senatum populumque Senesem scripti*. Strasbourg, 1594.

Pearson, John, ed. *Critici sacri, sive, Doctissimorum virorum in ss. Biblia annotationes*. 9 vols. London, 1660.

Petrarch, Francesco. *Letters of Old Age*. 2 vols. Trans. Aldo S. Bernardo, Saul Levin, and Reta A. Bernardo. New York, 2005.

Philodemius, Eleutherius. *The armies vindication . . . in reply to Mr. William Sedgwick*. London, 1649.

Philo of Alexandria. *Philo*. 11 vols. Ed. and trans. F. H. Colson and G. H. Whitaker. Cambridge, MA, 1929–1962.

Pico della Mirandola. *Conclusiones nongentae: Le novecento tesi dell'anno 1486*. Ed. and trans. Albano Biondi. Florence, 1995.

Pirke de Rabbi Eliezer, 4th ed. Ed. and trans. George Friedlander. New York, 1981.

[*Pirkei de Rabbi Eliezer*]. *Chronologia sacra-profana . . . Cui addita sunt Pirke vel Capitula R. Elieser*. Ed. and trans. G. H. Vorstius. Leiden, 1644.

Platina [Bartolomeo Sacchi]. *Platinae cremonensis de vita & moribus summarum pontificum historia . . . eiusdem de optimo cive*. Cologne, 1529.

Plutarch. *Moralia*. 17 vols. Ed. and trans. Harold North Fowler. Cambridge, MA, 1936.

———. *Lives*. 11 vols. Ed. and trans. B. Perrin. Cambridge, MA, 1914.

Pseudo-Jerome. *Quaestiones on the Book of Samuel*. Ed. Avrom Saltman. Leiden, 1975.

Raleigh, Sir Walter. *The Works of Sir Walter Raleigh, Kt*. 8 vols. Ed. T. Birch and W. Oldys. Oxford, 1829.

Rashi [Rabbi Solomon ben Isaac of Troyes]. *Hamishah humshe Torah 'im kol ha-haftarot: The Rashi Chumash* [Hebrew]. Ed. and trans. Shraga Silverstein. Jerusalem, 1997.

Rawls, John. *A Theory of Justice*. Oxford, 1972.

Reimer, Joachim Ludwig. *Respublica Ebraeorum, ex Sigonio, Bertramo, Cunaeo aliisque concinnata*. Leipzig, 1657.

Rousseau, Jean-Jacques. *The Social Contract*. Trans. Maurice Cranston. Harmondsworth, U.K., 1968.

Saint-Simon, Claude Henri de Rouvroy, comte de. *The Political Thought of Saint-Simon.* Ed. Ghita Ionescu. Oxford, 1976.

Saumaise, Claude de [Salmasius]. *C. L. Salmasii Defensio pro Carolo I.* Cambridge, 1684.

Schickard, Wilhelm. *Mishpat ha-melekh, Jus regium Hebraeorum e tenebris rabbinicis.* Strasbourg, 1625.

Sefer haHinnuch. Ed. and trans. Charles Wengrov. Jerusalem, 1984.

Sefer Rabot: . . . midrashot 'al Hamishah Humshe Torah. 2 vols. Amsterdam, 1640.

Selden, John. *Opera omnia.* 3 vols. Ed. David Wilkins. London, 1726.

———. *De synedriis & praefecturis iuridicis veterum Ebraeorum.* 3 vols. London, 1650–1655.

———. *De jure naturali et gentium iuxta disciplinam Ebraeorum.* London, 1640.

———. *The Historie of Tithes That is, The Practice of Payment of them, The Positiue Laws made for them, The Opinions touching the Right of them.* London, 1618.

Sidney, Algernon. *Court Maxims.* Ed. Hans Blom, Eco Haitsma Mulier, and Ronald Janse. Cambridge, 1996.

———. *Discourses Concerning Government.* Ed. Thomas G. West. Indianapolis, 1996.

Sigonio, Carlo. *Caroli Sigonii de republica Hebraeorum libri VII, ad Gregorium XIII pontificem maximum.* Frankfurt, 1585.

———. *De republica Hebraeorum libri VII: Ad Gregorium XIII pontificem maximum.* Bologna, 1582.

———. *De antiquo iure civium Romanorum, Italiae, provinciarum: Romanae iurisprudentiae iudiciis, tum privatis, tum publicis, eorumque ratione libri XI.* Paris, 1576.

———. *De republica Atheniensium libri IV.* Bologna, 1564.

Spinoza, Baruch. *A theologico-political treatise and A political treatise.* Ed. and trans. R. H. M. Elwes. New York, 1951.

———. *Opera quae supersunt omnia.* 3 vols. Ed. Carl Hermann Bruder. Leipzig, 1843–1846.

Stephani, Joachim. *De iurisdictione Judaeorum, Graecorum, Romanorum et Ecclesiasticorum libri IV.* Frankfurt, 1604.

Stubbe, Henry. *An Essay In Defence of the Good Old Cause, or A Discourse concerning the Rise and Extent of the power of the Civil Magistrate in reference to Spiritual Affairs.* London, 1659.

Surenhuis, Willem, ed. and trans. *Mischna: Sive totius Hebraeorum juris, rituum, antiquitatum, ac legum oralium systema.* 6 vols. Amsterdam, 1698–1703.

[Talmud]. *Soncino Hebrew-English Edition of the Babylonian Talmud.* 30 vols. Ed. Isidore Epstein. London, 1994.

Uytenbogaert, Jan. *Tractaet van't Ampt ende Authoriteyt eener hooger Christelijcker Overheydt in Kercklycke Saeken.* s'Graven-Haghe, 1610.

Velleius Paterculus. *Res gestae divi Augusti.* Ed. and trans. Frederick W. Shipley. New York, 1924.

Voltaire. *Oeuvres complètes.* 52 vols. Ed. Louis Moland. Paris, 1877–1885.

Waller, Edmund. *A Speech Made by Master Waller Esquire . . . Concerning Episcopacie.* London, 1641.

Weemes, John. *An explication of the iudiciall lavves of Moses.* London, 1636.

Wellwood, William. *Juris divini Judaeorum ac juris civilis Romanorum parallela.* Leiden, 1594.

Winstanley, Gerrard. *The Law of Freedom in a Platform, or, True Magistracy Restored.* London, 1652.

SECONDARY SOURCES

Albertone, Manuela, ed. *Il repubblicanesimo moderno: L'idea di repubblica nella riflessione storica di Franco Venturi.* Naples, 2006.

Allen, Michael J. B., Rees, Valery, and Davies, Martin, eds. *Marsilio Ficino: His Theology, His Philosophy, His Legacy.* Leiden, 2002.

Anderson, Gary A. "Redeem Your Sins by the Giving of Alms: Sin, Debt, and the 'Treasury of Merit' in Early Jewish and Christian Tradition." *Letter & Spirit* 3 (2007): 39–69.

Annas, Julia. "Cicero on Stoic Moral Philosophy and Private Property." In *Philosophia Togata,* vol. 1: *Essays on Philosophy and Roman Society,* ed. Miriam Griffin and Jonathan Barnes. Oxford, 1989, pp. 151–173.

Badian, Ernst. "Tiberius Gracchus and the Beginning of the Roman Revolution." In *Aufstieg und Niedergang der römische Welt,* 37 vols. Ed. Hildegard Temporini. Berlin, 1972, vol. 1:1, pp. 668–731.

———. "From the Gracchi to Sulla: 1940–59." *Historia* 11 (1962): 197–245.

———. *Foreign Clientelae.* Oxford, 1958.

Barbour, Reid. *John Selden: Measures of the Holy Commonwealth in Seventeenth-Century England.* Toronto, 2003.

Baron, Salo Wittmayer. "The Council of Trent and Rabbinic Literature." In *Ancient and Medieval Jewish History.* New Brunswick, NJ, 1972, pp. 353–371.

Bartolucci, Guido. "Carlo Sigonio and the Respublica Hebraeorum: A Re-evaluation." *Hebraic Political Studies* 3 (2008): 19–59.

———. *La repubblica ebraica di Carlo Sigonio: Modelli politici dell'età moderna.* Florence, 2007.

Bergsma, John S. *The Jubilee from Leviticus to Qumran: A History of Interpretation.* Leiden, 2007.

Bernstein, A. H. *Tiberius Gracchus: Tradition and Apostasy.* Ithaca, NY, 1978.

Blair, Ann. "Mosaic Physics and the Search for a Pious Natural Philosophy in the Late Renaissance." *Isis* 91 (2000): 32–58.

Blidstein, Gerald. "The Monarchic Imperative in Rabbinic Perspective." *Association for Jewish Studies Review* 7–8 (1982–1983): 15–39.

Blythe, James. "'Civic Humanism' and Medieval Political Thought." In *Renaissance Civic Humanism,* ed. James Hankins. Cambridge, 2000, pp. 30–74.

Bock, Gisela, Quentin Skinner, and Maurizio Viroli, eds. *Machiavelli and Republicanism.* Cambridge, 1990.

Boralevi, Lea Campos. "Classical Foundational Myths of European Republicanism: The Jewish Commonwealth." In *Republicanism: A Shared European Heritage,* vol, 1, ed. Martin van Gelderen and Quentin Skinner. Cambridge, 2002, pp. 247–261.

Botley, Paul. *Latin Translation in the Renaissance: The Theory and Practice of Leonardo Bruni, Giannozzo Manetti, Erasmus.* Cambridge, 2007.

Burke, Peter. "A Survey of the Popularity of Ancient Historians, 1450–1700." *History and Theory* 5 (1966): 135–152.

Burmeister, K. H. *Sebastian Münster: Versuch eines biographischen Gesamtbildes.* Basel, 1963.

Burnett, Stephen G. "Christian Aramaism: The Birth and Growth of Aramaic Scholarship in the Sixteenth Century." In *Seeking Out the Wisdom of the Ancients: Essays Offered to Honor Michael V. Fox on the Occasion of His Sixty-Fifth Birthday,* ed. Ronald L. Troxel, Kelvin G. Friebel, and Dennis R. Magary. Winona Lake, IN, 2005, pp. 421–436.

———. "The Regulation of Hebrew Printing in Germany, 1555–1630: Confessional Politics and the Limits of Jewish Toleration." In *Infinite Boundaries: Order, Dis-order, and Re-order in Early Modern German Culture,* ed. M. Reinhart and T. Robisheaux. Kirksville, MO, 1998, pp. 329–348.

———. *From Christian Hebraism to Jewish Studies: Johannes Buxtorf (1564–1629) and Hebrew Learning in the Seventeenth Century.* Leiden, 1996.

Busi, Giulio. *Hebrew to Latin, Latin to Hebrew: The Mirroring of Two Cultures in the Age of Humanism.* Berlin, 2006.

Carcopino, Jérome. *Autour des Gracques: Études critiques.* Paris, 1967.

Cardinali, Giuseppe. *Studi Graccani.* Rome, 1965.

Champion, Justin. *Republican Learning: John Toland and the Crisis of Christian Culture, 1696–1722.* Manchester, U.K., 2003.

———. "'Le culte privé est libre quand il est rendu dans le secret': Hobbes, Locke at les limites de la tolérance, l'athéisme et l'hétérodoxie." In *Les fondements philosophiques de la tolérance en France et en Angleterre au xviie siècle,* ed. Yves Charles Zarka, Franck Lessay, and John Rogers. Paris, 2002, pp. 221–253.

Chernaik, Warren. "Biblical Republicanism." *Prose Studies* 23 (2000): 147–160.

Cohen, Jeremy. *Living Letters of the Law: Ideas of the Jew in Medieval Christianity.* Berkeley, 1999.

Cohen, Kitty. *The Throne and the Chariot: Studies in Milton's Hebraism.* The Hague, 1975.

Cohen, Shaye J. D. *Josephus in Galilee and Rome: His Vita and Development as a Historian.* Leiden, 1979.

Collins, Jeffrey. "Interpreting the Religion of Thomas Hobbes: An Exchange. Interpreting Hobbes in Competing Contexts." *Journal of the History of Ideas* 70 (2009): 165–188.

———. *The Allegiance of Thomas Hobbes.* Oxford, 2005.

Conti, Vittorio. *Consociatio civitatum: Le reppubliche nei testi elzeviriani (1625–1649).* Politeia: Scienza e Pensiero 4. Florence, 1997.

Copenhaver, Brian. "The Secret of Pico's Oration: Cabala and Renaissance Philosophy." *Midwest Studies in Philosophy* 26 (2002): 56–81.

———. "Number, Shape, and Meaning in Pico's Christian Cabala: The Upright *Tsade,* The Closed *Mem,* and The Gaping Jaws of Azazel." In *Natural Particulars: Nature and the Disciplines in Renaissance Europe,* ed. Anthony Grafton and Nancy Siraisi. Cambridge, MA, 1999, pp. 25–76.

Corns, Thomas N. "Milton and the characteristics of a Free Commonwealth." In *Milton and Republicanism,* ed. David Armitage, Armand Himy, and Quentin Skinner. Cambridge, 1995, pp. 25–42.

Curley, Edwin. "Hobbes and the Cause of Religious Toleration." In *The Cambridge Companion to Hobbes's* Leviathan, ed. Patricia Springborg. Cambridge, 2007, pp. 309–334.

———. "Calvin and Hobbes, or, Hobbes as an Orthodox Christian." *Journal of the History of Philosophy* 34 (1996): 257–283.

Dienstag, J. I. "Christian Translators of Maimonides' *Mishneh Torah* into Latin." In *Salo Wittmayer Baron Jubilee Volume*. Ed. Saul Lieberman. New York, 1974, pp. 287–310.

Dzelzainis, Martin. "Milton's Classical Republicanism." In *Milton and Republicanism*, ed. David Armitage, Armand Himy, and Quentin Skinner. Cambridge, 1995, pp. 3–24.

Eisenach, Eldon. "Hobbes on Church, State, and Religion." *History of Political Thought* 3 (1982): 215–243.

———. *Two Worlds of Liberalism: Religion and Politics in Hobbes, Locke, and Mill*. Chicago, 1981.

Eyffinger, Arthur. Introduction to Petrus Cunaeus, *The Hebrew Republic,* ed. Arthur Eyffinger, trans. Peter Wyetzner. Jerusalem, 2006.

Farr, James. "Atomes of Scripture: Hobbes and the Politics of Biblical Interpretation." In *Thomas Hobbes and Political Theory*, ed. Mary Dietz. Lawrence, KS, 1990, pp. 172–196.

Figgis, John Neville. "Erastus and Erastianism." *Journal of Theological Studies* 2 (1900): 66–101.

Fletcher, Harris. *Milton's Rabbinical Readings*. Urbana, IL, 1930.

Frei, Hans. *The Eclipse of Biblical Narrative*. Princeton, NJ, 1982.

Friedman, Jerome. *The Most Ancient Testimony: Sixteenth-Century Christian Hebraica in the Age of Renaissance Nostalgia*. Athens, OH, 1983.

Froehlich, Karlfried. "Walafrid Strabo and the Glossa Ordinaria: The Making of a Myth." *Studia Patristica* 28 (1993): 192–196.

Fubini, Riccardo. *Storiografia dell'Umanesimo in Italia: Da Leonardo Bruni ad Annio da Viterbo*. Rome, 2003.

Funkenstein, Josef. *Das Alte Testament im Kampf von regnum und sacerdotium zur Zeit des Investiturstreits*. Dortmund, Germany, 1938.

Garin, Eugenio. *Italian Humanism: Philosophy and Civic Life in the Renaissance*. Trans. Peter Munz. Oxford, 1965.

Gaus, Gerald F. "Backwards into the Future: Neorepublicanism as a Postsocialist Critique of Market Society." *Social Philosophy & Policy* 20: 59–92.

Geiger, Ludwig. *Das Studium der hebräischen Sprache in Deutschland vom Ende des XV bis Mitte des XVI Jahrhunderts*. Breslau, 1870.

Gillespie, Michael Allen. *The Theological Origins of Modernity*. Chicago, 2008.

Goldie, Mark. "Civil Religion and the English Enlightenment." In *Politics, Politeness, and Patriotism,* ed. Gordon Schochet. Washington, DC, 1993, pp. 31–46.

———. "The Civil Religion of James Harrington." In *The Languages of Political Theory in Early-Modern Europe*, ed. Anthony Pagden. Cambridge, 1987, pp. 197–222.

Grafton, Anthony. *Joseph Scaliger: A Study in the History of Classical Scholarship*, vol. 2: *Historical Chronology*. Oxford, 1983.

Gulak, Asher. *Prolegomena to the study of the History of Jewish Law in the Talmudic Age. Part I: The Law of Immoveable Property*. Jerusalem, 1929.

Güldner, G. *Das Toleranz-Problem in den Niederlanden im Ausgang des 16. Jahrhunderts.* Lübeck, Germany, 1968.

Hankins, James. "Rhetoric, History, and Ideology: The Civic Panegyrics of Leonardo Bruni." In *Renaissance Civic Humanism,* ed. James Hankins. Cambridge, 2000, pp. 151–178.

———. *Plato in the Italian Renaissance.* Leiden, 1991.

———. "Exclusivist Republicanism and the Non-Monarchical Republic." Forthcoming in *Political Theory* 38 (2010).

Hardin, Richard F. *Civil Idolatry: Desacralizing and Monarchy in Spenser, Shakespeare, and Milton.* London, 1992.

Harrison, Peter. *The Bible, Protestantism, and the Rise of Natural Science.* Cambridge, 1998.

Harvey, Warren Zev. "The Israelite Kingdom of God in Hobbes's Political Thought." *Hebraic Political Studies* 1 (2006): 310–327.

Hoffmann, F. L. "Hebräische Grammatiken Christlicher Autoren bis Ende des XVI Jahrh. in der Hamburger Stadtbibliothek." *Jeschurun* 6 (1868).

Hsia, R. Po-Chia, and Van Nierop, H. F. K., eds. *Calvinism and Religious Toleration in the Dutch Golden Age.* Cambridge, 2002.

Hübener, Wolfgang. "Die verlorene Unschuld der Theokratie." In *Religionstheorie und politische Theologie,* vol. 3: *Theokratie,* ed. Jacob Taubes. Munich, 1987, pp. 29–64.

Idel, Moshe. "Prisca Theologia in Marsilio Ficino and in Some Jewish Treatments." In *Marsilio Ficino: His Theology, His Philosophy, His Legacy,* ed. Michael J. B. Allen, Valery Rees, and Martin Davies. Leiden, 2002, pp. 137–158.

———. "Jewish Mystical Thought in the Florence of Lorenzo il Magnifico." In *La cultura ebraica all'epoca di Lorenzo il Magnifico,* ed. Dora Liscia Bemporad and Ida Zatelli. Florence, 1998, pp. 17–42.

Israel, Jonathan. *Enlightenment Contested: Philosophy, Modernity, and the Emancipation of Man, 1670–1752.* Oxford, 2006.

———. "Religious Toleration and Radical Philosophy in the Later Dutch Golden Age (1668–1710)." In *Calvinism and Religious Toleration in the Dutch Golden Age,* ed. R. Po-Chia Hsia and H. F. K. Van Nierop. Cambridge, 2002, pp. 148–158.

———. *Radical Enlightenment: Philosophy and the Making of Modernity, 1650–1750.* Oxford, 2001.

———. "The Intellectual Debate about Toleration in the Dutch Republic." In *The Emergence of Tolerance in the Dutch Republic,* ed. C. Berkvens-Stevelinck, J. Israel, and G. H. M. Posthumus Meyjes. Leiden, 1997, pp. 3–36.

James, Susan. *Passion and Action: The Emotions in Seventeenth-Century Philosophy.* Oxford, 1997.

Johnston, William R. "Emphyteusis: A Roman 'Perpetual' Tenure." *University of Toronto Law Journal* 3 (1940): 323–347.

Katchen, Aaron. *Christian Hebraists and Dutch Rabbis: Seventeenth Century Apologetics and the Study of Maimonides' Mishneh Torah.* Harvard Judaic Texts and Studies 3. Cambridge, MA, 1984.

Kishlansky, Mark. "Turning Frogs into Princes: Aesop's Fables and the Political Culture of Early-Modern England." In *Political Culture and Cultural Politics in Early*

Modern England, ed. Susan Amussen and Mark Kishlansky. Manchester, U.K., 1995, pp. 338–360.

Klepper, Deeana Copeland. "Nicholas of Lyra and Franciscan Interest in Hebrew Scholarship." In *Nicholas of Lyra: The Senses of Scripture,* ed. Philip D. W. Krey and Lesley Smith. Leiden, 2000, pp. 289–312.

Klutstein, Ilana. *Marsilio Ficino et la théologie ancienne: Oracles chaldaïques, Hymnes orphiques, Hymnes de Proclus.* Florence, 1987.

Kokin, Daniel Stein. "The Hebrew Question in the Italian Renaissance: Linguistic, Cultural, and Mystical Perspectives." Unpublished PhD dissertation, Harvard University, 2006.

Kontchalkovsy, D. "Recherches sur l'histoire du mouvement agraire des Gracques." *Revue Historique* 153 (1926): 161–186.

Korshin, Paul. *Typologies in England, 1650–1820.* Princeton, NJ, 1982.

Kuntz, Marion. *Guillaume Postel: Prophet of the Restitution of All Things, His Life and Thought.* The Hague, 1981.

Lachs, Phyllis. "Hugo Grotius's Use of Jewish Sources in *On the Law of War and Peace.*" *Renaissance Quarterly* 30 (1977): 181–200.

Lamont, William. *Godly Rule: Politics and Religion, 1603–1660.* London, 1969.

Laplanche, François. "L'érudition Chrétienne aux XVIe et XVIIe siècles et l'état des Hebreux." In *L'écriture sainte au temps de Spinoza et dans le système Spinoziste.* Paris, 1992, pp. 133–147.

Laqueur, R. *Der jüdische Historiker Flavius Josephus.* Darmstadt, 1970.

Lauré, Martin John. *The Property Concepts of the Early Hebrews.* Studies in Sociology, Economics, Politics and History. Iowa City, IA, 1915.

Lefebvre, Jean-François. *Le jubilé biblique: Lev 25—exégèse et théologie.* Göttingen, Germany, 2003.

Lejosne, Roger. "Milton, Satan, Salmasius and Abdiel." In *Milton and Republicanism,* ed. David Armitage, Armand Himy, and Quentin Skinner. Cambridge, 1995, pp. 106–117.

Lelli, Fabrizio. *Yohanan Alemanno: Hay Ha-'Olamim (L'Immortale).* Florence, 1995.

Lewalski, Barbara. "Milton and Idolatry." *Studies in English Literature* 43 (2003): 213–232.

Ligota, C. R. "Histoire à fondement théologique: La république des Hebreux." In *L'écriture sainte au temps de Spinoza et dans le système Spinoziste.* pp. 149–167. Paris, 1992.

Liljegren, S. B. "Harrington and the Jews." *Bulletin de la societé royale des lettres de Lund* 4 (1931–1932): 656–692.

Lilla, Mark. *The Stillborn God: Religion, Politics, and the Modern West.* New York, 2007.

Lim, Walter S. H. *John Milton, Radical Politics, and Biblical Republicanism.* Newark, DE, 2006.

Lloyd Jones, Gareth. *The Discovery of Hebrew in Tudor England: A Third Language.* Manchester, U.K., 1983.

Löwith, Karl. *Meaning in History: The Theological Implications of the Philosophy of History.* Chicago, 1957.

Malcolm, Noel. "Jean Bodin and the Authorship of the *Colloquium Heptaplomeres.*" *Journal of the Warburg and Courtauld Institutes* 69 (2006): 95–150.

———. *Aspects of Hobbes*. Oxford, 2002.

Manuel, Frank. *The Broken Staff: Judaism through Christian Eyes*. Cambridge, MA, 1992.

Markish, Shimon. *Erasmus and the Jews*. Chicago, 1986.

Marshall, John. *John Locke, Toleration, and Enlightenment Culture*. Cambridge, 2006.

Martinich, A. P. "Interpreting the Religion of Thomas Hobbes: An Exchange. Hobbes's Erastianism and Interpretation." *Journal of the History of Ideas* 70 (2009): 143–164.

———. *The Two Gods of Leviathan: Thomas Hobbes on Religion and Politics*. Cambridge, 1992.

McCabe, David. "John Locke and the Argument against Strict Separation." *Review of Politics* 59 (1997): 233–258.

McCuaig, William. *Carlo Sigonio: The Changing World of the Late Renaissance*. Princeton, NJ, 1989.

McKane, William. *Selected Christian Hebraists*. Cambridge, 1989.

Meijer, J. "Hugo Grotius' Remonstrantie." *Jewish Social Studies* 17 (1955): 91–104.

Mendelsohn, Leonard R. "Milton and the Rabbis: A Later Inquiry." *Studies in English Literature* 18 (1978): 125–135.

Milhelic, Joseph L. "The Study of Hebrew in England." *The Journal of Bible and Religion* 14 (1946): 94–100.

Mitchell, Joshua. *Not by Reason Alone: Religion, History, and Identity in Early Modern Political Thought*. Chicago, 1993.

———. "Luther and Hobbes on the Question: Who Was Moses, Who Was Christ?" *Journal of Politics* 53 (1991): 676–700.

Morstein-Marx, Robert. *Mass Oratory and Political Power in the Late Roman Republic*. New York, 2004.

Nauta, Lodi. "Hobbes on Religion and the Church between *The Elements of Law* and *Leviathan*: A Dramatic Change of Direction?" *Journal of the History of Ideas* 63 (2002): 577–598.

Nederman, Cary. *Worlds of Difference: European Discourses of Toleration, c. 1100–c. 1550*. University Park, PA, 2000.

Nelson, Eric, ed. *Thomas Hobbes: Translations of Homer*. 2 vols. The Clarendon Edition of the Works of Thomas Hobbes. Oxford, 2008.

———. " 'Talmudical Commonwealthsmen' and the Rise of Republican Exclusivism." *The Historical Journal* 50 (2007): 809–835.

———. "Republican Visions." In *The Oxford Handbook of Political Theory*, ed. John Dryzek, Bonnie Honig, and Anne Phillips. Oxford, 2006, pp. 191–210.

———. *The Greek Tradition in Republican Thought*. Cambridge, 2004.

Neuman, Kalman. "Political Hebraism and the Early Modern 'Respublica Hebraeorum': On Defining the Field." *Hebraic Political Studies* 1 (2005): 57–70.

Nobbs, Douglas. *Theocracy and Toleration: A Study of the Disputes in Dutch Calvinism from 1600–1650*. Cambridge, 1938.

North, Robert, S.J. *Sociology of the Biblical Jubilee*. Rome, 1954.

Novak, B. C. "Giovanni Pico della Mirandola and Jochanan Alemanno." *Journal of the Warburg and Courtauld Institutes* 45 (1982): 125–147.

Oz-Salzberger, Fania. "The Jewish Roots of Western Freedom." *Azure* 13 (2002): 88–132.

Pelikan, Jaroslav. *The Reformation of the Bible, the Bible of the Reformation.* New Haven, CT, 1996.

Perl-Rosenthal, Nathan. "'The Divine Right of Republics': Hebraic Republicanism and the Legitimization of Kingless Government in America." *William and Mary Quarterly* 66 (2009): 535–564.

Pettit, Philip. *Republicanism: A Theory of Freedom and Government.* Oxford, 1997.

Pichetto, Maria Teresa. "La 'respublica Hebraeorum' nella rivoluzione americana." *Il pensiero politico* 35 (2002): 481–500.

Pocock, J. G. A. *Barbarism and Religion.* 4 vols. Cambridge, 1999–2005.

———. "Time, History and Eschatology in the Thought of Thomas Hobbes." In *Politics, Language, and Time: Essays on Political Thought and History.* New York, 1971, pp. 148–201.

Preus, J. Samuel. *Spinoza and the Irrelevance of Biblical Authority.* Cambridge, 2001.

Quaglioni, Diego. "L'iniquo diritto: 'Regimen regis' e 'ius regis' nell'esegesi di I *Sam.* 8, 11–17 e negli 'specula principum' del tardo Medioevo." In *Specula principum,* ed. Angela De Benedictis. Studien zur europäischen Rechtsgeschichte 117. Frankfurt, 1999, pp. 209–242.

Rabbie, Edwin. "Grotius and Judaism." In *Hugo Grotius, Theologian: Essays in Honour of G. H. M. Posthumus Meyjes,* ed. Henk J. M. Nellen and Edwin Rabbie. Leiden, 1994, pp. 99–120.

Rahe, Paul. *Against Throne and Altar: Machiavelli and Political Theory under the English Republic.* Cambridge, 2008,

———. "The Classical Republicanism of John Milton." *History of Political Thought* 25 (2004): 243–275.

———. "Antiquity Surpassed: The Repudiation of Classical Republicanism." In *Republicanism, Liberty, and Commercial Society,* ed. David Wootton. Stanford, CA, 1994, pp. 233–256.

Raz-Krakotzkin, Amnon. *The Censor, the Editor, and the Text: The Catholic Church and the Shaping of the Jewish Canon in the Sixteenth Century.* Trans. Jackie Feldman. Philadelphia, 2007.

Remer, Gary. "Machiavelli and Hobbes: James Harrington's Commonwealth of Israel." *Hebraic Political Studies* 4 (2006): 440–461.

———. "James Harrington's New Deliberative Rhetoric: Reflection of an Anti-Classical Republicanism." *History of Political Thought* 16 (1995): 532–557.

Reventlow, Henning Graf. *The Authority of the Bible and the Rise of the Modern World.* Philadelphia, 1985.

Ridley, Ronald T. "*Leges Agrariae:* Myths Ancient and Modern." *Classical Philology* 95 (2000): 459–467.

Rosenblatt, Jason. *John Selden: Renaissance England's Chief Rabbi.* Oxford, 2006.

———. "John Selden's *De Jure Naturali . . . Juxta Disciplinam Ebraeorum* and Religious Toleration." In *Hebraica Veritas? Christian Hebraists and the Study of Judaism in Early Modern Europe,* ed. Allison Coudert and Jeffrey Shoulson. Philadelphia, 2004, pp. 102–124.

———. *Torah and Law in* Paradise Lost. Princeton, NJ, 1994.

Rosenthal, Franz. *"Sedaqah,* Charity." *Hebrew Union College Annual* 23 (1950/1951): 411–430.

Rummel, Erika. *The Case against Johann Reuchlin: Religious and Social Controversy in Sixteenth-Century Germany.* Toronto, 2002.

Ryan, Alan. "A More Tolerant Hobbes?" In *Justifying Toleration,* ed. Susan Mendus. Cambridge, 1988, pp. 37–59.

Schmitt, Carl. *Positionen und Begriffe im Kampf mit Weimar–Genf–Versailles, 1923–1939.* 2nd ed. Berlin, 1988.

———. *Politische Theologie: Vier Kapitel zur Lehre von der Souveränität.* Berlin, 1979.

Schochet, Gordon et al., eds. *Political Hebraism: Judaic Sources in Early Modern Political Thought.* Jerusalem: Shalem Press, 2008.

Schoek, R. J. "More, Plutarch, and King Agis: Spartan History and the Meaning of *Utopia.*" *Philological Quarterly* 35 (1956): 366–375.

Schwartz, Seth. *Josephus and Judaean Politics.* Leiden, 1990.

Scott, Jonathan. "The Rapture of Motion: James Harrington's Republicanism." In *Political Discourse in Early Modern Britain,* ed. Nicholas Phillipson and Quentin Skinner. Cambridge, 1993, pp. 139–163.

Seck, Friedrich, ed. *Wilhelm Schickard: Briefwechsel.* 2 vols. Stuttgart–Bad Cannstatt, 2002.

———. *Zum 400. Geburtstag von Wilhelm Schickard: Zweites Tübinger Schickard-Symposion.* Sigmaringen, Germany, 1995.

———. *Wissenschaftsgeschichte um Wilhelm Schickard: Vorträge bei dem Symposion der Universität Tübingen im 500. Jahr ihres Bestehens.* Tübingen, 1981.

Shalev, Eran. " 'A Perfect Republic': The Mosaic Constitution in Revolutionary New England, 1775–1788." *The New England Quarterly* 82 (2009): 235–263.

Shoulson, Jeffrey S. *Milton and the Rabbis: Hebraism, Hellensim, & Christianity.* New York, 2001.

Singer, Michael A. "Polemic and Exegesis: The Varieties of Twelfth-Century Hebraism." In *Hebraica Veritas? Christian Hebraists and the Study of Judaism in Early Modern Europe,* ed. Allison Coudert and Jeffrey Shoulson. Philadelphia, 2004, pp. 21–32.

Skinner, Quentin. *Visions of Politics.* 3 vols. Cambridge, 2002.

———. *Reason and Rhetoric in the Philosophy of Hobbes.* Cambridge, 1996.

———. *Foundations of Modern Political Thought.* 2 vols. Cambridge, 1978.

Skinner, Quentin, and van Gelderen, Martin, eds. *Republicanism: A Shared European Heritage.* 2 vols. Cambridge, 2002.

Smith, Nigel. "The Uses of Hebrew in the English Revolution." In *Language, Self, and Society,* ed. Peter Burke and Roy Porter. Cambridge, 1991, pp. 51–71.

Sommerville, Johann. "Hobbes, Selden, Erastianism, and the History of the Jews." In *Hobbes and History,* ed. G. A. J. Rogers and Tom Sorell. New York, 2000, pp. 160–188.

———. *Thomas Hobbes: Political Ideas in Historical Context.* London, 1992.

Somos, Mark. "The History and Implications of Secularisation: The Leiden Circle, 1575–1618." Unpublished PhD dissertation, Harvard University, 2007.

Sorkin, David. *The Religious Enlightenment: Protestants, Jews, and Catholics from London to Vienna.* Princeton, NJ, 2008.

Spragens, Thomas A., Jr. "The Limits of Libertarianism." In *The Essential Communitarian Reader,* ed. Amitai Etzioni. Lanham, MD, 1998, pp. 21–30.

Stacey, Peter. *Roman Monarchy and the Renaissance Prince.* Cambridge, 2007.

Steinschneider, Moritz. *Christliche Hebraisten: Nachrichten über mehr als 400 Gelehrte, welche über nachbiblisches Hebraisch geschrieben haben.* Hildesheim, Germany, 1973.

Stockton, David. *The Gracchi.* Oxford, 1979.

Stow, Kenneth. *Catholic Thought and Papal Jewry Policy, 1555–1593.* New York, 1977.

———. "The Burning of the Talmud in 1553, in the Light of Sixteenth Century Catholic Attitudes toward the Talmud." *Bibliothèque d'Humanisme et Renaissance* 34 (1972): 435–459.

Strumia, Anna. *L'immaginazione repubblicana: Sparta e Israele nel dibattito filosofico-politico dell'età di Cromwell.* Turin, Italy, 1991.

Sunstein, Cass. *Free Markets and Social Justice.* Oxford, 1997.

Sutcliffe, Adam. *Judaism and Enlightenment.* New York, 2003.

Taylor, Charles. *A Secular Age.* Cambridge, MA, 2008.

Thompson, S. J. "Parliamentary Enclosure, Property, Population, and the Decline of Classical Republicanism in Eighteenth-Century Britain." *The Historical Journal* 51 (2008): 621–642.

Tibiletti, Gianfranco. "Il possesso dell'*ager publicus* e le norme *de modo agrorum* sino ai Gracchi." *Athenaeum* 26 (1948): 173–236; 27 (1949): 3–42.

Toomer, Gerald. *John Selden: A Life in Scholarship.* 2 vols. Oxford, 2009.

Trevor-Roper, Hugh. *The Crisis of the Seventeenth Century: Religion, the Reformation, and Social Change.* New York, 1967.

Tuck, Richard. "The Civil Religion of Thomas Hobbes." In *Political Discourse in Early Modern Britain,* ed. Nicholas Phillipson and Quentin Skinner. Cambridge, 1993, pp. 120–138.

———. *Philosophy and Government: 1572–1651.* Cambridge, 1993.

———. "Hobbes and Locke on Toleration." In *Thomas Hobbes and Political Theory.* ed. Mary Dietz. Lawrence, KS, 1990, pp. 153–170.

———. "Scepticism and Toleration in the Seventeenth Century." In *Justifying Toleration: Conceptual and Historical Perspectives,* ed. Susan Mendus. Cambridge, 1988, pp. 21–35.

———. *Natural Rights Theories.* Cambridge, 1979.

Van Liere, Frans. "The Literal Sense of the Books of Samuel and Kings: From Andrew of St. Victor to Nicholas of Lyra." In *Nicholas of Lyra: The Senses of Scripture,* ed. Philip D. W. Krey and Lesley Smith. Leiden, 2000, pp. 59–81.

Van Rooden, Peter. T. *Theology, Biblical Scholarship and Rabbinical Studies in the Seventeenth Century: Constantijn L'Empereur (1591–1648), Professor of Hebrew and Theology at Leiden.* Leiden, 1989.

Von Maltzahn, Nicholas. "Laureate, Republican, Calvinist: An Early Response to Milton and *Paradise Lost* (1667)." *Milton Studies* 29 (1993): 181–198.

Waldron, Jeremy. *God, Locke, and Equality: Christian Foundations in Locke's Political Thought.* Cambridge, 2002.

Walker, D. P. *The Ancient Theology: Studies in Christian Platonism from the Fifteenth to the Eighteenth Century.* Ithaca, NY, 1972.

Walzer, Michael, and Lorberbaum, Menachem, eds. *The Jewish Political Tradition*, vol. 1. New Haven, CT, 2000.

Weber-Möckl, Annette. *"Das Recht des Königs, der über euch herrschen soll": Studien zu I Sam 8, 11ff. in der Literatur der frühen Neuzeit.* Berlin, 1986.

Weiss, Roberto. *Medieval and Humanist Greek: Collected Essays by Roberto Weiss.* Padua, 1978.

Werman, Golda. *Milton and Midrash.* Washington, DC, 1995.

Wilkinson, Robert J. *Orientalism, Aramaic and Kabbalah in the Catholic Reformation: The First Printing of the Syriac New Testament.* Leiden, 2007.

Wirszubski, Chaim. *Pico della Mirandola's Encounter with Jewish Mysticism.* Cambridge, MA, 1989.

Wood, Neal. *Cicero's Social and Political Thought.* Berkeley, 1988.

———. "The Economic Dimension of Cicero's Political Thought: Property and State." *Canadian Journal of Political Science* 16 (1983): 739–756.

Wootton, David. "The True Origins of Republicanism: The Disciples of Baron and the Counter-example of Venturi." In *Il repubblicanesimo moderno: L'idea di repubblica nella riflessione storica di Franco Venturi,* ed. Manuela Albertone. Naples, 2006, pp. 271–304.

———, ed. *Republicanism, Liberty, and Commercial Society, 1649–1776.* Stanford, 1994.

———. *Paolo Sarpi: Between Renaissance and Enlightenment.* Cambridge, 1983.

Worden, Blair. *Literature and Politics in Cromwellian England: John Milton, Andrew Marvell, Marchamont Nedham.* Oxford, 2007.

———. "Milton's Republicanism and the Tyranny of Heaven." In *Machiavelli and Republicanism,* ed. Gisela Bock, Quentin Skinner, and Maurizio Viroli. Cambridge, 1990, pp. 225–245.

———. "Toleration and the Cromwellian Protectorate." In *Persecution and Toleration,* ed. W. J. Sheils. Studies in Church History 21. Oxford, 1984, pp. 199–233.

Zagorin, Perez. *How the Idea of Religious Toleration Came to the West.* Princeton, NJ, 2003.

Zambelli, Paola. *L'apprendista stregone: Astrologia, cabala e arte lulliana in Pico della Mirandola e seguaci.* Venice, 1995.

Ziskind, Jonathan. "Cornelius Bertram and Carlo Sigonio: Christian Hebraism's First Political Scientists." *Journal of Ecumenical Studies* 37 (2000): 381–401.

———. "Petrus Cunaeus on Theocracy, Jubilee and Latifundia." *Jewish Quarterly Review* 48 (1978): 235–254.

Zurbuchen, Simone. "Republicanism and Toleration." In *Republicanism: A Shared European Heritage,* vol. 2, ed. Martin Van Gelderen and Quentin Skinner. Cambridge, 2002, pp. 47–71.

Index